The Art and Science of Teaching

A COMPREHENSIVE FRAMEWORK FOR EFFECTIVE INSTRUCTION

ASCD MEMBER BOOK

Many ASCD members received this book as a
member benefit upon its initial release.

Learn more at: **www.ascd.org/memberbooks**

The Art
and Science
of
Teaching

A COMPREHENSIVE FRAMEWORK FOR EFFECTIVE INSTRUCTION

Robert J.
MARZANO

Alexandria, Virginia USA

1703 N. Beauregard St. • Alexandria, VA 22311 1714 USA
Phone: 800-933-2723 or 703-578-9600 • Fax: 703-575-5400
Web site: www.ascd.org • E-mail: member@ascd.org
Author guidelines: www.ascd.org/write

Gene R. Carter, *Executive Director;* Nancy Modrak, *Director of Publishing;* Julie Houtz, *Director of Book Editing & Production;* Ernesto Yermoli, *Project Manager;* Reece Quiñones, *Senior Graphic Designer;* Circle Graphics, *Typesetter;* Vivian Coss, *Production Specialist*

ASCD Member Book, No. FY07-8 (July 2007, PC). ASCD Member Books mail to Premium (P), Comprehensive (C), and Regular (R) members on this schedule: Jan., PC; Feb., P; Apr., PCR; May, P; July, PC; Aug., P; Sept., PCR; Nov., PC; Dec., P.

PAPERBACK ISBN: 978-1-4166-0571-3   ASCD product #107001
Also available as an e-book through ebrary, netLibrary, and many online booksellers (see Books in Print for the ISBNs).

Quantity discounts for the paperback edition only: 10–49 copies, 10%; 50+ copies, 15%; for 1,000 or more copies, call 800-933-2723, ext. 5634, or 703-575-5634. For desk copies: member@ascd.org.

Library of Congress Cataloging-in-Publication Data

Marzano, Robert J.
   The art and science of teaching : a comprehensive framework for
effective instruction / Robert J. Marzano.
      p. cm.
   Includes bibliographical references.
   ISBN 978-1-4166-0571-3 (pbk. : alk. paper) 1. Effective teaching—
United States. 2. Classroom management—United States. 3. Teaching—
Aids and devices. 4. Learning, Psychology of. I. Title.

   LB1025.3M3387 2007
   371.102—dc22

                                                    2007005994

18 17 16 15   9 10 11 12

To Richard Strong:

The best teacher I ever saw

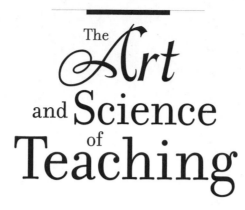

The Art and Science of Teaching

A COMPREHENSIVE FRAMEWORK FOR EFFECTIVE INSTRUCTION

Introduction: A Question Answered

Strange as it might sound to modern-day educators, there was a time in the not too distant past when people questioned the importance of schools and teachers. Specifically, the 1966 report entitled *Equality in Educational Opportunity* and commonly referred to as the Coleman report in deference to its senior author (Coleman et al., 1966) involved more than 640,000 students in grades 1, 3, 6, 9, and 12 and concludes the following: "Taking all these results together, one implication stands above all: that schools bring little to bear on a child's achievement that is independent of his background and general social context" (p. 235). This was a devastating commentary on the potential (or lack thereof) of schools and teachers to positively influence student achievement. In general, these results were interpreted as strong evidence that schools (and by inference the teachers within them) make little difference in the academic lives of students.

Since then a number of studies have provided evidence for a different conclusion (for a discussion, see Marzano, 2003b). Indeed, those studies demonstrate that effective schools can make a substantial difference in the achievement of students. In the last decade of the 20th century, the picture of what constitutes an effective school became much clearer. Among elements such as a well-articulated curriculum and a safe and orderly environment, the one factor that surfaced as the single most influential component of an effective school is the individual teachers within that school.

Many studies have quantified the influence an effective teacher has on student achievement that is relatively independent of anything else that occurs in the school (for discussions see Haycock, 1998; Marzano, 2003b; Nye, Konstantopoulos, & Hedges, 2004). Of these studies, the one by Nye, Konstantopoulos, and Hedges is the most compelling because it involved random assignment of students to classes controlled for factors such as the previous achievement of students, socioeconomic status, ethnicity, gender, class size, and whether or not an aide was present in class. The study involved 79 elementary schools in 42 school districts in Tennessee.

Among a number of findings, the study dramatically answers the question of how much influence the individual classroom teacher has on student achievement. Nye and colleagues (2004) summarize the results as follows:

> These findings would suggest that the difference in achievement gains between having a 25th percentile teacher (a not so effective teacher) and a 75th percentile teacher (an effective teacher) is over one-third of a standard deviation (0.35) in reading and almost half a standard deviation (0.48) in mathematics. Similarly, the difference in achievement gains between having a 50th percentile teacher (an average teacher) and a 90th percentile teacher (a very effective teacher) is about one-third of a standard deviation (0.33) in reading and somewhat smaller than half a standard deviation (0.46) in mathematics. . . . These effects are certainly large enough effects to have policy significance. (p. 253)

Figures I.1 and I.2 depict Nye and colleagues' findings.

Figure I.1 indicates that students who have a teacher at the 75th percentile in terms of pedagogical competence will outgain students who have a teacher at the 25th percentile by 14 percentile points in reading and 18 percentile points in mathematics. Figure I.2 indicates that students who have a 90th percentile teacher will outgain students who have a 50th percentile teacher by 13 percentile points in reading and 18 percentile points in mathematics. Again, Nye and colleagues (2004) note that these differences are significant enough to imply a need for policy changes. It is important to remember that the Nye study was conducted in lower elementary grades. However, given the statistical controls employed and the consistency of their findings with other studies at different grade levels, one can conclude that the question as to whether effective teachers make a significant difference in student achievement has been answered. They do!

Whereas Nye and colleagues' (2004) study was not intended to identify specific characteristics of effective teachers, this book is. However, just as Nye's team qualified its findings, I too must qualify the recommendations made in this book. Notice that it is titled *The Art and Science of Teaching*. In this text I present

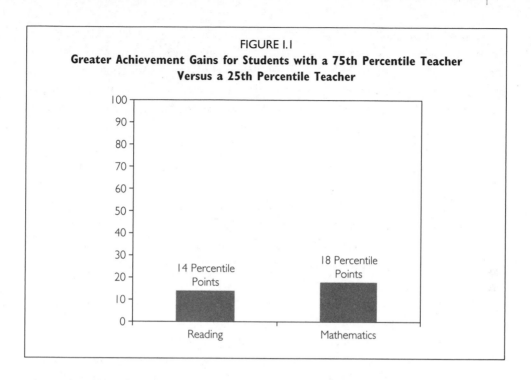

FIGURE I.1

Greater Achievement Gains for Students with a 75th Percentile Teacher Versus a 25th Percentile Teacher

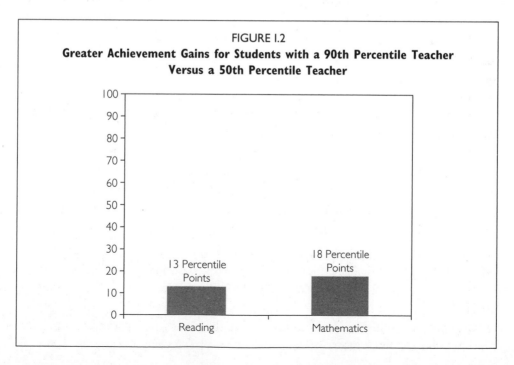

FIGURE I.2

Greater Achievement Gains for Students with a 90th Percentile Teacher Versus a 50th Percentile Teacher

a fair amount of research. One might conclude from this that I believe teaching to be a science. It is certainly true that research provides us with guidance as to the nature of effective teaching, and yet I strongly believe that there is not (nor will there ever be) a formula for effective teaching. This is not an unusual claim. Many researchers and those who try to apply research (a category into which I place myself) would probably agree. Commenting on educational research in the 1970s and 1980s, Willms (1992) notes, "I doubt whether another two decades of research will . . . help us specify a *model for all seasons*—a model that would apply to all schools in all communities at all times" (p. 65). A similar sentiment is credited to the famous mathematical statistician George Box, who is reported to have said that all mathematical models are false but some are useful (de Leeuw, 2004). In effect, Box warned that mathematical models that form the basis of all quantitative research are approximations only of reality, yet they can help us understand the underlying dynamics of a specific situation. Reynolds and Teddlie (2000) address the issue in the following way: "Sometimes the adoption of ideas from research has been somewhat uncritical; for example, the numerous attempts to apply findings from one specific context to another entirely different context when research has increasingly demonstrated significant contextual differences" (p. 216).

Even though the comments of Willms (1992) and Reynolds and Teddlie (2000) address the broader issue of school reform, they are quite applicable to research on classroom instruction. No amount of further research will provide an airtight model of instruction. There are simply too many variations in the situations, types of content, and types of students encountered across the K–12 continuum.

Riehl (2006) offers an interesting perspective as a result of her contrast of educational research with medical research. She notes that medical research employs a variety of methodologies that range from randomized clinical trials to single subject case studies. But the findings from these studies are anything but absolute. She explains: "Even the seemingly most determinant causal association in medicine (such as the relationship between smoking and lung cancer) is really just a probability" (p. 26). Riehl further comments:

> When reported in the popular media, medical research often appears as a blunt instrument, able to obliterate skeptics or opponents by the force of its evidence and arguments. . . . Yet repeated visits to the medical journals themselves can leave a much different impression. The serious medical journals convey the sense that medical research is an ongoing conversation and quest, punctuated occasionally by important findings that can and should alter practice, but more often characterized by continuing investigations. These investigations, taken cumulatively, can inform

the work of practitioners who are building their own local knowledge bases on medical care. (pp. 27–28)

The individual medical practitioner must sift through a myriad of studies and opinions to build a local knowledge base for interacting with patients. So too must the practitioner in education. Educational research is not a blunt instrument that shatters all doubt about best practice. Rather it provides general direction that must be interpreted by individual districts, schools, and teachers in terms of their unique circumstances.

In short, research will never be able to identify instructional strategies that work with every student in every class. The best research can do is tell us which strategies have a good chance (i.e., high probability) of working well with students. Individual classroom teachers must determine which strategies to employ with the right students at the right time. In effect, a good part of effective teaching is an art—hence the title, *The Art and Science of Teaching*.

Viewing teaching as part art and part science is not a new concept. Indeed, in his article entitled "In Pursuit of the Expert Pedagogue," Berliner (1986) ultimately concludes that effective teaching is a dynamic mixture of expertise in a vast array of instructional strategies combined with a profound understanding of the individual students in class and their needs at particular points in time. In effect, in different words, Berliner characterized effective teaching as part art and part science more than two decades ago.

A Confluence of Previous Works

To a great extent this text represents the confluence of suggestions from a number of previous works in which I have been involved. Specifically, the text *What Works in Schools* (Marzano, 2003b) presents a framework for understanding the characteristics of effective schools and effective teachers within those schools. Three general characteristics of effective teaching are articulated in that framework:

1. Use of effective instructional strategies
2. Use of effective classroom management strategies
3. Effective classroom curriculum design

The book *Classroom Instruction That Works* (Marzano, Pickering, & Pollock, 2001) and its related text *A Handbook for Classroom Instruction That Works* (Marzano, Norford, Paynter, Pickering, & Gaddy, 2001) address the first general characteristic. The book *Classroom Management That Works* (Marzano, 2003a) and its related text *A Handbook for Classroom Management That Works* (Marzano, Gaddy, Foseid, Foseid, & Marzano, 2005) address the second characteristic of effective teaching. The third characteristic is addressed in a chapter in *What Works in Schools* but not in a separate text. From the outset, I tried to acknowledge that these three characteristics are highly interdependent and that to separate them is an artificial distinction. As noted in the book *Classroom Instruction That Works,*

> We need to make one final comment on the limitations of the conclusions that educators can draw from reading this book. Although the title of this book speaks to instruction in a general sense, you should note that we have limited our focus to instructional strategies. There are certainly other aspects of classroom pedagogy that affect student achievement. In fact, we might postulate that effective pedagogy involves three related areas: (1) the instructional strategies used by the teacher, (2) the management techniques used by the teacher, and (3) the curriculum designed by the teacher. (Marzano, Pickering, & Pollock, 2001, pp. 9–10)

In short, the components of effective pedagogy can be symbolized in part as shown in Figure I.3.

This book combines my previous works on classroom instruction and management just cited along with information from *Classroom Assessment and Grading That Work* (Marzano, 2006). It does so in the context of a comprehensive framework of effective teaching. It is a framework offered as a model of what I believe every district or school should develop on its own. Specifically, I recommend that schools and districts generate their own models using this one as a starting point. There are other models, in addition to this one, districts and schools might consult in their efforts (see, for example, Good and Brophy, 2003; Mayer, 2003; Stronge, 2002).

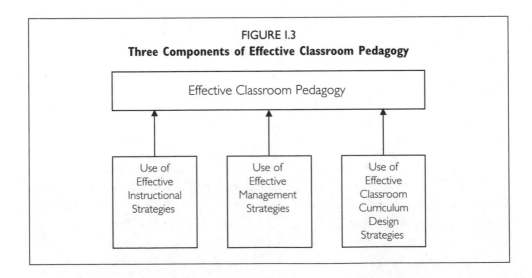

FIGURE I.3
Three Components of Effective Classroom Pedagogy

Effective Classroom Pedagogy

Use of Effective Instructional Strategies

Use of Effective Management Strategies

Use of Effective Classroom Curriculum Design Strategies

The comprehensive model offered in this book is articulated in the form of 10 design questions. They are listed in Figure I.4.

The remaining chapters address these questions in some detail. They represent a logical planning sequence for effective instructional design. Question 10 is an omnibus question in that it organizes the previous nine into a framework for thinking about units of instruction and the lessons within those units.

FIGURE I.4
Instructional Design Questions

1. What will I do to establish and communicate learning goals, track student progress, and celebrate success?

2. What will I do to help students effectively interact with new knowledge?

3. What will I do to help students practice and deepen their understanding of new knowledge?

4. What will I do to help students generate and test hypotheses about new knowledge?

5. What will I do to engage students?

6. What will I do to establish or maintain classroom rules and procedures?

7. What will I do to recognize and acknowledge adherence and lack of adherence to classroom rules and procedures?

8. What will I do to establish and maintain effective relationships with students?

9. What will I do to communicate high expectations for all students?

10. What will I do to develop effective lessons organized into a cohesive unit?

1

What will I do to establish and communicate learning goals, track student progress, and celebrate success?

Arguably the most basic issue a teacher can consider is what he or she will do to establish and communicate learning goals, track student progress, and celebrate success. In effect, this design question includes three distinct but highly related elements: (1) setting and communicating learning goals, (2) tracking student progress, and (3) celebrating success. These elements have a fairly straightforward relationship. Establishing and communicating learning goals are the starting place. After all, for learning to be effective, clear targets in terms of information and skill must be established. But establishing and communicating learning goals alone do not suffice to enhance student learning. Rather, once goals have been set it is natural and necessary to track progress. This assessment does not occur at the end of a unit only but throughout the unit. Finally, given that each student has made progress in one or more learning goals, the teacher and students can celebrate those successes.

In the Classroom

Let's start by looking at a classroom scenario as an example. Mr. Hutchins begins his unit on Hiroshima and Nagasaki by passing out a sheet of paper with the three learning goals for the unit:

- **Goal 1.** Students will understand the major events leading up to the development of the atomic bomb, starting with Einstein's publication of the theory of special relativity in 1905 and ending with the development of the two bombs Little Boy and Fat Man in 1945.

- **Goal 2.** Students will understand the major factors involved in making the decision to use atomic weapons on Hiroshima and Nagasaki.
- **Goal 3.** Students will understand the effects that using atomic weapons had on the outcome of World War II and the Japanese people.

At the bottom of the page is a line on which students record their own goal for the unit. To facilitate this step, Mr. Hutchins has a brief whole-class discussion and asks students to identify aspects of the content about which they want to learn more. One student says: "By the end of the unit I want to know about the Japanese Samurai." Mr. Hutchins explains that the Samurai were warriors centuries before World War II but that the Samurai spirit definitely was a part of the Japanese view of combat. He says that sounds like a great personal goal.

For each learning goal, Mr. Hutchins has created a rubric that spells out specific levels of understanding. He discusses each level with students and explains that these levels will become even more clear as the unit goes on. Throughout the unit, Mr. Hutchins assesses students' progress on the learning goals using quizzes, tests, and even informal assessments such as brief discussions with students. Each assessment is scored using the rubric distributed on the first day.

As formative information is collected regarding student progress on these goals, students chart their progress using graphs. At first some students are dismayed by the fact that their initial scores are quite low—1s and 2s on the rubric. But throughout the unit students see their scores gradually rise. They soon realize that even if you begin the unit with a score of 0 for a particular learning goal, you can end up with a score of 4.

By the end of the unit virtually all students have demonstrated that they have learned, even though everyone does not end up with the same final score. Progress is celebrated for each student. For each learning goal, Mr. Hutchins recognizes those students who gained one point on the scale, each student who gained two points on the scale, and so on. Virtually every student in class has a sense of accomplishment by the unit's end.

Research and Theory

As demonstrated by the scenario for Mr. Hutchins's class, this design question includes a number of components, one of which is goal setting. Figure 1.1 summarizes the findings from a number of synthesis studies on goal setting.

To interpret these findings, it is important to understand the concept of an effect size. Briefly, in this text an effect size tells you how much larger (or smaller) you might expect the average score to be in a class where students use a particular

FIGURE 1.1 **Research Results for Goal Setting**				
Synthesis Study	Focus	Number of Effect Sizes	Average Effect Size	Percentile Gain
Wise & Okey, 1983[a]	General effects of setting goals or objectives	3 25	1.37 0.48	41 18
Lipsey & Wilson, 1993[b]	General effects of setting goals or objectives	204	0.55	21
Walberg, 1999	General effects of setting goals or objectives	21	0.40	16

[a] Two effect sizes are listed because of the manner in which effect sizes are reported. Readers should consult that study for more details.

[b] The review includes a wide variety of ways and contexts in which goals might be used.

strategy as compared to a class where the strategy is not used. In Figure 1.1 three studies are reported, and effect sizes are reported for each. Each of these studies is a synthesis study, in that it summarizes the results from a number of other studies. For example, the Lipsey and Wilson (1993) study synthesizes findings from 204 reports. Consider the average effect size of 0.55 from those 204 effect sizes. This means that in the 204 studies they examined, the average score in classes where goal setting was effectively employed was 0.55 standard deviations greater than the average score in classes where goal setting was not employed. Perhaps the easiest way to interpret this effect size is to examine the last column of Figure 1.1, which reports percentile gains. For the Lipsey and Wilson effect size of 0.55, the percentile gain is 21. This means that the average score in classes where goal setting was effectively employed would be 21 percentile points higher than the average score in classes where goal setting was not employed. (For a more detailed discussion of effect sizes and their interpretations, see Marzano, Waters, & McNulty, 2005.)

One additional point should be made about the effect sizes reported in this text. They are averages. Of the 204 effect sizes, some are much larger than the 0.55 average, and some are much lower. In fact, some are below zero, which indicates that the classrooms where goals were not set outperformed the classrooms where goals were set. This is almost always the case with research regarding instructional strategies. Seeing effect sizes like those reported in Figure 1.1 tells us that goal setting has a general tendency to enhance learning. However, educators must remember that the goal-setting strategy and every other strategy mentioned in this book must be done well and at the right time to produce positive effects on student learning.

As illustrated in Mr. Hutchins's scenario, feedback is intimately related to goal setting. Figure 1.2 reports the findings from synthesis studies on feedback.

Notice that the effect sizes in Figure 1.2 tend to be a bit larger than those reported in Figure 1.1. This makes intuitive sense. Goal setting is the beginning step only in this design question. Clear goals establish an initial target. Feedback provides students with information regarding their progress toward that target. Goal setting and feedback used in tandem are probably more powerful than either one in isolation. In fact, without clear goals it might be difficult to provide effective feedback.

Formative assessment is another line of research related to the research on feedback. Teachers administer formative assessments while students are learning

FIGURE 1.2
Research Results for Feedback

Synthesis Study	Focus	Number of Effect Sizes	Average Effect Size	Percentile Gain
Bloom, 1976	General effects of feedback	8	1.47	43
Lysakowski & Walberg, 1981[a]	General effects of feedback	39	1.15	37
Lysakowski & Walberg, 1982	General effects of feedback	94	0.97	33
Haller, Child, & Walberg, 1988[b]	General effects of feedback	115	0.71	26
Tennenbaum & Goldring, 1989	General effects of feedback	16	0.66	25
Bangert-Drowns, Kulik, Kulik, & Morgan, 1991	General effects of feedback	58	0.26	10
Kumar, 1991[c]	General effects of feedback	5	1.35	41
Walberg, 1999	General effects of feedback	20	0.94	33
Haas, 2005	General effects of feedback	19	0.55	21

[a] Reported in Fraser, Walberg, Welch, & Hattie, 1987.

[b] Feedback was embedded in general metacognitive strategies.

[c] The dependent variable was engagement.

new information or new skills. In contrast, teachers administer summative assessments at the end of learning experiences, for example, at the end of the semester or the school year. Major reviews of research on the effects of formative assessment indicate that it might be one of the more powerful weapons in a teacher's arsenal. To illustrate, as a result of a synthesis of more than 250 studies, Black and Wiliam (1998) describe the impact of effective formative assessment in the following way:

> The research reported here shows conclusively that formative assessment does improve learning. The gains in achievement appear to be quite considerable, and as noted earlier, amongst the largest ever reported for educational interventions. As an illustration of just how big these gains are, an effect size of 0.7, if it could be achieved on a nationwide scale, would be equivalent to raising the mathematics attainment score of an "average" country like England, New Zealand, or the United States into the "top five" after the Pacific rim countries of Singapore, Korea, Japan, and Hong Kong. (p. 61)

One strong finding from the research on formative assessment is that the frequency of assessments is related to student academic achievement. This is demonstrated in the meta-analysis by Bangert-Drowns, Kulik, and Kulik (1991). Figure 1.3 depicts their analysis of findings from 29 studies on the frequency of assessments.

To interpret Figure 1.3, assume that we are examining the learning of a particular student who is involved in a 15-week course. (For a discussion of how this figure was constructed, see Marzano, 2006, Technical Note 2.2.) Figure 1.3 depicts the increase in learning one might expect when differing quantities of formative assessments are employed during that 15-week session. If five assessments are employed, a gain in student achievement of 20 percentile points is expected. If 25 assessments are administered, a gain in student achievement of 28.5 percentile points is expected, and so on. This same phenomenon is reported by

FIGURE 1.3
Achieved Gain Associated with Number of Assessments over 15 Weeks

Number of Assessments	Effect Size	Percentile Gain
0	0	0
1	0.34	13.5
5	0.53	20.0
10	0.60	22.5
15	0.66	24.5
20	0.71	26.0
25	0.78	28.5
30	0.82	29.0

Note: Effect sizes are from data reported by Bangert-Drowns, Kulik, & Kulik, 1991.

Fuchs and Fuchs (1986) in their meta-analysis of 21 controlled studies. They report that providing two assessments per week results in an effect size of 0.85 or a percentile gain of 30 points.

A third critical component of this design question is the area of research on reinforcing effort and providing recognition for accomplishments. Reinforcing effort means that students see a direct link between how hard they try at a particular task and their success at that task. Over the years, research has provided evidence for this intuitively appealing notion, as summarized in Figure 1.4.

Among other things, reinforcing effort means that students see a direct relationship between how hard they work and how much they learn. Quite obviously, formative assessments aid this dynamic in that students can observe the increase in their learning over time.

Providing recognition for student learning is a bit of a contentious issue—at least on the surface. Figure 1.5 reports the results of two synthesis studies on the effects of praise on student performance. The results reported by Wilkinson (1981) are not very compelling, in that praise does not seem to have much of an effect on student achievement. The 6 percentile point gain shown in those studies is not that large. On the other hand, the results reported by Bloom (1976) are noteworthy; a 21 percentile point gain is considerable. A plausible reason for the discrepancy is that these two studies were very general in nature, in that praise was defined in a wide variety of ways across studies.

FIGURE 1.4
Research Results for Reinforcing Effort

Synthesis Study	Focus	Number of Effect Sizes	Average Effect Size	Percentile Gain
Stipek & Weisz, 1981	Reinforcing effort[a]	17	0.54	21
Schunk & Cox, 1986	Reinforcing effort	3	0.93	32
Kumar, 1991[b]	Reinforcing effort	6	1.72	46
Hattie, Biggs, & Purdie, 1996[c]	Reinforcing effort	8 2 2 2	1.42 0.57 2.14 0.97	42 22 48 33

[a] These studies also dealt with students' sense of control.

[b] The dependent variable was engagement.

[c] Multiple effect sizes are listed because of the manner in which effect sizes are reported. Readers should consult that study for more details.

FIGURE 1.5 Research Results on Praise				
Synthesis Study	Focus	Number of Effect Sizes	Average Effect Size	Percentile Gain
Bloom, 1976	General effects of praise	12	0.54	21
Wilkinson, 1981[a]	General effects of praise	14	0.16	6

[a] Reported in Fraser et al., 1987.

Other synthesis studies—particularly research on the effects of reward on intrinsic motivation—have been more focused in their analyses. Figure 1.6 summarizes findings from two major synthesis studies on the topic.

Among other things, both studies in Figure 1.6 examined the impact of what is commonly referred to as *extrinsic rewards* on what is referred to as *intrinsic motivation*. Both are somewhat fuzzy concepts that allow significant variation in how they are defined. (For a discussion, see Cameron & Pierce, 1994.) Considered at face value though, external reward is typically thought of as some type of token or payment for success. Intrinsic motivation is necessarily defined in contrast to extrinsic motivation. According to Cameron and Pierce (1994):

> Intrinsically motivated behaviors are ones for which there is no apparent reward except the activity itself (Deci, 1971). Extrinsically motivated behaviors, on the other hand, refer to behaviors in which an external controlling variable [such as reward] can be readily identified. (p. 364)

The average effect sizes in Figure 1.6 show an uneven pattern—two effect sizes are below zero, and two effect sizes are above zero. However, the two effect

FIGURE 1.6 Research Results on Rewards				
Synthesis Study	Measure Used to Assess Intrinsic Motivation	Number of Effect Sizes	Average Effect Size	Percentile Gain
Cameron & Pierce, 1994	Free-choice behavior	57	−0.06	−2
	Interest/attitude	47	0.21	8
Deci, Koestner, & Ryan, 2001	Free-choice behavior	101	−0.24	−9
	Interest/attitude	84	0.04	2

sizes below zero are for studies that used free-choice behavior as the measure of intrinsic motivation. Typically these studies examine whether students (i.e., subjects) tend to engage in the task for which they are being rewarded even when they are not being asked to do the task. In both synthesis studies, the effect of extrinsic reward on free-choice behavior was negative. In contrast, positive effects (albeit small for the Deci, Koestner, & Ryan, 2001, study) are reported when the measure of intrinsic motivation is students' interest. Typically student interest is assessed by some form of self-report.

The contradictory findings for student interest versus student free-choice behavior do not provide any clear direction, but they do demonstrate the highly equivocal nature of the research on rewards and intrinsic motivation. A possible answer is found, however, by examining more carefully the distinction between free-time behavior and interest, as shown in Figure 1.7.

This research indicates that when verbal rewards are employed (e.g., positive comments about good performance, acknowledgments of knowledge gain) the trend is positive when intrinsic motivation is measured either by interest/attitude or by free-choice behavior. Even these results must be interpreted cautiously. Certainly, factors such as the age of students and the context in which rewards (verbal or otherwise) are given can influence their effect on students. It is safe to say, however, that when used appropriately verbal rewards and perhaps

FIGURE 1.7
Influence of Abstract Versus Tangible Rewards

Synthesis Study	Measure Used to Assess Intrinsic Motivation	Number of Effect Sizes	Average Effect Size	Percentile Gain
Cameron & Pierce, 1994	Verbal on interest/attitude	15	0.45	17
	Verbal on free time	15	0.42	16
	Tangible on interest/attitude	37	0.09	4
	Tangible on free time	51	−0.20	−8
Deci, Koestner, & Ryan, 2001	Verbal on interest/attitude	21	0.31	12
	Verbal on free time	21	0.33	13
	Tangible on interest/attitude	92	−0.34	−13
	Tangible on free time	70	−0.07	−3

also tangible rewards can positively affect student achievement. Deci, Ryan, and Koestner (2001) share the following observations:

> As our research and theory have always suggested, there are ways of using even tangible rewards that are less likely to have a negative effect and may, under limited circumstances, have a positive effect on intrinsic motivation. However, the use of rewards as a motivational strategy is clearly a risky proposition, so we continue to argue for thinking about educational practices that will engage students' interest and support the development of their self-regulation. We believe that it is an injustice to the integrity of our teachers and students to simply advocate that educators focus on the use of rewards to control behavior rather than grapple with the deeper issues of (a) why many students are not interested in learning within our educational system and (b) how intrinsic motivation and self-regulation can be promoted among these students. (p. 50)

Action Steps
Action Step 1. Make a Distinction Between Learning Goals and Learning Activities or Assignments

Even though the term *learning goal* is commonly used by practitioners, there appears to be some confusion as to its exact nature. For example, consider the following list, which typifies learning goals one might find in teachers' planning books:

- Students will successfully complete the exercises in the back of Chapter 3.
- Students will create a metaphor representing the food pyramid.
- Students will be able to determine subject/verb agreement in a variety of simple, compound, and complete sentences.
- Students will understand the defining characteristics of fables, fairy tales, and tall tales.
- Students will investigate the relationship between speed of air flow and lift provided by an airplane wing.

Some of these statements—the first, second, and last—involve activities as opposed to learning goals. As the name implies, activities are things students do. As we will see in Design Questions 2, 3, and 4, activities are a critical part of effective teaching. They constitute the means by which the ends or learning goals are accomplished. However, they are not learning goals.

A learning goal is a statement of what students will know or be able to do. For example, Figure 1.8 lists learning goals for science, language arts, mathematics, and social studies, which differ from the related activities.

The learning goals presented in Figure 1.8 have a distinct format that emphasizes the knowledge students would potentially gain. Teachers provide the related activities to help students attain those learning goals. I will explain how some

	FIGURE 1.8 **Learning Goals and Activities**	
Subject	Learning Goals	Activities
Science	Students will understand that • The sun is the largest body in the solar system. • The moon and earth rotate on their axes. • The moon orbits the earth while the earth orbits the sun.	Students will watch the video on the relationship between the earth and the moon and the place of these bodies in the solar system.
Language Arts	Students will be able to • Sound out words that are not in their sight vocabulary but are known to them.	Students will observe the teacher sounding and blending a word.
Mathematics	Students will be able to • Solve equations with one variable.	Students will practice solving 10 equations in cooperative groups.
Social Studies	Students will understand • The defining characteristics of the barter system.	Students will describe what the United Sates might be like if it were based on the barter system as opposed to a monetary system.

activities are designed to introduce students to new content in Chapter 2, how some activities are designed to help students practice and deepen their understanding of new content in Chapter 3, and how some activities are designed to help students generate and test hypotheses about content in Chapter 4.

Teachers would most likely use the science and language arts activities in Figure 1.8 to introduce new content to students. The mathematics activity would most likely serve as a practice activity. The social studies activity would most likely promote generating and testing hypotheses.

In general, I recommend that learning goals be stated in one of the following formats:

Students will be able to_____.

or

Students will understand_____.

These formats represent different types of knowledge and have been suggested by those who have constructed taxonomies of learning (Anderson et al., 2001; Marzano & Kendall, 2007). The reason for the two formats is that content knowledge can be organized into two broad categories: declarative knowledge and procedural knowledge.

Chapter 4 addresses these two types of knowledge in some depth. Briefly, though, declarative knowledge is informational in nature. Procedural knowledge involves strategies, skills, and processes. In Figure 1.8, the learning goals for science and social studies are declarative or informational in nature. Hence they employ the stem "students will understand. . . ." The mathematics and language arts goals are procedural or strategy oriented. Hence they employ the stem "students will be able to. . . ." Occasionally a learning goal involves a substantial amount of declarative and procedural knowledge. In such cases, the following format can be useful:

Students will understand _____ and be able to _____.

To illustrate, the following 3rd grade learning goal for number sense includes both declarative and procedural knowledge: "Students will understand the defining characteristics of whole numbers, decimals, and fractions with like denominators, and will be able to convert between equivalent forms as well as represent factors and multiples of whole numbers through 100."

Action Step 2. Write a Rubric or Scale for Each Learning Goal

Once learning goals have been established, the next step is to state them in rubric format. There are many different approaches to designing rubrics. The one presented here is explained in depth in the book *Classroom Assessment and Grading That Work* (Marzano, 2006) and has some research supporting its utility (see Flicek, 2005a, 2005b; Marzano, 2002). For reasons articulated in *Classroom Assessment and Grading That Work,* I prefer to use the term *scale* as opposed to the term *rubric.* Figure 1.9 shows what I refer to as the *simplified scale.*

FIGURE 1.9 **Simplified Scale**
Score 4.0: In addition to Score 3.0, in-depth inferences and applications that go beyond what was taught.
Score 3.0: No major errors or omissions regarding any of the information and/or processes (simple or complex) that were explicitly taught.
Score 2.0: No major errors or omissions regarding the simpler details and processes but major errors or omissions regarding the more complex ideas and processes.
Score 1.0: With help, a partial understanding of some of the simpler details and processes and some of the more complex ideas and processes.
Score 0.0: Even with help, no understanding or skill demonstrated.

The simplified scale contains five whole-point values only—4.0, 3.0, 2.0, 1.0, and 0.0—as contrasted with a more detailed scale that has half-point scores—3.5, 2.5, 1.5, and 0.5. Although the simplified scale is generally less precise than the complete scale, I have found it a good starting place for teachers who are not familiar with using scales of this design. Additionally, in some situations half-point scores are difficult to discern or simply do not make much sense.

To demonstrate how the scale shown in Figure 1.9 can be used, assume that a health teacher wishes to score an assessment on the topic of obesity. The lowest score value on the scale is a 0.0, representing no knowledge of the topic—even with help the student demonstrates no understanding. A score of 1.0 indicates that *with help* the student shows partial knowledge of the simpler details and processes as well as the more complex ideas and processes regarding obesity. To be assigned a score of 2.0, the student independently demonstrates understanding and skill related to the simpler details and processes but not the more complex ideas and processes regarding obesity. For example, the student knows the general definition of obesity and some of the more obvious causes. A score of 3.0 indicates that the student demonstrates understanding of the simple *and* complex content *that was taught in class.* For example, the student understands the relationship between obesity and the chances of developing diseases such as heart disease as an adult. Additionally, the student understands risk factors for becoming obese as an adult even if you are not obese as a child. Finally, a score of 4.0 indicates that the student demonstrates inferences and applications that *go beyond what was taught in class.* For example, the student is able to identify his or her risk for becoming obese and personal actions necessary to avoid obesity, even though those actions were not specifically addressed in class.

The simplified scale has intuitive appeal and is easy to use. However, measurement theory tells us that the more values a scale has, the more precise the measurement (Embretson & Reise, 2000). To illustrate, assume that a teacher used a scale with only two values—pass and fail—to score a test. Also assume that to pass the test students had to answer 60 percent of the items correctly. In this scenario, the student who answered all items correctly would receive the same score (pass) as the student who answered 60 percent of the items correctly. Similarly, the student who answered no items correctly would receive the same score (fail) as the student who answered 59 percent of the items correctly. In general, the more score points on a scale, the more precise that scale can be. Figure 1.10 presents the complete scale.

The scale in Figure 1.10 has half-point scores, whereas the scale in Figure 1.9 does not. The half-point scores are set off to the right to signify that they describe student response patterns between the whole-point scores and therefore allow for more

---

FIGURE 1.10
Complete Scale

Score 4.0: In addition to Score 3.0 performance, in-depth inferences and applications that go beyond what was taught.

Score 3.5: In addition to Score 3.0 performance, partial success at inferences and applications that go beyond what was taught.

Score 3.0: No major errors or omissions regarding any of the information and/or processes (simple or complex) that were explicitly taught.

Score 2.5: No major errors or omissions regarding the simpler details and processes and partial knowledge of the more complex ideas and processes.

Score 2.0: No major errors or omissions regarding the simpler details and processes but major errors or omissions regarding the more complex ideas and processes.

Score 1.5: Partial knowledge of the simpler details and processes but major errors or omissions regarding the more complex ideas and processes.

Score 1.0: With help, a partial understanding of some of the simpler details and processes and some of the more complex ideas and processes.

Score 0.5: With help, a partial understanding of some of the simpler details and processes but not the more complex ideas and processes.

Score 0.0: Even with help, no understanding or skill demonstrated.

---

precision in scoring an assessment. The half-point scores allow for partial credit to be assigned to items. To illustrate, a score of 3.0 indicates that a student has answered all items or tasks correctly that involve simpler details and processes as well as all items or tasks that involve more complex ideas and processes. A score of 2.0 indicates that the student has answered all items or tasks correctly that involve simpler details and processes but has missed all items or tasks that involve more complex ideas and processes. However, what score should be assigned if a student has answered all items or tasks correctly regarding simpler details and processes and *some* items or tasks correctly involving more complex ideas and processes or has received *partial credit* on those items or tasks? Using the simplified scale a teacher would have to assign a score of 2.0. Using the complete scale a teacher would assign a score value of 2.5. The second option allows for much more precision of measurement.

The complete scale, then, is a logical extension of the simplified scale. Teachers can use them interchangeably. When the type of assessment allows for determining partial credit, the teacher uses the complete scale. When the type of assessment does not allow for determining partial credit, the simplified scale is used.

The generic scales depicted in Figures 1.9 and 1.10 are easily translated into scales for specific learning goals. To illustrate, consider Figure 1.11, which shows a scale for the previously mentioned 3rd grade learning goal for number sense.

	FIGURE 1.11 **Scale for Number Sense in 3rd Grade**
Score 4.0	In addition to Score 3.0 performance, in-depth inferences and applications that go beyond what was taught.
Score 3.5	In addition to Score 3.0 performance, partial success at inferences and applications that go beyond what was taught.
Score 3.0	**The student demonstrates number sense by** • ordering and comparing whole numbers (millions), decimals (thousandths), and fractions with like denominators • converting between equivalent forms of fractions, decimals, and whole numbers • finding and representing factors and multiples of whole numbers through 100 **The student exhibits no major errors or omissions.**
Score 2.5	No major errors or omissions regarding the simpler details and processes and partial knowledge of the more complex ideas and processes.

Score 2.0	**The student exhibits no major errors or omissions regarding the simpler details and processes:**
	• basic terminology, for example—
	  • millions
	  • thousandths
	  • like denominator
	  • factor
	  • multiple
	• basic solutions, for example—
	  • 5.15 is greater than 5.005
	  • 3/4 is the same as 0.75
	  • 4 is a factor of 12
	However, the student exhibits major errors or omissions regarding the more complex ideas and processes stated in score 3.0.

Score 1.5	Partial knowledge of the simpler details and processes but major errors or omissions regarding the more complex ideas and processes.
Score 1.0	**With help, a partial understanding of some of the simpler details and processes and some of the more complex ideas and processes.**
Score 0.5	With help, a partial understanding of some of the simpler details and processes but not the more complex ideas and processes.
Score 0.0	**Even with help, no understanding or skill demonstrated.**

Source: Adapted from Marzano & Haystead, in press.

The scale in Figure 1.11 is basically identical to the generic form of the complete scale in Figure 1.10 except that the score values 3.0 and 2.0 identify specific elements. Although it is also possible to fill in specific elements for the score value of 4.0, I have found that many school and district leaders wish to leave this up to individual teachers. For a more detailed discussion, the reader should consult *Classroom Assessment and Grading That Work* (Marzano, 2006). When learner goals have been articulated in scale format as in Figure 1.11, the teacher and students have clear direction about instructional targets as well as descriptions of levels of understanding and performance for those targets.

Action Step 3. Have Students Identify Their Own Learning Goals

One way to enhance student involvement in an instructional unit's subject matter is to ask students to identify something that interests them beyond the teacher-identified learning goals. During a unit on habitats, for example, a particular student might decide that she wants to find out about a particular animal—the falcons she sometimes sees flying over the field next to her bedroom. Even though personal applications might not seem obvious to students at first, a little guidance can go a long way in demonstrating to students that they can relate their own interests to the content addressed in class. To illustrate, a teacher once shared with me a personal goal a student had identified during a mathematics unit on polynomials. The student wanted to know what types of polynomials were used when rating quarterbacks in football. As a result of some Internet research, the student identified and could explain three formulas for rating quarterbacks:

National Football League Quarterback Rating Formula

$a = (((\text{Comp/Att}) \times 100) - 30) / 20$
$b = ((\text{TDs/Att}) \times 100) / 5$
$c = (9.5 - ((\text{Int/Att}) \times 100)) / 4$
$d = ((\text{Yards/Att}) - 3) / 4$
a, b, c, and d cannot be greater than 2.375 or less than 0.
QB Rating $= (a + b + c + d) / 0.06$

Arena Football League Quarterback Rating Formula

$a = (((\text{Comp/Att}) \times 100) - 30) / 20$
$b = ((\text{TDs/Att}) \times 100) / (20/3)$
$c = (9.5 - ((\text{Int/Att}) \times 100)) / 4$
$d = ((\text{Yards/Att}) - 3) / 4$
a, b, c, and d cannot be greater than 2.375 or less than 0.
QB Rating $= (a + b + c + d) / 0.06$

National Collegiate Athletic League Quarterback Rating Formula

a = (Comp/Att) × 100
b = (TDs/Att) × 100
c = (Int/Att) × 100
d = Yards/Att
QB Rating = a + (3.3 × b) − (2 × c) + (8.4 × d)

Key: Comp = pass completions, Att = pass attempts, TDs = completed touchdown passes, Int = interceptions thrown, Yards = passing yards.

Once students have identified their personal goals, they should write them in a format similar to the one used by the teacher:

When this unit is completed I will better understand_____.

or

When this unit is completed I will be able to_____.

Students might also use a simplified version of the scale to keep track of their progress:

4. I did better than I thought I would do.
3. I accomplished my goal.
2. I didn't accomplish everything I want to, but I learned quite a bit.
1. I tried but didn't really learn much.
0. I didn't really try to accomplish my goal.

Action Step 4. Assess Students Using a Formative Approach

As described in the research and theory section, formative assessment is not only a powerful measurement tool but also a powerful instructional tool because it allows students to observe their own progress. As I explained, formative assessments are used while students are learning new content. In the case of a unit of instruction, formative assessments are used from the beginning to the end. The scale discussed in Action Step 2 is designed specifically for formative assessment because each score on the scale describes specific progress toward a specific learning goal. That is, a score of 4.0 indicates that the student has gone beyond the information and skill taught by the teacher. A score of 3.0 indicates that the student has learned the target knowledge as articulated by the teacher. A score of 2.0 indicates that the student understands or can perform the simpler information and skills relative to the learning goal but not the more complex information or processes. A score of 1.0 indicates that on his or her own the student does not demonstrate understanding of or skill regarding the learning goal, but with help the student does. Finally a score of 0.0 indicates that even with help the student does not demonstrate understanding or skill relative to the learning goal.

To design a formative assessment for a particular learning goal, a teacher must ensure that the assessment contains items or tasks that apply to levels 2.0, 3.0, and 4.0. For example, reconsider the scale for number sense reported in Figure 1.11. To design an assessment regarding this topic, the teacher would make sure she has items that represent score values of 4.0, 3.0, and 2.0. She would include some items or tasks on the test that require students to order and compare whole numbers to the millions, decimals to thousandths, and fractions with like denominators. She would include items or tasks that require students to convert between equivalent forms of fractions, decimals, and whole numbers. Likewise she would include some items or tasks that require students to represent factors and multiples of whole numbers through 100. Success on these tasks would indicate a score value of 3.0. To determine whether students should receive a score value of 2.0, the teacher would include items that address simpler aspects of the learning goal. She might assess knowledge of basic terminology such as *millions, thousandths, like denominator, factor,* and *multiple.* Finally, to determine whether students deserve a score value of 4.0, she would include items or tasks that go beyond what she had addressed in class. For example, she might include items or tasks that require students to convert composite numbers that had not been addressed in class.

Scoring assessments designed around the simplified or complete scale is a matter of examining the pattern of responses for each student. (For a detailed discussion, see *Classroom Assessment and Grading That Work* [Marzano, 2006].) In the beginning of the unit, students would most likely receive low scores on these assessments. However, by the end of the unit students should show growth in their scores. This is at the heart of formative assessment—examining the gradual increase in knowledge for specific learning goals throughout a unit.

Action Step 5. Have Students Chart Their Progress on Each Learning Goal

Because formative assessments are designed to provide a view of students' learning over time, one useful activity is to have students chart their own progress on each learning goal. To do so, the teacher provides a blank chart for each learning goal that resembles the one shown in Figure 1.12.

The chart in Figure 1.12 has already been filled out. The first column represents an assessment given by the teacher on October 5. This student received a score of 1.5 on that assessment. The second column represents the assessment on

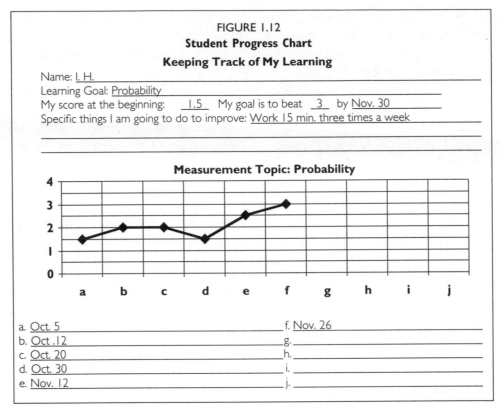

FIGURE 1.12
Student Progress Chart
Keeping Track of My Learning

Name: I. H.

Learning Goal: Probability

My score at the beginning: __1.5__ My goal is to beat __3__ by Nov. 30

Specific things I am going to do to improve: Work 15 min. three times a week

Measurement Topic: Probability

a. Oct. 5   f. Nov. 26
b. Oct .12   g.
c. Oct. 20   h.
d. Oct. 30   i.
e. Nov. 12   j.

Source: Reprinted from Marzano, 2006, p. 90.

October 12. This student received a score of 2.0 on that assessment; and so on. Having each student keep track of his or her scores on learning goals in this fashion provides them with visual views of their progress. It also allows for powerful discussions between teacher and students. The teacher can discuss progress with each student regarding each learning goal. Also, in a tracking system such as this one the student and teacher are better able to communicate with parents regarding the student's progress in specific areas of information and skill. Finally, note that the chart has places for students to identify the progress they wish to make and the things they are willing to do to make that progress.

Action Step 6. Recognize and Celebrate Growth

One of the most powerful aspects of formative assessment is that it allows students to see their progress over time, as depicted in Figure 1.12. In a system like this one, virtually every student will succeed in the sense that each student will increase his or her knowledge relative to specific learning goals. One student might have started with a score of 2.0 on a specific learning goal and then increased to a score of 3.5; another student might have started with a 1.0 and increased to a 2.5—both have learned. *Knowledge gain,* then, is the currency of student success in a formative assessment system. Focusing on knowledge gain also provides a legitimate way to recognize and celebrate—as opposed to reward—success. Recall the discussion in the research section regarding rewards and intrinsic motivation. Whereas tangible reward has weak support for its use, verbal reward has moderate support. That research notwithstanding, even verbal recognition when used as a way to control student behavior externally is questionable. This action step recommends that knowledge gain for each student be recognized and celebrated. Such behavior seems more directly aligned with Deci, Ryan, and Koestner's (2001) call to acknowledge students in a way that promotes self-regulation.

To illustrate, a chart like the one in Figure 1.13 can be constructed for each student. This figure indicates that the student has gained 2 points on learning goal 1, 0.5 points on learning goal 2, and 2.5 points on learning goal 3. When knowledge gain has been recognized, it can be legitimately celebrated. For example, teachers might hold informal and verbal celebrations by asking all students who gained 0.5 points for a specific learning goal to stand and be acknowledged by a

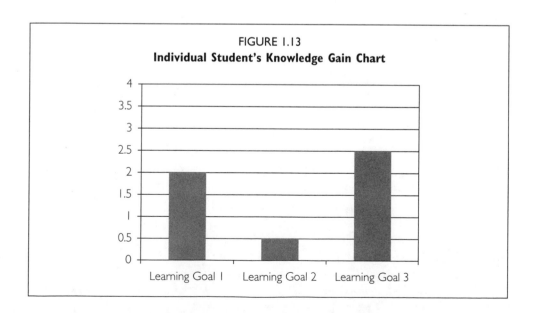

FIGURE 1.13
Individual Student's Knowledge Gain Chart

round of applause from their classmates, then all students who gained 1.0 points, and so on. Such celebrations could occur for each learning goal and at the end of each unit or grading period. In this context of recognition and celebration, teachers could also acknowledge those students who obtained high scores (i.e., scores of 3.0 and higher) on learning goals.

Summary

When considering the first instructional design question—What will I do to establish and communicate learning goals, track student progress, and celebrate success?—teachers should think about three basic elements. First, establishing and communicating learning goals involves distinguishing between learning goals and learning activities and then writing learning goals in a suitable format. Second, tracking student progress involves using formative assessments and a scale designed specifically for formative assessments. It also involves charting student progress on individual learning goals. Third, celebrating success involves recognizing and acknowledging students' knowledge gains.

2

What will I do to help students effectively interact with new knowledge?

Throughout a well-structured unit teachers are continually providing input to students regarding new content. Sometimes this occurs in the form of answers to questions, discussions with individual students, discussions with small groups of students, and other types of rather spontaneous interactions. At other times, input is planned as a part of the overall design of the unit. For example, a teacher might plan to have students engage in one or more of the following activities: read a section of the textbook, listen to a lecture, observe a demonstration, be part of a demonstration, or watch a video. I refer to these designed input activities as critical-input experiences. If students understand the content provided in these critical-input experiences, they have a good start toward the accomplishment of learning goals. To increase students' understanding of the content inherent in these experiences, teachers should facilitate students' actively processing the content.

In the Classroom

Let's return to the classroom scenario described in the previous chapter. One of the first things Mr. Hutchins asks students to do is view a video on Hiroshima and Nagasaki. Prior to showing the video, he asks students if they have ever seen or read anything about these two cities in Japan and what happened to them at the end of World War II. He emphasizes that he does not expect them to know anything yet but wonders if some students have ideas about what occurred. As students volunteer responses, Mr. Hutchins summarizes them briefly on the whiteboard. He then organizes students into groups of three. Each member of the group is assigned a letter—A, B, or C. Mr. Hutchins tells students that they should feel free to record ideas in their academic notebooks as they watch, but he cautions that they should not try to take notes per se. He says:

> Just watch the video and try to understand what is being presented. We'll watch this in small bits or chunks about four minutes each, and you will have time to talk about each little bit as we go through it. You'll also have time to take notes later when you have a better understanding of the information.

After students have viewed the first four-minute chunk, Mr. Hutchins turns off the video and asks Student A in each group to summarize what he or she remembers from the four-minute interval. The other two students in each group are invited to add to what Student A has said. Mr. Hutchins also asks if any students have questions about what they viewed. He answers these questions briefly and then allows a few moments for students to record ideas in their notebooks. Again, he cautions them not to spend too much energy on these notes because they will have time for notes later. He then turns the video back on for another four minutes and repeats the process with Student B in each group. This is done one more time until all three students have had a chance to be the one who summarizes the content.

Next Mr. Hutchins asks students some inferential questions that require them to go beyond what was presented in the video. This step is done as a whole-class activity. After the inferential questions have been addressed, Mr. Hutchins provides each group time to summarize what they have learned. He explains to students that now is a good time to make more detailed entries in their academic notebooks. He also asks each group to design a graphic representation depicting what they have learned. Groups are invited to present their graphic representations and summaries to the whole class. Finally, each student is asked to respond to the following question: What were you right about in terms of your initial understanding of the events at Hiroshima and Nagasaki? These answers are recorded in their academic notebooks.

Research and Theory

Over the years there have been many discussions regarding the need for students to process new information in ways that make personal sense. Under such banners as constructivism and brain research, books have discussed the need for active processing on the part of students (Berman, 2001; Brandt, 1998; Brooks & Brooks, 1999, 2001; Caine & Caine, 1991, 1997; Jensen, 2005; Sousa, 2001; Sylwester & Margulies, 1998; Wolfe, 2001). These works have provided useful insights into the nature of learning. The basic generalization has been that learners must be actively engaged in the processing of information and that the teaching and learning process involves an interaction among the teacher, the students, and the content. Researchers Cobb, Yackel, and Wood (1992) describe the process in the following way: "The teaching–learning process is interactive in nature and involves the implicit and explicit negotiation of . . . meanings" (p. 5). However, knowledge construction or the negotiation of meaning is not done in isolation. Indeed, a number of cognitive psychologists offer support for the position that teachers must provide guidance as to the important aspects of the new content as well as facilitate the processing of that content by students (Anderson, Greeno, Reder, & Simon, 2000; Anderson, Reder, & Simon, 1995, 1996; Bruer, 1993, 1997). What is needed then is a comprehensive approach that allows for student construction of meaning while interacting with the content, the teacher, and other students. Fortunately, research and theory provide guidance as to the components of such an approach.

Critical-Input Experiences

One aspect of a comprehensive approach is the identification on the teacher's part of critical-input experiences—those experiences that present important new content to students. The work of Nuthall and his colleagues (Nuthall, 1999; Nuthall & Alton-Lee, 1995) is particularly relevant here. Nuthall studied the learning of elementary students who had been exposed to the same learning experiences regarding science and social studies in terms of their depth of understanding and the longevity of their understanding. Even though all students had the same basic experiences, they recalled different things, and for those things they recalled in common they demonstrated different levels of understanding. Some of the reasons for these differences were variations in the types of optional activities students selected and levels of engagement in the key learning experiences. One inference that can be made from Nuthall's work is that those learning experiences that are critical to understanding new content should be identified and highlighted by teachers. This also makes sense from the perspective of the work on comprehending written material (Kintsch, 1974, 1979; van Dijk, 1977, 1980; van Dijk & Kintsch, 1983). Information can be organized many different ways. If one particular way provides the highest utility in terms of students' understanding of the content, then guidance should be provided to students as to the critical aspects of the information.

Interestingly, Nuthall (Nuthall, 1999; Nuthall & Alton-Lee, 1995) found that different types of critical-input experiences produced different effects on students.

These findings are depicted in Figure 2.1, which indicates that visual instruction, dramatic instruction, and verbal instruction all enhance learning when done effectively. However, one is struck by the superior findings reported for visual and dramatic instruction over verbal instruction in terms of the percentage of information recalled by students one year after the completion of the unit. In simple terms, visual instruction involves helping students generate mental pictures for the information being taught. Dramatic instruction includes anything that dramatizes content. Nuthall further explains that narratives or stories involve both visual and dramatic instructional techniques. About the use of narratives, Nuthall (1999) notes the following:

FIGURE 2.1	
Effects of Different Types of Learning Experiences in Nuthall's Research	
Type of Experience	Percent of Information Recalled One Year After Completion of Unit
Visual Instruction	77
Dramatic Instruction	57
Verbal Instruction	53

Source: Data from Nuthall, 1999; Nuthall & Alton-Lee, 1995.

> Our studies suggest that narratives provide powerful structures for organization and storage of curriculum content in memory. . . . Stories often contain a rich variety of supplemental information and connect to personal experiences, as well as being integrated and held together by a familiar structure. (p. 337)

Previewing

A second characteristic of a comprehensive approach to student interaction with content is that students are involved in some form of previewing activity prior to the actual presentation of content. Previewing refers to any activity that starts students thinking about the content they will encounter in a critical-input experience. These activities appear particularly useful for students who do not possess a great deal of background knowledge about the topic (Mayer, 1979; West & Fensham, 1976). Mayer (2003) explains that advance organizers are well-researched types of preview techniques. Ausubel (1968) is credited with much of the original research on advance organizers.

Closely related to advance organizers are cues. With cues, teachers provide students with direct links between new content and content previously taught.

As demonstrated in the action steps in this chapter, cues can be used as a form of advance organizer. Figure 2.2 reports the findings from a number of synthesis studies on advance organizers and cues.

Mayer (2003) reviews several types of advance organizers and extends the concept well beyond those listed in Figure 2.2. He also notes that advance organizers not only enhance comprehension but aid transfer.

FIGURE 2.2
Research Results for Advance Organizers and Cues

Synthesis Study	Focus	Number of Effect Sizes	Average Effect Size	Percentile Gain
Luiten, Ames, & Ackerson, 1980	General effects of advance organizers	110	0.21	8
Lott, 1983[a]	General effects of advance organizers	17 5	0.09 0.77	3 28
Stone, 1983	Expository advance organizers	44	0.80	29
	Narrative advance organizers	12	0.53	20
	Illustrated and written advance organizers	15	0.52	20
Hattie, 1992	General effects of advance organizers	387	0.37	14
Walberg, 1999[a]	General effects of advance organizers	29 16	0.45 0.24	17 9
	Cues	— —	0.75 0.71	27 26
Bloom, 1976	Cues	20	0.90	32
Wise & Okey, 1983	Cues	11	0.56	21
Crismore, 1985	Cues	231	0.60	23
Ross, 1988[b]	Cues	6	0.41	16
Guzzetti, Snyder, Glass, & Gamas, 1993	Cues	14	0.08	3

[a] Two effect sizes are listed because of the manner in which effect sizes are reported. Readers should consult these studies for more details.

[b] Effect size computed using data reported by Ross, 1988.

Small Chunks

Once students preview content, they can engage in a critical-input experience. Of vital importance to the success of critical-input experiences is the extent to which the teacher organizes the experience into small chunks (Linden et al., 2003). Rosenshine (2002) refers to this practice as teaching in small steps. Discussing the findings from a number of studies of effective teachers, he makes the following observation:

> When the most effective teachers in these studies taught new material, they taught it in "small steps." That is, they only presented small parts of new material at a single time. . . . The importance of teaching in small steps fits well with the findings from cognitive psychology on the limitations of our working memory. Our working memory, the place where we process information, is small. It can only handle a few bits of information at once—too much information swamps our working memory. (2002, p. 7)

Although they use different terminology, Good and Brophy (2003) and Mayer (2003) also acknowledge the importance of organizing input experience into digestible chunks for students. It is important to recognize that the teacher is most probably the only one who can determine the nature and size of these chunks because the teacher knows his students and their level of understanding of the content in the input experience. It is also important to recognize that breaking input experiences into small chunks is useful regardless of whether an input experience involves students listening to a lecture, reading a section of a text, observing a demonstration, observing a video, and so on.

Active Processing Using Macrostrategies

Small chunks of content must still be actively processed by students. This requires the use of a set of interacting instructional strategies. In effect, no single instructional strategy will suffice to meet the demands of actively processing content during a critical-input experience. Rather, what might be thought of as *macrostrategies* must be employed. For example, reciprocal teaching (Palincsar & Brown, 1984) is one such macrostrategy. Reciprocal teaching is explained later in this chapter, in Action Step 4. In very simple terms, it integrates the more specific strategies of summarizing, questioning, clarifying, and predicting. Students employ the strategy in groups and rotate the position of student leader. The research on reciprocal teaching is quite encouraging. For example, in a review of the research on reciprocal teaching, Rosenshine and Meister (1994) found the average effect size to be 0.88 when experimenter-designed assessments were used to measure comprehension. This translates into a 31 percentile point gain in achievement. In a related study, Rosenshine, Meister, and Chapman (1996) found that the question-generation component of reciprocal teaching is powerful in its own right. The overall effect size with experimenter-developed assessments was 0.86, which also translates into a 31 percentile point gain.

Although they use different terminology, Barley and her colleagues (2002) identify several macrostrategies particularly useful for students at risk. They observe that these strategies are "designed to increase student abilities to (1) cumulatively review information read, (2) sequence information, (3) summarize paragraphs and issues, (4) state main ideas in as few words as possible, and (5) predict and check outcomes" (2002, p. 84). In short, there are a number of techniques that might be classified as macrostrategies as defined here. (For other examples of macrostrategies, see Good & Brophy, 2003; Mayer, 2003.) Typically, macrostrategies involve specific components that have a good deal of research supporting their use even in isolation. At least five specific strategies are common subcomponents of a good macrostrategy: (1) summarizing and note taking, (2) nonlinguistic representations, (3) questions, (4) reflection, and (5) cooperative learning.

Summarizing and Note Taking

Summarizing requires students to create a personalized, parsimonious account of the information gleaned from a critical-input experience (Kintsch, 1979; van Dijk, 1980). Anderson and Hidi (Anderson & Hidi, 1988/1989; Hidi & Anderson, 1987) have provided comprehensive reviews of the research and theory on summarizing. Note taking is closely related to summarizing in that it requires students to translate information from a critical-input experience into their own abbreviated form. Figure 2.3 presents some of the research findings on summarizing and note taking.

Nonlinguistic Representations

Both summarizing and note taking are linguists' ways of synthesizing information. That is, both use language. Information also can be encoded in nonlinguistic or imagery form. Paivio (Paivio, 1969, 1971, 1990; Sadoski & Paivio, 2001) provides a detailed explanation of the dynamics of this type of processing. The linguistic aspect of processing is most observable as the ability to talk about what one has read, heard, or experienced. The nonlinguistic aspect of information processing is most observable as the mental images associated with one's experiences. For example, a student who has studied and understands the defining characteristics of the cell will have mental images associated with this information. Activities that aid students in the nonlinguistic processing of information include creating graphic representations (Alvermann & Boothby, 1986; Armbruster, Anderson, & Meyer, 1992; Darch, Carnine, & Kameenui, 1986; Griffin, Simmons, & Kameenui, 1992; Horton, Lovitt, & Bergerud, 1990; McLaughlin, 1991; Robinson & Keiwra,

FIGURE 2.3
Research Results for Summarizing Strategies and Note Taking

Synthesis Study	Focus	Number of Effect Sizes	Average Effect Size	Percentile Gain
Pflaum, Walberg, Karegianes, & Rasher, 1980[a]	Summarizing strategies	2 2	0.62 0.73	23 27
Crismore, 1985	Summarizing strategies	100	1.04	35
Raphael & Kirschner, 1985	Summarizing strategies	3	1.80	47
Hattie, Biggs, & Purdie, 1996	Summarizing strategies	15	0.88	31
	Note taking	3	1.05	35
Bangert-Drowns, Hurley, & Wilkinson, 2004[b]	Summarizing strategies	(math) 27 (science) 7 (social studies) 6	0.33 0.24 0.13	13 9 5
Ganske, 1981	Note taking	24	1.16	38
Henk & Stahl, 1985[a]	Note taking	25 11	0.34 1.56	13 44
Marzano, Gnadt, & Jesse, 1990	Note taking	3	1.26	40

[a] Two effect sizes are listed because of the manner in which effect sizes are reported. Readers should consult these studies for more details.

[b] The study focused on students summarizing and describing content in written form within different subject areas.

1996), making physical models (Corkill, 1992; Welch, 1997), generating mental pictures (Muehlherr & Siermann, 1996; Willoughby, Desmarias, Wood, Sims, & Kalra, 1997), drawing pictures and pictographs (Macklin, 1997; Newton, 1995; Pruitt, 1993), and engaging in kinesthetic representations of the content (Aubusson, Foswill, Barr, & Perkovic, 1997; Druyan, 1997).

Again, a fair amount of research supports the efficacy of processing information in nonlinguistic ways. Figure 2.4 reports some of this research.

One aspect of nonlinguistic processing that is often overlooked is memory devices that employ some type of nonlinguistic representations. Typically, these devices fall under the general category of mnemonic strategies. Mayer (2003) describes mnemonic strategies as follows:

FIGURE 2.4
Research Results for Nonlinguistic Representation

Synthesis Study	Focus	Number of Effect Sizes	Average Effect Size	Percentile Gain
Powell, 1980[a]	General nonlinguistic techniques	13 6 4	1.01 1.16 0.56	34 38 21
Stahl & Fairbanks, 1986[a]	General nonlinguistic techniques	2 8	0.92 1.23	32 39
Mayer, 1989[a]	General nonlinguistic techniques	6 16	1.47 1.20	43 39
Guzzetti et al., 1993	General nonlinguistic techniques	3	0.51	20
Hattie et al., 1996	General nonlinguistic techniques	9	0.91	32
Haas, 2005	General nonlinguistic techniques	5	0.38	15
Lovelace, 2005[a]	General nonlinguistic techniques	— — —	0.82 0.92 0.42	29 32 16
Nesbit & Adesope, 2006	Concept maps, grades 4–8	4	0.91	32
	Concept maps, grades 9–12	7	0.17	7

[a] Multiple effect sizes are listed because of the manner in which effect sizes are reported. Readers should consult these studies for more details.

> Mnemonic strategies are techniques that help students memorize material such as facts. Memorization means that you are able to remember and use material without conscious mental effort. . . . Mnemonic strategies involve time tested activities that help the learner to remember material. (pp. 364–365)

It is important to recognize that when used effectively mnemonic strategies are not lower order in nature. In fact, when used appropriately, memory techniques involve higher-level thought processes (see Hayes, 1981). Unfortunately some educators tend to equate memory techniques with rote memorization, which in fact violates most principles of the effective use of mnemonics. Specifically, students must understand information before a memory technique is employed.

Memory techniques should help not only the recall of information but also the understanding of that information.

Questioning

Questions are another important aspect of effective macrostrategies. Figure 2.5 presents research findings regarding questioning in general.

The study by Redfield and Rousseau (1981) is particularly germane to the discussion here because it contrasted the effects of higher-level questions versus lower-level questions. The researchers conclude that "the results of this meta-analysis indicate a positive overall effect (+.7292) for prominent use of higher cognitive questions in the classroom" (1981, p. 243). They also note that this finding contradicts an earlier study by Winne (1979).

By definition, inferential questions require students to elaborate on information they have experienced (see Reder, 1980). One particularly effective type of inferential question is "elaborative interrogation" (Ozgungor & Guthrie, 2004). Elaborative interrogation has been described as questions that have the basic design: Why would that be true? (Pressley et al., 1992; Willoughby & Wood, 1994). Fishbein, Eckart, Lauver, Van Leeuwen, and Langmeyer (1990) found that questions of this ilk can greatly enhance students' comprehension.

Reflection

Reflection is another aspect of many macrostrategies. Although the term is used in many different ways, here it refers to students reviewing a critical-input experience and identifying points of confusion, the level of certainty they have about content,

FIGURE 2.5
Research Results for Questions

Synthesis Study	Focus	Number of Effect Sizes	Average Effect Size	Percentile Gain
Redfield & Rosseau, 1981	Questions	7	0.76	28
Wise & Okey, 1983	Questions	11	0.56	21
Hamaker, 1986	Questions	100	0.75	27
Guzzetti et al., 1993	Questions	11	0.80	29
Walberg, 1999	Questions	14	0.26	10

preconceptions that were accurate, and preconceptions that were inaccurate. Some of the research supporting reflection is found in the literature on assessment. Specifically, it has been reported that asking students to identify and record their areas of confusion not only enhances their learning but also provides the teacher with valuable diagnostic information (Butler & Winne, 1995; Cross, 1998).

Cooperative Learning

One final but critical aspect of macrostrategies as defined here is that students interact in groups about the content. There has been a great deal of research on the positive effects of cooperative learning. Figure 2.6 reports the findings from some of that research.

Although cooperative learning as defined by Johnson and Johnson (1999) has many benefits, one that is most germane to this discussion is that it allows students to experience content as viewed from multiple perspectives. McVee, Dunsmore, and Gavelek (2005) review the research on the sociolinguistic aspects

FIGURE 2.6
Research Results for Cooperative Learning

Synthesis Study	Focus	Number of Effect Sizes	Average Effect Size	Percentile Gain
Johnson, Maruyama, Johnson, Nelson, & Skon, 1981	Cooperative learning (general)	122	0.73	27
	Cooperative vs. intergroup competition	9	0.00	0
	Cooperative vs. individual competition	70	0.78	28
	Cooperative vs. individual student tasks	104	0.78	28
Hall, 1989	Cooperative learning (general)	37	0.30	12
Lipsey & Wilson, 1993	Cooperative learning (general)	414	0.63	23
Walberg, 1999	Cooperative learning (general)	182	0.78	28
Bowen, 2000	Cooperative learning (general), high school & college chemistry	30	0.37	14
Haas, 2005	Cooperative learning (general)	3	0.34	13

of knowledge (i.e., schema) development and note that group interaction not only facilitates knowledge development but also creates awareness that is difficult if not impossible without such interaction. O'Donnell and colleagues (1990) report that cooperative interactions facilitate the learning of complex procedures. The research by Lou and colleagues (1996) illustrates that group size might moderate the effects of learning in groups. This is depicted in Figure 2.7, which implies that groups should be kept relatively small. In fact, I recommend pairs and triads for most types of interactions described in the action steps that follow.

	FIGURE 2.7 Size of Groups		
Group Size	Number of Effect Sizes	Average Effect Size	Percentile Gain
2	13	0.15	6
3–4	38	0.22	9
5–7	17	−0.02	−1

Action Steps

Action Step 1. Identify Critical-Input Experiences

Teachers provide input to students regarding academic content on a daily basis. Much of this input is serendipitous and informal. However, there are times when the input is planned as a critical aspect of a unit of instruction. For example, a teacher might plan for students to read a specific section in the textbook that explains and exemplifies information about right triangles. Understanding the content in this section is a vital first step on the way to meeting a learning goal about angles. Additionally, the teacher might plan for students to watch a video, or listen to a lecture, or watch a demonstration, or engage in a simulation as a vital step in accomplishing that same learning goal. Again, I refer to these situations as critical-input experiences. To illustrate, assume that a physical education teacher has identified the learning goal that students will be able to demonstrate proper technique for doing lunges as an overall exercise for the legs. She identifies two critical-input experiences pertaining to this goal. The first is a lecture she delivers along with a brief demonstration. The second is a video of athletes from multiple sports engaging in various types of lunges that emphasize different muscles in the legs.

In effect, this action step requires a teacher to single out a few well-structured input experiences as critical to students' learning. Each learning goal might involve two or three such experiences. Thus, a unit with two learning goals might have four to six critical-input experiences. The identification of these experiences provides focus for students as well as the teacher. Students know that it is important to pay particular attention to these experiences; the teacher knows that adequate time must be taken during these experiences to ensure that students process the content deeply and comprehensively.

Action Step 2. Preview the Content Prior to a Critical-Input Experience

When a teacher previews the information that will be addressed in a critical learning experience, by definition she helps students activate prior knowledge relative to that information. Even if a student has little or no prior knowledge relative to a specific topic, he will at least activate related knowledge that will allow him to make important linkages. There are a variety of ways that previewing might occur. Many of them are grounded in the foundational research and theory on advance organizers.

What Do You Think You Know?

The simplest way to preview new content is to ask students what they think they know about a topic. This, of course, is an adaptation of a more general strategy developed by Ogle (1986). For example, prior to watching a computer-generated simulation of a tidal wave, a teacher asks students what they think they know about tidal waves. She emphasizes the fact that students do not have to be sure about their information. All that is required is to share what they think they know.

Overt Linkages

As a previewing technique, overt linkages point out the connections between content previously addressed in class and content that is about to be presented in a critical-input experience. For example, prior to demonstrating how to read a contour map, a teacher explains to students that they will see similarities between reading a contour map and a regular map. The teacher then lists on the blackboard those aspects of reading a regular map that students should keep in mind.

Preview Questions

Questions can be used as a powerful previewing activity when they are asked prior to a critical-input experience. For example, prior to showing students a documentary on Hurricane Katrina in 2005, a teacher asks students to keep the following questions in mind as they watch the documentary:

- What errors in judgment were made by the city government of New Orleans?

- What errors in judgment were made by the state government?
- What errors in judgment were made by the federal government?

These questions warn students that errors in judgment were made at multiple levels and focus their attention on specific aspects of the documentary.

Brief Teacher Summary
A brief summary can be used as an effective previewing tool. This can be done orally or in written form. To illustrate, prior to reading a section in the textbook on weather patterns, the teacher briefly describes the highlights of what students will be reading.

Skimming
Skimming can be employed as a previewing activity. Obviously, skimming is most effective with print material. If students are not adept at the strategy of skimming, then the teacher provides them with an explicit strategy such as the following:

- Read the section heading and ask yourself what it tells you about the overall passage.
- Next, read all the subheadings and a few sentences within each sub-heading.
- Finally, briefly summarize what you think the passage is about.

The teacher writes each student's summary statement on the whiteboard and then discusses with students the similarities and differences in these statements.

Teacher-Prepared Notes
Teacher-prepared notes are the most elaborate type of previewing activity. With this technique the teacher provides students with an outline of the important content within an upcoming critical-input experience. The teacher reviews the notes with the class, and students refer to the notes throughout the critical-input experience. Figure 2.8 depicts notes a teacher might distribute before students read a section in the textbook about the Bill of Rights. The outline in this figure is quite extensive and might cover the content in two or more critical-input experiences.

Action Step 3. Organize Students into Groups to Enhance the Active Processing of Information
Throughout this book, grouping students is mentioned a number of times simply because it has benefits for many aspects of teaching. One of those benefits is that

---

FIGURE 2.8
Teacher-Prepared Notes: The Bill of Rights

I. What It Is
The Bill of Rights is the first 10 amendments to the U.S. Constitution. It protects fundamental individual rights and liberties.

II. The History of the Bill of Rights
A. James Madison, congressman from Virginia, proposed a series of amendments to the Constitution. Madison introduced these amendments in the House of Representatives in May 1789.
B. Committees of the House of Representatives and the Senate rewrote the amendments.
C. The House and Senate approved 12 amendments in September 1789.
D. Ten of the 12 proposed amendments were ratified on December 14, 1791.
   1. "Ratification" is the name of the process by which constitutional amendments are approved. To be adopted, an amendment must be passed by two-thirds of each house of Congress and then by three-fourths of the state legislatures.
   2. The state legislatures voted on each of the 12 amendments separately. The first two proposed amendments were not ratified by three-quarters of the states.

III. Rights Protected by the Bill of Rights
A. More than 30 liberties and rights are protected by the 10 amendments that make up the Bill of Rights.
B. Each amendment protects specific rights:
   1. Protects freedom of speech, press, assembly, and religious belief; prohibits the government from creating a state religion or giving support to any or all religions.
   2. Protects the right to bear arms.
   3. Prohibits the government, even the military, from invading our homes.
   4. Prohibits unreasonable searches and arrests; declares that there must be probable cause for a search or arrest warrant to be issued.
   5. Prohibits double jeopardy; protects right to remain silent; prohibits government from taking away anyone's life, liberty, or property without due process of law.
   6. Protects right to a fair trial, including right to be represented by counsel in a speedy trial before an impartial jury.
   7. Protects right to trial by jury; prohibits courts from reexamining facts tried by a jury.
   8. Prohibits excessive bail or fines, or the infliction of cruel and unusual punishment.
   9. Preserves any individual rights or liberties not specifically mentioned in the Constitution.
   10. Preserves the power of the states.

Source: Marzano, Pickering, & Pollock, 2001, p. 45.

---

it can enhance the processing of new information because interacting in groups provides students with multiple reference points. It allows each student to see how others process information, and it allows each student to see how others react to his or her processing of information. I will address other ways grouping might be used in Chapters 3 and 4. Here, though, the generalization is that groups should be established to facilitate active processing of information during a critical-input experience. Those groups might be as small as two or as large as five. As mentioned previously, for the purposes of this action step I recommend groups of two or three. Given that the basic purpose of these groups is to enhance the processing of information, operating rules such as the following should be established:

- Be willing to add your perspective to any discussion.
- Respect the opinions of other people.
- Make sure you understand what others have added to the conversation. Be willing to ask questions if you don't understand something.
- Be willing to answer questions other group members ask you about your ideas.

Teachers should explicitly discuss these behaviors with students. For example, at the beginning of the year the teacher informs students that they will be working in groups quite frequently. Because the purpose of these groups is to facilitate the understanding of new content, everyone in a group must be willing to add to the conversation. The teacher then presents the operating rules to students, provides examples, and has students practice carrying out the rules.

Action Step 4. Present New Information in Small Chunks and Ask for Descriptions, Discussion, and Predictions

There is only so much new information that a learner can ingest at one time. Learning proceeds more efficiently if students receive information in small chunks that are processed immediately. To facilitate this technique, the teacher identifies the chunks within a critical-input experience ahead of time. There are no set rules regarding how large or small a chunk should be. The teacher is the only one who can make this determination. The more students know about the content, the larger the chunks can be.

If a critical-input experience involves a demonstration, then the teacher identifies the strategic stopping points during the demonstration. For example, assume that a teacher is providing a demonstration of the interaction between the moon and the earth and the earth and the sun. She uses a physical model of the three spheres. She first describes the relationship between the moon and the earth, demonstrating the rotation of the moon using the physical models. This takes a few minutes. She then stops her presentation and asks student groups to discuss the information.

She has organized students into groups of three and assigned each student in each group the letter A, B, or C. After this first chunk of new information has been demonstrated she asks member A of each group to briefly summarize the information. After member A has summarized the content, members B and C add to what A has said. Each group also identifies elements about which they are confused. Next, the teacher takes questions from the whole class that help clarify the confusions identified in each group. Finally, she asks the whole class whether they have any predictions about what they might see in the next chunk.

Next, the teacher presents another small chunk of information and asks member B of each group to summarize the content. Groups identify confusing parts and ask the teacher questions regarding these parts. Then, the teacher elicits predictions. Finally, a third chunk of information is provided, and member C of each group takes the lead.

This type of information about the moon, earth, and sun is declarative in nature. When a critical learning experience involves procedural knowledge, this action step is modified somewhat. Recall from the earlier discussion that declarative knowledge is informational. Procedural knowledge relates to skill, strategy, or process. To illustrate, assume that a physical education teacher provides a critical-input experience about the proper technique for shooting a free throw. The teacher has organized the demonstration into small chunks. The first chunk involves proper stance, with feet shoulder-width apart, and proper hand placement on the basketball—shooting hand on top, with the thumb and index finger making a Y shape, the bottom hand below the ball acting as a holder, and the outer edge of each palm close to or slightly touching. The teacher stops after demonstrating and talking through this part of the procedure. Student A in each group then summarizes the information for B and C, and B and C add to this summary. Before another chunk is presented, each member of each group briefly attempts to execute the procedure. Again each group generates questions regarding confusing aspects of the procedure, and the teacher addresses the questions in a whole-class manner. The teacher elicits predictions about what might be presented in the next segment and then presents the next chunk.

To use another procedural example, assume that a teacher has taught a specific strategy for editing an expository compare-and-contrast composition for overall logic. That strategy involves the following components:

1. In your own words try to state the two things you are comparing.
2. Look over your composition and make sure that the elements being compared are clear to the reader. If not, make the necessary changes.
3. Next, state the specific characteristics on which the elements are compared.
4. Look over your composition and make sure these characteristics are clear to the reader and that you have clearly described how the elements being compared are similar and different on these characteristics. If not, make the necessary changes.

5. Next, state the overall conclusion you came to as a result of your comparison.
6. Look over your composition and make sure this is clear to the reader. If not, make the necessary changes.

The teacher designs a critical-input experience for students using two unedited compare-and-contrast compositions from two anonymous students from the previous year. Steps 1 and 2 constitute the first chunk. One of the sample essays is placed on the overhead projector and used as the composition with which the teacher demonstrates the procedure. Each student has a copy of the second composition. Also each student has a copy of the six-step process.

Using the composition on the overhead, the teacher talks through the first two steps, verbalizing her thoughts as she executes the steps. She then asks the groups to address these steps. All members of the group try the first two steps. Member A summarizes his experience and elicits input from members B and C. Groups also identify confusions that one or more of the group members have. These are addressed by the teacher in front of the entire class. Conjectures about the other parts of the procedure are elicited, and a new chunk of information is presented.

As the examples regarding free throws and editing compare-and-contrast compositions illustrate, when procedural knowledge is the focus of a critical-input experience, students have the opportunity to try each aspect of the procedure addressed in each chunk.

Although the general technique described in this action step works quite well, a teacher may wish to use other more formal strategies. There are at least three formal instructional strategies that fit nicely within this action step: reciprocal teaching, jigsaw, and concept attainment. Any of these could be substituted for this action step because all involve discussion, summarizing, prediction, and clearing up confusing elements to one degree or another in the context of group learning. For each of these three macrostrategies, I now briefly describe how they might be used within this action step.

Reciprocal teaching is a technique designed by Palincsar and her colleagues (Palincsar & Brown, 1984; Palincsar & Herrenkohl, 2002). O'Donnell (2006) describes reciprocal teaching in the following way:

> During reciprocal teaching a group of students generate predictions about the text. After reading a portion of the text, the discussion leader [in each group] raises questions about the text and members of the group discuss these questions. Someone

from the group summarizes the content read up to this point, and the group members then clarify difficult concepts and then continue to make predictions about the next portion of the text. (p. 787)

As described by O'Donnell, reciprocal teaching employs many of the general elements outlined in this action step, although in a slightly different order. Students read a section of the text. The student leader does not initially summarize the text but raises questions that the group discusses. A summary of the discussion is presented not by the group leader but by some other member of the team.

Jigsaw was designed by Aronson, Blaney, Stephan, Sikes, and Snapp (1978). O'Donnell (2006) notes that it is one of the original cooperative learning techniques. She describes it in the following way:

Students are assigned to four-person heterogeneous groups that are assigned topics on which they are to become experts. For example, if the group were learning about the rainforest, each member of the group would be responsible for becoming an expert on a subtopic (e.g., birds and animals of the rainforest, people who live in the rainforest, plants, and the destruction of the rainforest). Students with the same "expert topic" from different teams meet in groups to discuss their topic. Their task is to become as knowledgeable as possible about the topic. They then return to their groups and teach the material to other students in their groups. (2006, p. 792)

Clarifying and predicting are not formal aspects of jigsaw but can be easily incorporated. For example, each expert group can generate questions that are clarified by the teacher on a group-by-group basis. Additionally, each expert group can generate predictions about what will be disclosed when the information from all expert groups is combined in the base group.

Concept attainment is a strategy based on the work of Bruner (1973). It was popularized by Joyce and Weil (1986). Although there are many techniques referred to as concept attainment (see Silver, Strong, & Perini, in press), Joyce and Weil describe its critical attributes as follows: "This model is designed to lead students to a concept by asking them to compare and contrast examples (called exemplars) that contain the characteristics (called attributes) of the concept with examples that do not contain those attributes" (1986, p. 27). To illustrate, Joyce and Weil provide an example of an 8th grade social studies teacher whose class has been studying the characteristics of the 14 largest cities in the United States. Students have been provided with data on the size, ethnicity of population, types of industry, location, and proximity to natural resources. This information has been organized into charts for each city, which are displayed around the classroom for all students to see.

With this setting as a backdrop, the teacher explains to the class that she is going to present information a bit differently. She tells students that some of the cities represent certain concepts, whereas others do not. She explains that she will provide one concept at a time. With each concept she will provide examples and nonex-amples. She starts by saying, "Houston, Texas, is an example of the concept I'm thinking of. It's a yes." The students immediately look at the chart for Houston to examine its characteristics. The teacher then points to the chart for Baltimore, Maryland, and says that it is a no. She also points to the chart for San Jose, Cali-fornia, and says it is a yes.

Next the teacher asks if anyone has a guess as to what she is thinking about. A few students raise their hands. The teacher acknowledges their progress but tells them to keep their guesses private for a while. Rather, she asks them to test their guesses using the next examples and nonexamples she provides. She then explains that Seattle, Washington, is a yes, but Detroit, Michigan, is a no, and Miami, Florida, is a yes. She continues until all students think they know the con-cept. Only after every student thinks he or she has the answer does the teacher ask students to share their ideas regarding the characteristics that link all the "yes" cities. This sharing is done in groups of three. Students come to a common understanding that the concept is rapidly growing cities that have relatively mild climates. Students are then asked to state this new concept in their own words. The process is repeated two more times for two additional concepts about large cities in the United States.

Action Step 5. Ask Questions That Require Students to Elaborate on Information

Elaborative questions can be organized into two broad categories: general infer-ential questions and elaborative interrogations.

General Inferential Questions

In its simplest form, inference involves asking students questions that require them to go beyond what was presented in a critical-input experience. There are two basic types of such questions (Marzano, 2001). One type of inferential ques-tion requires students to use their background knowledge to fill in information implied but not explicit in the input experience. These are called "default" inferen-tial questions because to answer them students must default to their background knowledge. For example, assume that students have watched a video about how the U.S. Senate functions; however, the video does not focus much on senators per se. Default inferential questions would take the following form:

- How long do you think a person can be a member of the Senate?
- How many senators are there?

To answer these questions, students must draw on their existing knowledge about senators.

Another type of inferential question requires students to use the information provided in the critical-input experiences to infer what must be true or is likely to be true. To answer these questions, students must use their ability to reason logically with the information presented. Hence, they are called "reasoned" inferences. For example, assume that within a critical-input experience students have listened to a lecture about how flowering plants reproduce sexually by relying on birds and insects to transfer pollen. Insects and birds are intermediaries in the sexual reproduction of plants. Asking students what would happen if the number of insects and birds servicing a given field of flowers suddenly dropped dramatically is an example of a question demanding reasoned inferences. To answer this question, students must use what is explicitly stated in the input experience to generate conclusions about what might happen.

Elaborative Interrogations

Elaborative interrogations begin with simple inferential questions such as the one just described. In addition, when a student provides an answer, the teacher asks: "Why do you believe this to be true?" or "Tell me why you think that is so." For example, after a student has provided an answer to the inferential questions about U.S. senators or flowering plants, the teacher asks the student to explain why she believes her response is true. This requires some skillful interaction with students, in that the teacher tries to make explicit the thinking the student is using to generate her answer. Typically, during such interactions the teacher uses phrases such as "It seems to me that you are saying. . . ." Such phrasing allows the teacher to restate the student's thinking so the student can reexamine her logic.

Elaborative interrogation might be approached quite informally by adding the tag question (or some variant of it), Why do you believe this to be true? At a more formal level it is useful to think in terms of two basic formats that can be used to ask beginning inferential questions. One format is

What are some typical characteristics or behaviors you would expect of
_____?

To illustrate, assume that a teacher has asked students to watch a video about Mahatma Gandhi. After students have processed the information in small chunks (see Action Step 4), the teacher asks the following question: Based on what we saw in the video about Gandhi, what are some characteristics you might expect of him? Given the type of question he has asked, the teacher understands that to answer it, students must associate Gandhi with some general type or category of people. For example, a particular student might associate Gandhi with the category of "people who make big changes in society." This leads the student to respond to the question in the following way: "I think he would be very brave."

Again the teacher asks the student why she thinks this is so. Based on the student's response and the teacher's understanding of the requirements of the question, the teacher says: "So, it seems like you are saying that people like Gandhi are very brave. You are thinking of Gandhi as belonging to a certain category of people. How would you describe that type of person?" This type of questioning would eventually lead to the generalization from which the student is generating her inferences: "What I hear you saying is you consider Gandhi to be the type of person who makes big changes in society and people in that category are typically brave." The intent is to articulate the basic generalizations that student has about the content.

In the example about Gandhi, the inferential question had the following form:

What are some typical characteristics or behaviors you would expect of _____?

Elaborative interrogations also apply to a second format:

What would you expect to happen if_____?

To illustrate, assume that a critical-input experience involved a combined demonstration and lecture regarding specific aspects of the Bernoulli principle as it pertains to lift and the design of airplane wings. In very brief and simple terms, this principle states that the shape of an airplane wing viewed from the cross-section (thick at the front and then tapering to very narrow at the end) makes air molecules move more quickly over the top of the wing than the bottom because the molecules must cover a greater distance to get around the top of the wing than to get around the bottom. This makes the molecules "spread out" over the top of the wing, lessening the density of the air over the wing as compared with the density of the air underneath the wing. Lift is created because the air above the wing is "thinner" (so to speak) than the air beneath the wing.

As described in Action Step 4, during the lecture and demonstration the teacher would have periodically stopped and asked students to restate or paraphrase the content. After sufficient processing of appropriately small chunks, the teacher asks the following inferential question: "What do you think would happen if we kept the wing the same shape but increased the speed of the air going over the wing?" A specific student responds by saying that more lift would be created. Again the teacher asks, "why do you think this is so?" The student responds, and the teacher tries to articulate the generalizations from which the student is reasoning. Knowing the requirements of the question, the teacher restates the student's thinking as follows: "It seems to me you are saying that increased air speed also spreads out the air molecules moving over the wing. If you increase the speed, you get more lift even if the wing doesn't change."

This type of elaborative interrogation helps make clear "if/then" generalizations from which students are reasoning. The previous example about Gandhi helps make clear generalizations about categories of persons, places, things, and events.

Action Step 6. Have Students Write Out Their Conclusions or Represent Their Learning Nonlinguistically

Although there are many ways to address this action step, five are presented here: notes, graphic organizers, dramatic enactments, mnemonics, and academic notebooks.

Notes

Notes have been a staple of classroom practice for decades. Taking notes requires students to differentiate between information that is considered important and information that is considered supplemental to the topic addressed in a critical-input experience. It is not advisable for students to take detailed notes during the small chunks presented in a critical-input experience because this might distract their attention from the content. However, they can jot down words and phrases that represent key ideas. A more appropriate time to take detailed notes is after the small chunks of information have been processed.

There are many forms in which notes can be taken. A particularly flexible form is shown in Figure 2.9. This form of notes requires students to record their thoughts in written form on the left and represent their thoughts on the right as graphic representations, pictographs, and pictures. The system requires students to process the new knowledge in two different modalities—linguistic and nonlinguistic. On the left-hand side of the page important ideas are recorded in linguistic form; on the right-hand side these ideas are represented in nonlinguistic form.

Although it is true that notes can be generated by a group, I recommend that each student in a group create his or her own notes and then compare the notes with others from the group. This ensures that each student processes the information from the critical-input experience in his or her own unique way.

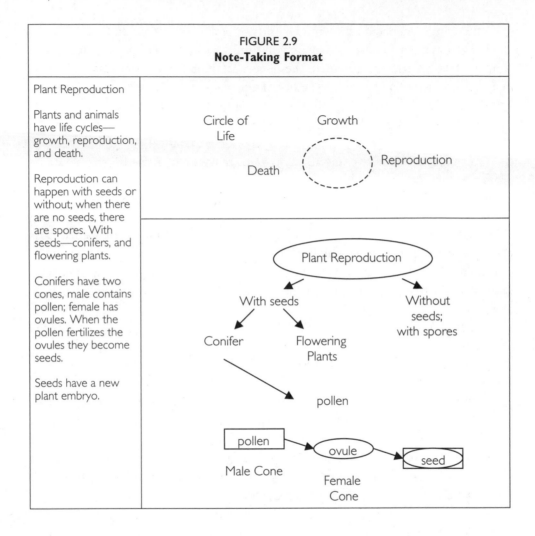

FIGURE 2.9
Note-Taking Format

Graphic Organizers

Graphic organizers are one of the most popular ways for students to represent the knowledge they have encountered in a critical-input experience. A variety of graphic organizers have been described by Hyerle (1996) and Marzano and Kendall (2007). Some of the more popular ones are shown in Figure 2.10.

Graphic organizers can be used as a form of nonlinguistic representation in the right-hand column of the two-column notes format shown in Figure 2.9. They can also be used in isolation. For example, a teacher might have individual students or groups of students create detailed graphic organizers for the information encountered

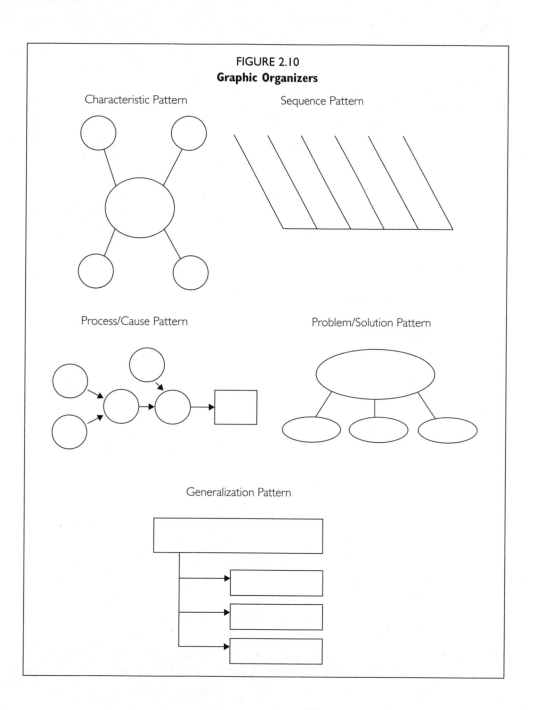

FIGURE 2.10
Graphic Organizers

Characteristic Pattern

Sequence Pattern

Process/Cause Pattern

Problem/Solution Pattern

Generalization Pattern

in an input experience and then share those representations with the entire class, while orally explaining the ideas and relationship depicted in the graphic organizer.

Dramatic Enactments

When engaged in dramatic enactments, groups of students physically act out or symbolize the content from a critical-input experience. Assume that a critical-input experience has provided information about the process of percolation, which is the movement and filtering of fluids through porous material. Within a group, some students might play the role of water droplets, while others play the role of a porous material such as tissue paper. Such enactments tend to be highly engaging to students. However, they take time and can be superficial unless the teacher asks students to explain how their enactments represent the important information from the critical-input experience.

Mnemonic Devices Employing Imagery

There are many mnemonic devices teachers can use (for a detailed discussion, see Hayes, 1981; Lindsay & Norman, 1977). Here two mnemonic strategies that emphasize the nonlinguistic processing of information are reviewed briefly (for a more detailed discussion of these and other strategies, see Marzano, Paynter, & Doty, 2003). Again it is important that teachers employ mnemonic devices only after students have processed information thoroughly and have a good, albeit incomplete, understanding of the content.

Before presenting students with mnemonic techniques, it is useful to introduce the concepts of symbols and substitutes. It is easy to create images for some types of information and difficult to do so for others. Creating images for factual information is fairly easy because it is easy to imagine. For example, it is fairly easy to mentally picture information about Abraham Lincoln with his tall top hat and long beard, the log cabin where he grew up, the theater in which he was assassinated, and so on. But it is more difficult to create images for abstract information, such as the basic elements of water: two hydrogen atoms and one oxygen atom.

If you use symbols and substitutes, however, it becomes relatively easy to create images for even abstract concepts such as these. A symbol is something that suggests or reminds the student of the information he is trying to remember. For example, an oxygen tank might symbolize oxygen. A substitute is a word that is easy to picture and sounds like information. For hydrogen the word *hydrant* might be used. The symbol for oxygen and the substitute for hydrogen can now be combined to create an image for the information that water is made of two parts hydrogen and one part oxygen. A student would simply create a mental image of two hydrants placed atop an oxygen tank. With the concepts of symbols and substitutes established, mnemonic devices are readily applied to a variety of types of content.

The *rhyming pegword method* is a simple system that can be used to remember information organized in a list format (Miller, Galanter, & Pribram, 1960). The method uses a set of words easily remembered because they rhyme with the numbers 1 through 10:

1 is a bun
2 is a shoe
3 is a tree
4 is a door
5 is a hive
6 is a stack of sticks
7 is heaven
8 is a gate
9 is a line
10 is a hen

The pegwords *bun, shoe, tree,* and so on are easy to remember and are also concrete and easy to picture. If a student wanted to connect information to pegword 1 (the bun), she would form a mental image of the bun interacting with that information. For example, assume the student wanted to remember the following information about the Incas of Peru:

- They had complex irrigation systems.
- They were skilled surgeons and dentists.
- They cultivated their crops and developed new kinds of vegetables and fruits.

To remember this, the student would picture a hot dog bun with a faucet tapped into it (representing irrigation); or a doctor might be sitting on the bun examining the faucet (surgeons and dentists) while fruits and vegetables pour out of the faucet (modern agriculture). Similar images would be used to connect information to each of the other pegwords. Though students could associate one element of information with each pegword, associating multiple elements with each pegword allows for the storage of more information.

The link strategy is a common approach, which involves linking symbols and substitutes together in a chain of events or narrative story. To illustrate, assume that a unit of instruction focuses on the 13 original colonies: Georgia, New Jersey, Delaware, New York, North Carolina, South Carolina, Virginia, New Hampshire, Pennsylvania, Connecticut, Rhode Island, Maryland, and Massachusetts. Throughout the unit the teacher has provided a number of critical-input experiences about each colony. She wants students to recall the colonies right from the outset. Because it is difficult to mentally picture the actual states, the teacher guides students through the use of the link strategy using symbols and substitutes.

A football jersey represents New Jersey, and the Empire State Building is used as a symbol for New York. The name George Washington sounds like Georgia, and the words *Christmas carols* provide good reminders for the two Carolinas. Dinnerware is used as a symbol for Delaware, and so on. Students link the mental images for each of the 13 original colonies into one story. For example, students picture George Washington (Georgia) wearing a football jersey (New Jersey). Next students imagine George holding dinnerware (sounds like Delaware) as he stands on top of the Empire State Building (New York) and sings two Christmas carols (North and South Carolina). With his left hand George is using the dinnerware to cut into a Virginia ham (Virginia and New Hampshire). In his right hand, George is holding a pen (Pennsylvania) and connecting dots (Connecticut) on a puzzle. These dots join to form a picture of a road (Rhode Island), and Marilyn Monroe (Maryland) is riding on this road on her way to Mass (Massachusetts).

Academic Notebooks

As defined here, academic notebooks are adaptations of the time-honored science notebooks (a.k.a. lab notebooks, science journals; see Hargrove & Nesbit, 2003, for a discussion). Ruiz-Primo, Li, and Shavelson (2001) define science notebooks as "a compilation of entries that provide partial records of the instructional experiences a student had in her or his classroom for a certain period of time" (p. 2). One of the powerful features of academic notebooks is that they can be used as permanent records of students' thinking during critical-input experiences. Students date each entry so as to document the chronology of their experiences. Notes (e.g., the two-column notes described in Figure 2.9) and graphic organizers would be recorded in these notebooks. As discussed in the next chapter, academic notebooks allow students to make corrections in their thinking because they provide a sequential record of students' understanding of the content.

Action Step 7. Have Students Reflect on Their Learning

The final step in a comprehensive approach to actively processing information is to have students reflect on their experiences at the completion of a critical-input experience. There are at least three reflection questions students might address (see Cross, 1998; Ross, Hogaboam-Gray, & Rolheiser, 2002):

- What they were right about and wrong about.
- How confident they are about what they have learned.
- What they did well during the experience and what they could have done better.

Every question would not be asked after every critical-input experience. Rather, the teacher selects one question to be addressed after each input experience. For example, after a critical-input experience in science involving solar energy, an elementary teacher asks students to respond to the following question: "What are you the least sure about, and what are you the most sure about?" Students write their comments in their academic notebooks. Alternatively, they might write their comments on a loose sheet of paper and turn it in to the teacher, who uses it as a form of evaluation regarding how much students have learned that class period.

Summary

In considering the second design question—What will I do to help students effectively interact with new knowledge?—it is key for the teacher to identify critical-input experiences. Teachers can take the following actions to approach critical-input experiences in a systematic fashion: preview information; divide students into small groups; organize the critical-input experience into small chunks of information that students describe, discuss, and use to make predictions; ask students questions that require elaborations; have students record their conclusions in linguistic and nonlinguistic formats; and finally, ask students to reflect on their learning.

3

What will I do to help students practice and deepen their understanding of new knowledge?

The last chapter emphasized the importance of having students actively process information during well-structured critical-input experiences. If a teacher uses the techniques presented in that chapter, the chances are good that students will walk away from those experiences with an understanding of the content presented. However, this initial understanding, albeit a good one, does not suffice for learning that is aimed at long-term retention and use of knowledge. Rather, students must have opportunities to practice new skills and deepen their understanding of new information. Without this type of extended processing, knowledge that students initially understand might fade and be lost over time.

In the Classroom

Remember, in our classroom example Mr. Hutchins presents a video on Hiroshima and Nagasaki. The next day he briefly summarizes the content from the video. He then introduces students to a metaphor activity regarding Hiroshima and Nagasaki. Previously he has discussed metaphors with students, so they understand that a metaphor links two things that do not seem related on the surface but are related at a more abstract level. In a whole-class discussion, Mr. Hutchins and his students identify some general characteristics of the events at Hiroshima and Nagasaki that students can use in their metaphors. He explains that they will begin the activity in class and finish it as homework.

The next day Mr. Hutchins begins by reviewing the homework with students. He organizes students into groups of five. Each student presents his or her metaphor assignment to the other members of the group. When all students have reported on the homework in their small groups, Mr. Hutchins leads a whole-class discussion on the insights students gained from the activity.

Throughout the unit, Mr. Hutchins engages students in a variety of activities that help them examine the content in new ways. Frequently, he asks students to return to their academic notebooks and make changes and additions. In some cases, students add information. In other cases students correct initial misconceptions in their knowledge.

Research and Theory

Actively processing information is the beginning point of learning. This is addressed in the second design question, discussed in Chapter 2. As Pressley (1998) notes, "Explicit teaching of skills is the beginning of a constructivist process for your learners" (p. 186). Although Pressley is referring to a particular type of knowledge—skills—his comments apply to all knowledge. Students must have a sound foundation on which to build new awareness. New awareness is forged through repeated exposure to knowledge. Exposures involving practice and knowledge-deepening activities are the focus of this design question.

The research and theory underlying this design question come from a variety of areas that might appear disparate on the surface. Four such areas are discussed here: schema development, development of procedural knowledge, development of declarative knowledge, and homework.

Schema Development

A schema is a concept typically associated with cognitive psychology. Arguably it has some roots in (or at least is similar to) the work of Piaget. Piaget (1971) makes a distinction between two types of knowledge development: assimilation and accommodation. He describes the process of assimilation as that of gradually integrating new knowledge into a learner's existing knowledge base. In general, assimilation involves making linkages between old knowledge and new knowledge. Multiple exposures over time facilitate the assimilation process. Accommodation is a more radical change in knowledge. It involves changing existing knowledge structures as opposed to simply adding information to them. For accommodation, interaction with content must challenge existing perceptions.

Schema theory provides another perspective on the nature of learning. Roughly speaking, schemata are the packets in which knowledge is organized and stored (Anderson, 1995; Bransford & Johnson, 1973; Winograd, 1975). Initially, schemata were thought of as idiosyncratic mental representations of phenomena by individuals. Currently, there is some agreement that schemata are shared by and created by groups as they interact around a common topic (McVee, Dunsmore, & Gavelek, 2005).

Three types of schema development are typically identified: (1) accretion, (2) tuning, and (3) restructuring. Accretion and tuning refer to the gradual accumulation or addition of knowledge over time and the expression of that knowledge in more parsimonious packages. In a sense, accretion and tuning are akin to Piaget's notion of assimilation. Restructuring involves reorganizing knowledge so that it might produce new insights. In a sense, restructuring is akin to Piaget's notion of accommodation.

Developing Procedural Knowledge

The concept of practicing and deepening knowledge is brought into focus by the distinction between declarative and procedural knowledge (for a discussion, see Anderson, 1983, 1995). Procedural knowledge is oriented toward skills, strategies, or processes. The following are examples of procedural knowledge commonly taught in school:

- Performing long division
- Reading a contour map
- Shooting a free throw
- Editing a composition for overall logic
- Editing a composition for mechanics
- Sounding out an unrecognized word while reading

Frequently, a number of procedures are embedded within a robust, complex macroprocedure (Marzano & Kendall, 2007). For example, the macroprocedure of writing has embedded procedures for planning, drafting, editing for overall logic, editing for mechanics, and so on.

Declarative knowledge is informational in nature. The following are examples of declarative knowledge:

- Events during the Normandy invasion in World War II
- Characteristics of different types of genre in literature
- Rules of basketball
- Characteristics of the cell
- Characteristics of the process of percolation

Procedural knowledge develops in different ways from declarative knowledge. Over time procedural knowledge is shaped by the learner. This reshaping involves adding steps, changing steps, and deleting steps. When fully developed, procedural knowledge can be performed at a level of automaticity or controlled processing (Fitts & Posner, 1967; LaBerge & Samuels, 1974). Automaticity means that the learner can execute the process without consciously thinking about the parts of the process. An example would be the skill of sounding out a word not recognized by sight. Once this process is learned, the student can execute it without much conscious thought. Other processes such as editing a composition require a little more thought. That is, even when a student knows how to edit, he must typically think about the process to execute the steps effectively. This is called controlled processing as opposed to automatic processing. Frequently, the term *fluency* is used to describe the development of a skill or process to the level of automaticity or controlled processing.

For procedural knowledge to develop, it must be practiced. For example, Rosenshine (2002) notes the following:

> The most effective teachers presented only small amounts of material at a time. After this short presenting, these teachers then guided student practice . . . guided practice is the place where students—working alone, with other students, or with the teacher—engage in the cognitive processing activities of organizing, reviewing, rehearsing, summarizing, comparing, and contrasting. However, it is important that all students engage in these activities. (p. 7)

Rosenshine's comments about the importance of practice are supported by the research reported in Figure 3.1.

FIGURE 3.1
Research Results for Practice

Synthesis Study	Focus	Number of Effect Sizes	Average Effect Size	Percentile Gain
Bloom, 1976[a]	General effects of practice	13 8	0.93 1.47	32 42
Feltz & Landers, 1983	Mental practice on motor skills	60	0.48	18
Ross, 1988	General effects of practice	12	1.26	40
Kumar, 1991[b]	General effects of practice	5	1.58	44

[a]Multiple effect sizes are listed because of the manner in which effect sizes are reported. Readers should consult that study for more details.

[b]This study used student engagement as the dependent measure.

Unfortunately, there has been a popular trend toward de-emphasizing the need for practice (see National Council of Teachers of Mathematics, 2000, p. 21). Arguments against practice typically focus on its perceived lockstep, didactic nature, providing little opportunity for student exploration. Some cognitive psychologists have expressed severe concerns about the trend against practice. As Anderson, Reder, and Simon (1995) note, "In denying the critical role of practice one is denying children the very thing they need to achieve real competence" (p. 7).

Perhaps the concern about practice stems from improper use of practice as simply drill, during which students mechanically execute steps that have been memorized. To the contrary, effective practice involves students examining and shaping the initial steps. Recall Rosenshine's comments that during guided practice students engage in high-level cognitive processes such as organizing, reviewing, rehearsing, summarizing, comparing, and contrasting. Note Rosenshine's use of the well-accepted term *guided practice,* which communicates the notion that the teacher does not simply turn students loose on practice activities but designs practice sessions that provide well-structured guidance. In short, effective practice is not unthinking execution of a set of steps or algorithms. Rather, it involves the gradual shaping of a procedure facilitated by teacher guidance (Anderson, 1982, 1995; Fitts & Posner, 1967).

Developing Declarative Knowledge

Although the term *practice* is used ubiquitously, it is more appropriate with procedural knowledge. With declarative knowledge, *reviewing* and *revision* are more accurate terms for the processes by which it is developed. Building on the research of Rovee-Collier (1995), Nuthall (1999) found that students require about four exposures to new informational knowledge to adequately integrate it into their existing knowledge base. He notes that these exposures should not be spaced too far apart: "We found that it took a minimum of three to four exposures with no more than a two-day gap or 'time window' (Rovee-Collier, 1995) between each one for these experiences to become integrated as a new knowledge structure" (1999, p. 305). This observation makes intuitive sense and is supported in part by some of the brain research as reported by Jensen (2005). Specifically, Jensen cites research indicating that students need time to think about new insights and awarenesses (Collie, Maruff, Darby, & McStephen, 2003; Stickgold, James, & Hobson, 2000).

Not only is time needed between exposures to declarative content, but the activities engaged in during these exposures should possess certain characteristics.

Here we consider three activities that qualify as useful ways to deepen students' understanding of declarative knowledge.

Revision

Much of the research on revising is focused on writing tasks (see Hillocks, 1986; Mayer, 2003). Revising a composition is obviously a critical step in the generation of an effective essay. Unfortunately, without structure and guidance students' revisions can be highly superficial (Fitzgerald, 1987). Revision is also important to the development of declarative knowledge. The learner begins with a fuzzy, partial knowledge. Over time with extended exposure, the learner sharpens and adds to his or her knowledge base (Hofstetter, Sticht, & Hofstetter, 1999; Schwanenflugel, Stahl, & McFalls, 1997; Stahl, 1999). To this end, revision activities should require students to add new information to the topic being revised as well as correct errors and clarify distinctions.

Error Analysis

Brown and Burton (1978) liken knowledge development to debugging a computer routine. They note that students' understanding of mathematics content is particularly susceptible to bugs, which are best corrected by continual examination of the conceptual accuracy of the content (Clement, Lockhead, & Mink, 1979; Tennyson & Cocchiarella, 1986). A number of researchers and theorists have demonstrated the tendency to use inefficient thinking (Abelson, 1995; Johnson-Laird, 1985; Perkins, Allen, & Hafner, 1983). On the lighter side of this issue, Gilovich (1991) identifies examples of erroneous thinking from those otherwise known for their rigorous academic logic. For example, Francis Bacon is reported to have believed that warts could be cured by rubbing them with pork. Aristotle thought that babies were conceived in a strong north wind.

The academic domain of philosophy identifies specific types of errors people make in their thinking (Johnson-Laird, 1983; Johnson-Laird & Byrne, 1991; Toulmin, Rieke, & Janik, 1981). Action Step 2 in this chapter describes some of these types in depth. Briefly though, types of errors or informal fallacies include faulty logic (such as assuming that something that has occurred once will occur on a systematic basis), attack (trying to disprove a point by discrediting the person making the point), weak references (using sources that have no credibility), and misinformation (confusing the facts). Many who advocate teaching and reinforcing critical thinking skills view error analysis as a primary intellectual skill (Costa, 2001; Halpern, 1996a, 1996b).

Identifying Similarities and Differences

Identifying similarities and differences is a common instructional activity that appears to pay dividends in terms of knowledge development. Apparently, this process is basic to human thought (see Gentner & Markman, 1994; Markman & Gentner, 1993a, 1993b; Medin, Goldstone, & Markman, 1995). Figure 3.2 presents findings from some of the studies on similarities and differences.

There are at least four general types of tasks that facilitate the identification of similarities: comparing, classifying, creating metaphors, and creating analo-

FIGURE 3.2
Selected Research Results for Identifying Similarities and Differences

Synthesis Study	Focus	Number of Effect Sizes	Average Effect Size	Percentile Gain
Alexander, White, Haensly, & Crimmins-Jeans, n.d.	Identifying similarities and differences	3	0.68	25
Lee, n.d.	Identifying similarities and differences	2	1.28	40
Gick & Holyoak, 1980	Identifying similarities and differences	2	1.70	46
Gick & Holyoak, 1983	Identifying similarities and differences	2	1.30	40
Stone, 1983	Identifying similarities and differences	22	0.88	31
Raphael & Kirschner, 1985	Identifying similarities and differences	2	1.13	37
Ross, 1988[a]	Identifying similarities and differences	2	1.65	45
Halpern, Hansen, & Reifer, 1990	Identifying similarities and differences	6	1.03	35
Baker & Lawson, 1995	Identifying similarities and differences	1	0.61	23
McDaniel & Donnelly, 1996	Identifying similarities and differences	1	0.30	12

[a]Effect size computed from data reported in Ross, 1988.

gies. The action steps in this chapter provide examples of these four processes. Briefly, though, *comparing* is the process of identifying similarities and differences among or between things and ideas. Technically, comparison involves identifying similarities, and contrast involves identifying differences. However, the term *comparing* is commonly used to indicate both. (For discussions of various approaches to comparison, see Chen, 1996, 1999; Chen, Yanowitz, & Daehler, 1996; Flick, 1992; Ross, 1987; Solomon, 1994.) *Classifying* is the process of grouping things that are alike into categories based on their characteristics. (For discussions of various approaches to classifying, see Chi, Feltovich, & Glaser, 1981; English, 1997; Newby, Ertmer, & Stepich, 1995; Ripoll, 1999.) *Creating metaphors* is the process of identifying a general or basic pattern that connects information that is not related on the literal or surface level. (For discussions of various approaches to creating metaphors, see Chen, 1999; Cole & McLeod, 1999; Dagher, 1995; Gottfried, 1998; Mason, 1994, 1995; Mason & Sorzio, 1996.) *Creating analogies* is the process of identifying the relationship between two sets of items—in other words, identifying similarities and differences between relationships. (For discussions of various approaches to analogies, see Alexander, 1984; Lee, n.d.; Ratterman & Gentner, 1998; Sternberg, 1977, 1978, 1979.)

Homework

The final area that relates to practicing and deepening knowledge is homework. Homework is typically defined as any teacher-assigned task intended for students to perform outside school hours (Cooper, 1989a). Cooper, Robinson, and Patall (2006) provide a brief but panoramic account of the history of homework. They explain that attitudes toward homework have been cyclical (Gill & Schlossman, 2000). Prior to the 20th century and into the first few decades of that century, the common belief was that homework helped create a disciplined mind. By 1940, a reaction against homework was established because of a growing concern that it intruded on other home activities. This trend was reversed in the late 1950s when the Soviets launched Sputnik. Americans became concerned that U.S. education lacked rigor and viewed homework as a partial solution to the problem. By 1970 the trend had reversed again, with some learning theorists claiming that homework can be detrimental to students' mental health. Since then, impassioned arguments for and against homework have proliferated (see Corno, 1996; Kralovec & Buell, 2000). Indeed, some arguments against homework have gone so far as to assert that educational researchers are trying to impose a useless practice on U.S.

students and parents (see Kohn, 2006). Many of the arguments against homework and the errors in those arguments have been addressed by Marzano and Pickering (2007a, 2007b, 2007c).

One of the most common reasons cited for homework is that it extends learning opportunities beyond the school day. This logic might have merit in U.S. K–12 education because "schooling occupies only about 13 percent of the waking hours of the first 18 years of life," which is less than the amount of time spent watching television (Fraser, Walberg, Welch, & Hattie, 1987, p. 234). A number of synthesis studies have been conducted on homework. Some of the more well-known studies are reported in Figure 3.3.

FIGURE 3.3
Synthesis Studies on Homework

Synthesis Study	Focus	Number of Effect Sizes	Average Effect Size	Percentile Gain
Graue, Weinstein, & Walberg, 1983[a]	General effects of homework	29	0.49	19
Bloom, 1984	General effects of homework	—	0.30	12
Paschal, Weinstein, & Walberg, 1984[b]	Homework vs. no homework contrasts	47	0.28	11
Cooper, 1989a	Homework vs. no homework contrasts	20	0.21	8
Hattie, 1992; Fraser et al., 1987	General effects of homework	110	0.43	17
Walberg, 1999	With teacher comments	2	0.88	31
	Graded	5	0.78	28
	Assigned	47	0.28	11
Cooper et al., 2006	Homework vs. no homework contrasts	6	0.60	23

Note: The Cooper (1989a) meta-analysis included over 100 empirical research reports (p. 41), and the Cooper, Robinson, & Patall (2006) meta-analysis included about 50 empirical research reports. Figure 3.3 reports only those results from experimental/control (i.e., homework versus no homework) contrasts.

[a]Reported in Fraser et al., 1987.

[b]Reported in Kavale, 1988.

Of these synthesis studies, the studies by Cooper (1989a) and by Cooper, Robinson, and Patall (2006) are the most robust and rigorous. The 2006 study reviewed the research literature from 1987 to 2003. The 1989 synthesis reviewed prior research. It is important to realize that the two meta-analyses conducted by Cooper (Cooper, 1989a; Cooper et al., 2006) reviewed a wide array of studies. Figure 3.3 reports only on those homework versus no homework contrasts that were used to generate causal inferences. Commenting on those studies that attempted to examine the causal relationship between homework and student achievement, Cooper, Robinson, and Patall (2006) note the following:

> With only rare exceptions, the relationship between the amount of homework students do and their achievement outcomes was found to be positive and statistically significant. Therefore, we think it would not be imprudent, based on the evidence in hand, to conclude that doing homework causes improved academic achievement. (p. 48)

With this generalization as a backdrop, a number of issues regarding homework should be addressed.

Grade Level

Although homework is prevalent across the K–12 spectrum, there is still no clear-cut consensus on the benefits of homework at lower grade levels. In his 1989 meta-analysis, Cooper reports the following effect sizes (p. 71):

Grades 4–6	ES = 0.15 (Percentile gain = 6)
Grades 7–9	ES = 0.31 (Percentile gain = 12)
Grades 10–12	ES = 0.64 (Percentile gain = 24)

The clear pattern is that homework has less effect at the lower grade levels. Interestingly, even though Cooper (1989a) found little effect for homework at the elementary level, he still recommends homework for elementary students:

> First, I recommend that elementary students be given homework even though it should not be expected to improve test scores. Instead, homework for young children should help them develop good study habits, foster positive attitudes toward school, and communicate to students the idea that learning takes work at home as well as at school. (1989b, p. 90)

In the Cooper, Robinson, and Patall (2006) meta-analysis, the issue of grade level is still not resolved. Depending on how the data are analyzed, different interpretations can be justified. Perhaps the most significant analysis is one involving studies that compared homework with no homework. In effect, this is the set of studies Cooper, Robinson, and Patall used to compute their overall effect size for homework reported in Figure 3.3. Six studies contrasted the achievement of students in classes where homework was assigned versus the achievement of students in classes where homework was not assigned. These results are summarized in Figure 3.4.

Note that in Figure 3.4 effect sizes were not computed for two studies, one with 4th graders and one with 3rd graders. The plus symbol indicates that the homework group outperformed the no-homework group on unit tests. From this pattern one might conclude that homework has a positive effect across all grade levels when student achievement is measured by unit tests covering the content actually taught.

However, when one considers studies that examined the amount of time spent on homework and student achievement, the findings are quite different. Specifically the correlation between time spent on homework and student achievement was 0.25 for secondary students and –0.04 for elementary students. One factor that seems to moderate the relationship between homework and achievement at the lower grade levels is whether researchers used the amount of homework assigned or the amount of homework actually completed as a predictor of student achievement. To illustrate, Cooper, Lindsay, Nye, and Greathouse (1998) found that in lower grade levels (i.e., 2 and 4) amount of homework assigned (as reported by parents) had a negative correlation (–0.12) with student achievement as measured by state tests and standardized tests. However, when they used the proportion of homework actually completed as reported by parents, the correlation with achievement was positive (0.22). The same pattern was observed when student grades were used as the measure of student achievement. The amount of homework assigned (as reported by parents) had a negative correlation (–0.22). The proportion of homework completed had a positive correlation (0.31). These findings and others led Cooper, Lindsay, Nye, and Greathouse (1998) to the following conclusion:

> Our results suggest that the benefits of homework for young children may not be immediately evident but exist nonetheless. . . . Further, to the extent that homework helps young students develop effective study habits, our results suggest that homework

FIGURE 3.4
Homework Versus No Homework Contrasts by Grade Level

Grade Level	Effect Size	Percentile Gain
9–12	0.46 0.39	18 15
5	0.90	32
4	+	+
3	0.71 +	26 +
2	0.97	33

Note: Computed from data reported by Cooper, Robinson, & Patall, 2006, p. 18. The dependent measure in these studies was unit tests. The plus sign indicates that no effect size was computed but that the homework group outperformed the no-homework group.

in early grades can have a long-term developmental effect that reveals itself as an even stronger relationship between completion rates and grades when the student moves into secondary school. (p. 82)

Time Spent on Homework

One of the more contentious issues is the amount of time students should spend on homework. The Cooper (1989a) synthesis reports that for secondary students the benefit of homework continued up to one to two hours per night. After that the benefits decreased. Similar findings are reported in the Cooper, Robinson, and Patall (2006) study. Specifically, the authors report on one study indicating that 7 to 12 hours per week produced the largest effect size. After that the benefits decreased. Although there are no clear guidelines regarding how much homework should be assigned at specific grade levels, education researchers make various recommendations. Bennett, Finn, and Cribb (1999) recommend 10 minutes per night, per grade level. This means that 1st graders would have 10 minutes of homework per night (including all subject areas), 2nd graders would have 20 minutes, 3rd graders would have 30 minutes, and so on. Good and Brophy (2003) provide the following recommendation:

> The same guidelines that apply to assignments done in the classroom also apply to homework assignments, but with the additional constraint that the homework must be realistic in length and difficulty given the students' abilities to work independently. Thus, 5 to 10 minutes per subject might be appropriate for fourth graders, whereas 30 to 60 minutes might be appropriate for college-bound high school students. (p. 394)

Good and Brophy caution that the amount of homework per night should not become inordinate. This, of course, requires coordination among teachers. In the final analysis, discussions about optimum amounts of homework are still speculative. As Cooper, Robinson, and Patall (2006) note, "There is still much guess work in these estimates, and optimum amounts of homework likely will be dependent on many factors. . . . Even for [the] oldest students, too much homework may diminish its effectiveness, or even become counter productive" (pp. 52–53).

It is also important to remember that the amount of time spent at homework is fairly meaningless in itself. As the previous discussion illustrates, it is not time per se that has a positive effect on student achievement. Rather, it is the proportion of homework completed that appears to produce the strongest achievement gains. By inference, large amounts of poorly structured homework will not be beneficial and may in fact be detrimental. Small amounts of well-structured homework, on the other hand, may produce the desired effect.

Parent Involvement

Another point of much discussion regarding homework is the extent to which parents should be involved. Some studies have reported minimal and even negative effects for parental involvement (see Balli, 1998; Balli, Demo, & Wedman, 1998; Balli, Wedman, & Demo, 1997; Perkins & Milgram, 1996). Additionally many parents report that they help their children with homework even though they feel unprepared and the subsequent interactions with their children frequently cause stress (Corno, 1996; Hoover-Dempsey, Bassler, & Burow, 1995).

Based on a series of studies designed to identify the conditions under which parental involvement enhances homework, Epstein and her colleagues (Epstein, 1988, 1991, 2001; Epstein & Becker, 1982; Van Voorhis, 2003) promote the notion of interactive homework. Following are some general features of interactive homework:

- Parents are provided with clear guidelines as to their role.
- Parents are not expected to act as experts regarding content.
- Parents ask clarifying questions and questions that help students summarize what they have learned.

Good and Brophy (2003) provide the following recommendations regarding interactive homework:

> Especially useful for parent–child relations purposes are assignments calling for students to show or explain their written work or other products completed at school to their parents and get their reactions (Epstein, 2001; Epstein, Simon, & Salinas, 1997) or to interview their parents to develop information about parental experiences or opinions relating to topics studied in social studies (Alleman & Brophy, 1998). Such assignments cause students and their parents or other family members to become engaged in conversations that relate to the academic curriculum and thus extend the students' learning. Furthermore, because these are likely to be genuine conversations rather than more formally structured teaching/learning tasks, both parents and children are likely to experience them as enjoyable rather than threatening. (p. 395)

Conclusions About Homework

One conclusion that can be supported is that research over the years has demonstrated an overall positive effect of homework on student achievement. Witness the effect sizes for the synthesis studies reported in Figure 3.3 and Cooper, Robinson, and Patall's (2006) statement that it would not be imprudent to conclude that homework causes improved achievement. Noting these findings, many issues still remain. The following cautions and recommendations seem appropriate given the current research on homework:

- Homework should be structured to ensure high completion rates.
- The amount of time assigned for homework should be carefully considered as well as the grade levels at which homework is assigned. The research on the differential effects at different grade levels and the diminishing returns for homework when time becomes excessive are compelling. No clear rules have emerged from that research, other than these:
  — The younger the student, the less homework teachers should assign.
  — The amount of homework that is assigned should not present a burden to parents or students.
- Homework should have a well-articulated purpose. Epstein (Epstein, 2001; Epstein & Van Voorhis, 2001) identifies a number of reasons why homework is commonly assigned and discusses the legitimacy of each. She emphasizes that homework assigned for punishment or to demonstrate to the public that a school is a serious place of study is not very defensible. Commenting on Epstein's work, Good and Brophy (2003) note that they believe that the most defensible purposes for homework are practice, preparation, and parent–child relations (p. 395).
- Homework should relate directly to identified learning goals. As discussed in Chapter 1, every unit of instruction should have a small set of clear learning goals. Each homework assignment should be directly and explicitly tied to these learning goals.
- Homework should be designed so that students can perform it independently. By definition homework is meant to be done by students without the help of a teacher overseeing the process.
- Homework should involve parents and guardians in appropriate ways. Operationally, this means that parents and guardians should be provided with guidelines regarding how to help with homework. Roderique and colleagues (1994) report that only 35 percent of school districts have written homework policies that provide even general guidelines.

Action Steps
Action Step 1. Provide Students with Tasks That Require Them to Examine Similarities and Differences
There are four basic types of tasks that focus on identifying similarities and differences: comparing, classifying, creating metaphors, and creating analogies.

Comparing is the process of identifying similarities and differences among or between things and ideas. Marzano and Pickering (2005) provide a variety of options for designing comparison tasks. With young students or when introducing students to comparison tasks, they recommend the use of sentence stems such as those depicted in Figure 3.5.

FIGURE 3.5
Sentence Stem for Comparing

_____and_____ are *similar* because they both
_____.
_____.
_____.
_____and_____ are *different* because
_____is_____, but _____is_____.
_____is_____, but _____is_____.
_____is_____, but _____is_____.

Source: Reprinted from Marzano & Pickering, 2005, p. 40.

To illustrate how sentence stems might be used, assume that a teacher has provided a series of critical-input experiences on the topics of monarchies and dictatorships. As a result of using the sentence stem, a student might provide the response depicted in Figure 3.6.

The Venn diagram is another popular format for comparison tasks. A Venn diagram used to compare monarchy and dictatorship is presented in Figure 3.7.

FIGURE 3.6
Complete Sentence Stems

Monarchy and *dictatorship* are *similar* because they both
• Are forms of government.
• Are governments with major power given to one person.
• Have examples from history in which the powerful person was a tyrant.

Monarchy and *dictatorship* are *different* because
• In a *monarchy*, the ruler is often in power because of heritage, but in a dictatorship, the ruler often comes to power through force or coercion.
• In *monarchies* today, the rulers are often perceived to be loved by the people, but in *dictatorships*, the rulers are often feared and hated by the people.
• A *monarchy* can coexist with a representative government, but a *dictatorship* often is a police state.

Source: Reprinted from Marzano & Pickering, 2005, p. 41.

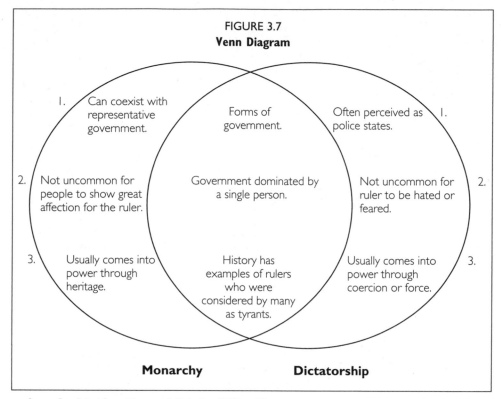

FIGURE 3.7
Venn Diagram

1. Can coexist with representative government.

Forms of government.

Often perceived as police states. 1.

2. Not uncommon for people to show great affection for the ruler.

Government dominated by a single person.

Not uncommon for ruler to be hated or feared. 2.

3. Usually comes into power through heritage.

History has examples of rulers who were considered by many as tyrants.

Usually comes into power through coercion or force. 3.

Monarchy   **Dictatorship**

Source: Reprinted from Marzano & Pickering, 2005, p. 42.

In his book *Visual Tools for Constructing Knowledge,* Hyerle (1996) recommends the double-bubble diagram for comparison tasks. This method is depicted in Figure 3.8.

A final variation on the theme is the comparison matrix, which is depicted in Figure 3.9. The advantage of the comparison matrix is that it can be easily expanded to include added elements to compare and more characteristics on which elements are compared.

Classifying is the process of grouping things that are alike into categories based on their characteristics. In the simplest form, classifying tasks present students with predetermined categories and require them to sort content into those categories. For example, assume that an art teacher has provided critical-input experiences regarding the following concepts and processes: overlapping, adding as it relates to sculpture, shading, clay, oil paint, subtracting in sculpture, charcoal, varying size, use of pencil, varying color, perspective, glaze as a medium,

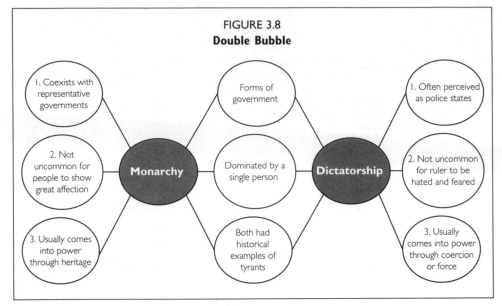

FIGURE 3.8
Double Bubble

Source: Reprinted from Marzano & Pickering, 2005, p. 43.

and stippling. The teacher asks students to sort these elements into three categories—art materials, art techniques, and art processes—using the chart in Figure 3.10. In this task, the categories are provided for students. To correctly complete the task, students must know the characteristics associated with each category and the characteristics associated with each element.

At a more advanced level, students are provided with a list of elements and asked to organize them into two or more categories of their own design. This task is more challenging because students must form categories based on their knowledge of the characteristics of the elements provided. They must explain the defining features of the categories they have constructed and then defend why each element belongs in a specific category. To illustrate, a history teacher provides students with the following list of historic figures: Joseph Stalin, Napoleon Bonaparte, Nero, Paul the Apostle, Scipio Africanus, Solomon, Socrates, and Benito Mussolini. Students are asked to organize these eight people into two or more categories. They are judged on the extent to which they explain the defining characteristics of each category and defend why specific people are assigned to specific categories.

Creating metaphors is the process of identifying a general or basic pattern that connects information that is not related on the literal or surface level. For example,

	Monarchy	Dictatorship	Democracy	
FIGURE 3.9 **Comparison Matrix**				
How the leaders come to power	King or queen gains throne out of heritage. Sometimes a monarch takes over country by force. Often a leader for life.	The dictator usually takes power through coercion or force. Often is leader for life.	Leaders are elected by the people, sometimes influenced by others. The leader doesn't have total power. May be voted out of office.	**Similarities & Differences** Actually, monarchy and dictatorship are more alike and democracy is different. Monarchs and dictatorships are similar in that power over people is taken by, or given to, an individual, but in a democracy, the people decide who will have the power. Even though monarchy and dictatorship are somewhat similar, they are also different in that the dictator takes over by force, but the monarch is usually designated as a result of heritage.
The reaction from the people	Throughout history are examples of monarchs loved by the people, but some were hated by certain persecuted groups.	Often in history the dictator is hated or feared by most people.	People are often split on their reactions but accept the elected leader, knowing they can try to elect a new one before too long.	**Similarities & Differences**
The role of the people	People are generally expected to obey the rule of the monarch. Monarch holds power and can change laws. Can become like dictators.	People must obey the dictator. Often there are serious consequences to not being loyal.	Generally the people are seen to have power through their votes. If they don't like what's happening, they can elect new leaders.	**Similarities & Differences**

Source: Reprinted from Marzano & Pickering, 2005, p. 45.

love is a rose is a metaphoric statement. On the surface, *love* and *rose* have little in common. However, at an abstract level, they are related. Both are alluring and enticing. Both can be prickly if grasped too tightly. One way to highlight the importance of the general characteristics that unite the two seemingly unrelated elements of a metaphor is

FIGURE 3.10 Classification Chart		
Art Materials	Art Techniques	Art Processes

to use a chart such as the one in Figure 3.11, which focuses on Frederick Douglass and Helen Keller. On the surface, Frederick Douglass and Helen Keller have little in common. Frederick Douglass was a slave; Helen Keller was born to rich parents and became blind and deaf. However, as the middle column of Figure 3.11 illustrates, at an abstract level they share common characteristics.

Creating analogies is the process of identifying the relationship between two sets of items. Typically an analogy has the form A is to B as C is to D. When analogies are presented to students, it is common for the teacher to exclude one or two elements that students are expected to fill in. The following are examples of analogy problems with one term missing:

Bone is to skeleton as word is to _____.
Inch is to foot as millimeter is to _____.
Martin Luther King Jr. is to civil rights as _____ is to women's rights.

FIGURE 3.11 Metaphor Example		
Element 1	Common Abstract Characteristics	Element 2
Frederick Douglass		*Helen Keller*
Was a slave as a young boy.	Had a rough beginning.	Got sick as a baby, which left her deaf and blind.
Learned to read and write anyway.	Achieved goals even when difficult.	Learned how to read Braille, write; also went to college.
Wrote books and gave speeches against slavery.	Worked to help other people who suffered like him/her.	Through her speech tours and writing, she inspired others to overcome their disabilities.

Source: Reprinted from Marzano & Pickering, 2005, p. 52.

Examples of analogy problems with two missing terms are

Harry Truman is to World War II as _____ is to _____.

Rhythm is to music as _____ is to _____.

Bury My Heart at Wounded Knee is to Native Americans as _____ is to
_____.

Hyerle (1996) recommends the use of the graphic representation in Figure
3.12 as a way of depicting the relationships in an analogy. Here the students must
actually state the relationship that ties the two sets of items together. In Figure
3.12, oxygen and people and carbon dioxide and plants have the same relationship, which is one of need.

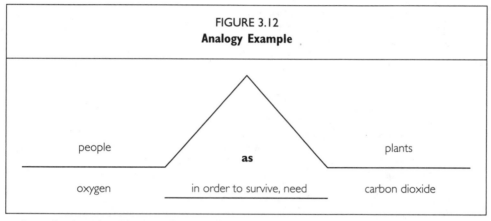

FIGURE 3.12
Analogy Example

people   plants
                              as
oxygen   in order to survive, need   carbon dioxide

Source: Reprinted from Marzano & Pickering, 2005, p. 50.

Action Step 2. Help Students Identify Errors in Thinking

Analyzing errors is a powerful way to deepen students' understanding of declarative knowledge. Figure 3.13 lists four categories of common errors in thinking.

These types of errors must be directly taught to students and exemplified
in concrete terms. With this knowledge in hand, students have a powerful set
of tools with which to analyze the validity of information. This type of analysis
is particularly useful when information is designed to persuade. For example, a
science teacher has students read an article on global warming. After reading the
article, the teacher organizes students into groups of five. Each group examines
the article for its overall logic. After adequate time has been spent analyzing
the article, group members discuss the case presented for global warming and
whether they believe it to be a strong argument. As described in the next chapter,

---

FIGURE 3.13
Four Categories of Errors

Faulty logic can occur in seven different ways:
1. *Contradiction*—presenting conflicting information. If a politician runs on a platform supporting reducing taxes, then states that she would vote for a bill designed to increase taxes, that politician has committed the error of contradiction.
2. *Accident*—failing to recognize that an argument is based on an exception to a rule. For example, if a student concludes that his friend always goes to an amusement park on the first Saturday each summer because he saw his friend go once to celebrate a cousin's graduation, that student has committed the error of accident.
3. *False cause*—confusing a temporal (time) order of events with causality or oversimplifying the reasons behind some event or occurrence. For example, if a person concludes that his favorite team won a game because the game was sold out, he is guilty of ascribing a false cause. The sell-out crowd may have contributed to his team winning the game, but there were also many other contributing factors.
4. *Begging the question*—making a claim and then arguing for the claim by using statements that are simply the equivalent of the original claim. For example, if a person says that a personal computer he built for himself is better than any other computer being sold and then backs up this statement by simply saying that it is superior to other computers, he is begging the question.
5. *Evading the issue*—changing the topic to avoid addressing the issue. For example, a person is evading the issue if she begins talking about high salaries for professional athletes when asked about her opinions on insurance fraud.
6. *Arguing from ignorance*—arguing that a claim is justified simply because its opposite has not been proven true. For example, if a person argues that there is no life after death because there is no proof of such existence, he is arguing from ignorance.
7. *Composition/division*—asserting something about a whole that is really only true of its parts is *composition*; on the flip side, *division* is asserting about all of the parts something that is generally, but not always, true of the whole. For example, if a person asserts that all police officers use excessive force because one police officer is found to have used excessive force, she is committing the error of composition. If a person states that a particular reporter supports liberal causes simply because reporters are generally known for being liberal, he is committing the error of division.

Attacks can occur in three ways:
1. *Poisoning the well*—being so completely committed to a position that you explain away absolutely everything that is offered in opposition to your position. This type of attack represents a person's unwillingness to consider anything that may contradict his or her opinion. For example, if a researcher argues against the findings of 10 studies proposing a contrary position by claiming that each study was based on flawed methodology without offering proof for these claims, she is poisoning the well.
2. *Arguing against the person*—rejecting a claim using derogatory facts (real or alleged) about the person who is making the claim. If a person argues against another person's position on morality by alleging he accepted a bribe, she is arguing against the person.
3. *Appealing to force*—using threats to establish the validity of a claim. If a person threatens to report a lie you told to a person because you disagree with her on a social issue, she is appealing to force.

FIGURE 3.13
Four Categories of Errors (Continued)

Weak reference occurs in five ways:
1. *Sources that reflect biases*—consistently accepting information that supports what we already believe to be true or consistently rejecting information that goes against what we believe to be true. For example, a person is guilty of bias if he rejects evidence supporting claims of faith simply because he does not believe in faith.
2. *Sources that lack credibility*—using a source that is not reputable for a given topic. Determining credibility can be subjective, but there are some characteristics that most people agree damage credibility, such as when a source is known to be biased or has little knowledge of the topic. A person is guilty of using a source that lacks credibility when he supports his claims by citing research from an individual known for questionable methodology.
3. *Appealing to authority*—invoking authority as the last word on an issue. If a person claims that a local government policy is valid and supports this claim by saying the city council said so, she is appealing to authority.
4. *Appealing to the people*—attempting to justify a claim based on its popularity. For example, if a boy tells his parents that he should have a television in his room because all his friends have one, he is appealing to the people.
5. *Appealing to emotion*—using a "sob story" as proof for a claim. For example, if someone uses the story of a tragic illness as a means to convince people to agree with her opinion on health care reform, she is appealing to emotion.

Misinformation occurs in two different ways:
1. *Confusing the facts*—using information that seems to be factual but that has been changed in such a way that it is no longer accurate. For example, a person is confusing the facts if he backs up his claim by telling a recent news story with key details missing.
2. *Misapplying a concept or generalization*—misunderstanding or wrongly applying a concept or generalization to support a claim. For example, if someone argues that a person should be arrested after losing a civil case, the person has misunderstood the concept of civil law.

---

knowledge of the types of errors listed in Figure 3.13 also helps students construct valid support for their own conclusions.

Action Step 3. Provide Opportunities for Students to Practice Skills, Strategies, and Processes

The activities discussed in Action Steps 1 and 2 are more applicable to declarative knowledge. The activities addressed in this action step are more applicable to procedural knowledge—skills, strategies, and processes. For some types of procedural knowledge taught in school the end goal is that students can execute them with very little or no conscious thought. This is referred to as fluency. Without fluency, procedural knowledge is not very useful. To illustrate, imagine a student's discomfort if she had to remind herself how to decode an unrecognized word every time she performed the task. Effective practice transforms procedural knowledge that must be laboriously executed to procedural knowledge that is executed fluently. There are at least three characteristics of effective practice.

Initially Provide Structured Practice Sessions Spaced Close Together

When first learning new procedural knowledge, students have little or no ability to practice on their own. During a well-structured critical-input experience for procedural knowledge, students should be provided a clear model of the procedure and even a chance or two to try it themselves. Very soon after the initial input experience students should be involved in structured opportunities to practice the procedure. *Structured* means that the practice tasks are designed in such a way as to maximize students' success rates. Frequently, the practice session focuses on a small part of an overall procedure. For example, assume that during a critical-input experience a teacher has provided a clear model of the following sounding and blending strategy:

- Look at the first few letters and the last few letters and guess what the word is.
- If that doesn't work, then look at the letters in the middle and look for familiar letter patterns.
- If that doesn't work, skip the word and move on unless you can't understand the passage without understanding the word. In that case, look up the word in the glossary or dictionary or ask someone about the word.

These elements have been exemplified and discussed during the critical-input experience. A practice session is scheduled soon after that initial experience, preferably within a day or two. The teacher introduces the practice session with a brief review of the procedure. The teacher again models the procedure for students to give them a sense of how it works. Students are presented with a few sentences that have words specifically selected because they can be decoded relatively easily by examining the first and last letters. In effect, the practice exercise requires students to use the first step only in the overall procedure. Students are asked to read the sentences on their own, paying attention to the target words that require the strategy. After each student has had time to read the passage and try the strategy, volunteers are asked to describe how they used the strategy with the target words. In short, the practice session is structured so that a few well-crafted examples are addressed and discussed. Additionally, students experience a high rate of success during the practice session.

Provide Practice Sessions That Are Gradually Less Structured and More Varied

As time goes on, more and more practice sessions are provided for students that gradually require more examples to be worked on and that gradually become more complex. To illustrate, assume a teacher has taught a particular procedure for reading a contour map. During the critical-input experience, the teacher has presented a clear model and allowed students brief chances to try the model. The first few practice sessions are designed in such a way that very simple versions of contour maps are used. To read these maps, students must know very general characteristics of contour maps, such as the following:

- Contour lines are curves that connect contiguous points of the same altitude.
- Contour maps show general topography.

In later practice sessions, more complex aspects of contour maps are required for success, such as the following:

- To determine differences in elevation between two points, the contour interval—the distance in altitude between two adjacent contour lines—must be known, and this information is typically provided at the bottom of the page.
- Close contours indicate a steep slope and distant contours indicate a shallow slope. Two or more contour lines merging indicate a cliff.

At the end of each practice session, the teacher asks students to share their new awareness regarding the strategy. This helps students shape the procedure to meet their individual needs. As indicated in the Research and Theory section of this chapter, during the shaping phase of learning a new procedure, students change, add, and delete elements. Procedures are not learned in a rote manner.

When Appropriate, Provide Practice Sessions That Help Develop Fluency

The final phase of learning a procedure is to develop it to the level of fluency. It is important to keep in mind that not all procedures presented to students are intended to be learned to this level. For example, a mathematics teacher presents students with a procedure for using a protractor. However, the teacher is aware that using a protractor is not a skill all students will require for success later on in school or in life. In such cases, it is appropriate to cease the formal instruction and the practice once students have a general sense of its execution. However, if a procedure is necessary for students' future success in school or in life, enough practice must be provided for students to develop the procedure to a level of fluency.

Practice for the purpose of developing fluency should include a fairly wide array of exercises so as to expose students to different contexts in which the procedure might be executed. Additionally, the teacher should consider accuracy and speed in these practice sessions along with further shaping of the procedure.

At this level of learning, students should be able to engage in the procedure independently. Thus practice activities can be assigned as homework when appropriate. To emphasize accuracy and speed, the teacher might have students keep track of their progress as depicted in Figure 3.14.

Students construct a chart like the one in Figure 3.14 over a number of practice sessions, with some done in class and some done as homework. This tracking allows students to see their progress over time and helps them pinpoint whether they need to

FIGURE 3.14
Example of Student Progress-Tracking Chart

Progress Measurement	Practice Session				
	1	2	3	4	5
Number of items in my practice set	5	5	5	10	10
Number of items performed correctly	2	3	4	7	9
Number of minutes to complete the items	3	3	2	5	4

focus on accuracy, speed, or both. For example, the student in Figure 3.14 is becoming proportionally more accurate over the five practice sessions (except in the fourth session) and is taking proportionally less time (except in the fourth session).

Action Step 4. Determine the Extent to Which Cooperative Groups Will Be Used

Cooperative learning techniques can be employed in a wide variety of instructional situations. The tasks mentioned in Action Step 1—comparison, classification, metaphor, and analogy activities—can be executed individually by students or in small groups. The same may be said for Action Step 2; identifying errors in information can be accomplished individually or in groups. Using cooperative groups for practice activities (Action Step 3) typically occurs after students have engaged in some form of individual practice. After individual students have worked through a practice activity, they meet in small groups to check their work for accuracy and describe their personal approaches to the exercises. For example, after students have worked through exercises on balancing equations with one variable individually, the teacher organizes them into groups of three. Each student explains how he or she approached the exercises. Through dialogue, students discover what led to their correct and incorrect answers.

Action Step 5. Assign Purposeful Homework That Involves Appropriate Participation from the Home

When considering the recommendations for effective use of homework, teachers should keep in mind the cautions and suggestions in the research and theory section. I recommend three general types of homework.

Homework That Helps Students Deepen Their Knowledge

In Action Steps 1 and 2, we saw that declarative knowledge can be deepened by tasks involving comparing, classifying, creating metaphors, creating analogies, and analyzing errors. Many times such tasks are begun in class. However, because of their length, their completion is sometimes assigned as homework. For example, assume a teacher begins the following assignment in class:

> A number of expeditions took place in the early 19th century that marked the early stages of the expansion into the western regions of the United States. Perhaps the best-known expedition was that undertaken by army officers Meriwether Lewis and William Clark. About the same time, another army officer, Zebulon Pike, explored the American Southwest—one of Pike's expeditions in the Southwest was known as the Arkansas River Expedition of 1806.
>
> Using a comparison matrix, compare these two expeditions on the following characteristics: who ordered the expedition, purpose of the expedition, areas explored, and outcomes of the expedition.

Students work on this assignment in class but then complete it at home. Before the end of class, the teacher makes sure that all students have the resources necessary to complete the assignment. In this case, students might need a specific section of the textbook. The involvement of parents and guardians in this homework is guided by the following directions:

> Your son or daughter has homework this evening. It requires them to compare two expeditions we have been studying. The resource students need to complete this homework is pages 78–84 of the textbook. The homework should take no more than 30 minutes to complete. You can help clarify your son's or daughter's thinking by asking the following questions before and after the homework is completed:
>
> - Who ordered each expedition?
> - What areas were explored in each expedition?
> - What happened as a result of each expedition?

Homework That Enhances Students' Fluency with Procedural Knowledge

A second type of homework is designed to develop fluency for procedural knowledge. Parent involvement for homework designed for fluency is typically focused on helping students keep track of their accuracy and speed. Directions to parents and guardians regarding homework designed to enhance fluency might be worded as follows:

> The homework your son or daughter is being asked to do tonight is designed to help the child solve multiplication problems quickly without making a great deal of errors. You can help by timing your son or daughter as he or she works through the 10 exercises. Your child will tell you when to start and when to stop timing. You might remind

your child that there is no expectation that he or she get all exercises correct. This isn't a test. Rather, it's practice to help them get better. It is very important that they engage in this practice.

Homework That Introduces New Content

One use of homework is to introduce new content to students. This homework commonly takes the form of students reading sections in a textbook that the teacher has not addressed but will address the next day. Variations of this type of homework include watching a DVD, videotape, or television program that presents content that the teacher will address or has addressed. Parent and guardian involvement typically includes asking students what they learned from the homework or questions that might have surfaced for them. Directions sent home to parents and guardians might resemble the following:

> The homework tonight is to introduce your child to food chains before we study them tomorrow in class. The assignment is to read pages 56 to 62 in the textbook. Remind your child that the content in those pages will be covered in class tomorrow. However, also remind him or her that it is important to complete the assignment so that he or she has some basic understanding of food chains. You can help by asking your child to summarize what he or she learned as a result of reading those pages. You can also ask your child to write out at least two questions he or she has about what was read.

Action Step 6. Have Students Systematically Revise and Make Corrections in Their Academic Notebooks

The previous action steps should provide students with multiple exposures to content. Those exposures can help them shape and sharpen their knowledge. However, students must periodically reexamine their understanding of content. Academic notebooks, introduced earlier, are particularly useful to this end. There are some advantages to students keeping their academic notebooks in class (i.e., not taking them home); the biggest one is that students will not lose them if they are always kept in class. In a self-contained elementary classroom, an academic notebook might be a three-ring binder with tabs for the various subject areas. If a teacher has 30 students, then she will need to find storage space for only 30 binders. With secondary teachers who have 30 different students in five classes, storage can be more of an issue. However, this challenge can be easily solved if the notebooks are relatively small (e.g., 100 to 150 pages). Inexpensive composition books sold at most school supply stores will suffice. They can be stored in plastic bins or tubs at the end of class and distributed to each student at the beginning of class. In this way, a teacher will be assured that all students have their academic notebooks for class every day.

With this assurance, students can make new entries in their notebooks after homework has been corrected and discussed. Students can reexamine the entries in their notebooks at any point in time—not just after a homework assignment. That is, periodically students are asked to review what they have recorded in their notebooks with an emphasis on identifying those things about which they were accurate initially and those things about which they were inaccurate initially. They also make additions to their notebooks, capturing awareness and insights they might not have recorded before. One variation on this process is to organize students into groups of two or three. Periodically, group members compare the entries in their notebooks. Members of each group identify what they agree on as a group, what they disagree on, and questions they still have about the content. Groups report out to the whole class, and the teacher addresses common agreements, disagreements, and questions.

Summary

When considering the third design question—What will I do to help students practice and deepen their understanding of new knowledge?—teachers should distinguish between declarative and procedural knowledge. Practice is more appropriate for procedural knowledge. Activities such as identifying similarities and differences and error analysis are more appropriate for declarative knowledge. Use of cooperative groups, homework, and revision activities apply well to both types of knowledge.

4

What will I do to help students generate and test hypotheses about new knowledge?

When executed well, the three design questions discussed thus far move students to a point at which they have a good understanding of new information (declarative knowledge) and can perform new skills, strategies, and processes (procedural knowledge) with some fluency. These are noteworthy accomplishments. If the teacher wishes to move students beyond these levels of knowing, then students should be engaged in tasks that require them to experiment with the new knowledge. In the vernacular of this design question, students must generate and test hypotheses about the new knowledge.

In the Classroom

Let's look in again on our classroom scenario. After students have some basic information about Hiroshima and Nagasaki, Mr. Hutchins assigns the following task:

> You are observing the interactions of those individuals who made the ultimate decision to drop the atomic bomb on Hiroshima and Nagasaki. What are some of the other alternatives the committee probably considered? What criteria did they use to evaluate the alternatives they were considering, and what value did they place on those criteria that led them to their final decision? Before you gather information about this issue, make your best guess at the alternatives and criteria you think they were considering. Then reexamine your guess after you have collected information on the topic.

Given its complexity, the assignment will last the remainder of the unit. Mr. Hutchins organizes students into groups of five to gather data on the task. Each group will report on its findings at the end of the unit. However, Mr. Hutchins explains that each student will turn in a written description of his or her findings, which can differ from those of other group members. In effect, there is a group component to the assignment and an individual component. Throughout the unit students are provided time to meet in their groups to collect data and organize the data around the task.

Research and Theory

Recall that the research and theory section of the previous chapter addressed the issue of knowledge change, and the chapter emphasized the gradual shaping and tuning of knowledge. This chapter addresses the type of knowledge change associated with what Piaget refers to as *accommodation* and what schema theorists refer to as *restructuring*—the more radical reorganization of knowledge.

The dynamics of knowledge restructuring or accommodation (or whatever name is applied to dramatic changes in knowledge structures) implies tasks that require students to question their knowledge. To illustrate, consider the task Mr. Hutchins assigned to his class. Students were required to make a prediction regarding the decision to use atomic weapons and then reexamine their predictions in light of what they discovered from their research. This type of activity is at the heart of what is referred to as problem-based learning. According to Gijbels, Dochy, Van den Bossche, and Segers (2005), problem-based learning originated in Canada in the 1950s and 1960s in medical education. Since then problem-based learning (or PBL, as it is known today) has been used in a variety of disciplines, although primarily at the postsecondary level (Gijselaers, 1995). Barrows and Tamblyn (1980) define PBL as "the learning that results from the process of working toward the understanding or resolution of a problem" (p. 18). Boud (1987) notes that "the starting point for learning should be a problem, a query, or a puzzle that the learner wishes to solve" (p. 13).

The use of PBL in postsecondary education has produced promising results, as depicted in Figure 4.1. The results reported from the meta-analysis by Gijbels, Dochy, Van den Bossche, and Segers (2005) are quite revealing. PBL demonstrated a rather weak effect on students' ability to produce examples, which Gijbels and colleagues refer to as lower-level, factual type of understanding. However, PBL exhibited a strong effect on understanding of principles and a moderate effect on applying knowledge to new situations.

As noted, PBL is employed primarily in postsecondary education. Research in K–12 contexts, however, supports a central component of PBL, the generation

FIGURE 4.1
Meta-analysis of Problem-Based Learning

Outcome	Number of Effect Sizes	Average Effect Size	Percentile Gain
Producing examples	21	0.07	3
Understanding principles	15	0.80	29
Applying knowledge	13	0.34	13

Note: Computed from data reported by Gijbels, Dochy, Van den Bossche, & Segers, 2005.

and testing of hypotheses. Bruner (1973) posits that making predictions and then trying to confirm or disconfirm those predictions is a powerful learning experience for students. Other researchers and theorists add support and clarity to this notion (Hayes, Foster, & Gadd, 2003; Linn & Eylon, 2006; McClelland, 1994; White & Gunstone, 1992). Figure 4.2 reports some of the findings regarding hypothesis-generation and -testing tasks.

FIGURE 4.2
Research on Generating and Testing Hypotheses

Synthesis Study	Focus	Number of Effect Sizes	Average Effect Size	Percentile Gain
El-Nemr, 1980[a]	General effects of generating and testing hypotheses	250	0.38	15
Sweitzer & Anderson, 1983[a]	General effects of generating and testing hypotheses	19	0.43	17
Ross, 1988[b]	General effects of generating and testing hypotheses	57	0.79	29
Hattie, Biggs, & Purdie, 1996	General effects of generating and testing hypotheses	2	0.79	29
Walberg, 1999[c]	General effects of generating and testing hypotheses	38 68	0.41 0.43	16 17

[a]Reported in Fraser, Walberg, Welch, & Hattie, 1987.

[b]Computed from data reported in Ross, 1988.

[c]Two effect sizes are listed because of the manner in which effect sizes are reported. Readers should consult this study for more details.

Mergendoller, Markham, Ravitz, and Larmer (2006) suggest that activities involving the generation and testing of hypotheses are best organized as comprehensive projects with the teacher serving as a guide. A perspective on these types of tasks is provided in the meta-analysis by Guzzetti, Snyder, Glass, and Gamas (1993), which is reported in Figure 4.3.

The Guzzetti and colleagues (1993) study addressed science textbooks and the types of activities that accompany them. They examined the effects of various activities on knowledge change in science. As indicated in Figure 4.3, simply activating prior knowledge had little effect on knowledge change. The biggest effect involved activities designed to produce cognitive dissonance—discrepancies between what students believed to be accurate and what is presented as accurate. Discussions regarding a central question showed a moderate effect.

By definition, generating and testing hypotheses involve providing support for a conclusion. This constitutes a foundational skill for generating and testing hypotheses. There are at least two major schools of thought regarding support. One comes from the field of statistical inferences. This is not to say that K–12 students must understand principles of statistical hypothesis testing. But it is reasonable to expect students to understand general guidelines regarding the use of data to support a claim. Abelson (1995) has outlined the general conventions used in this approach. Halpern (1984, 1996a, 1996b) has translated many of these principles into rules and generalizations that can be adapted for middle and high school students. Additionally, the field of philosophy provides guidelines for the effective presentation of an argument (Toulmin, Rieke, & Janik, 1981). Again, Halpern (1984, 1996a, 1996b) has presented these guidelines in ways that can be adapted for middle and high school students.

FIGURE 4.3
Research on Activities for Promoting Knowledge Change in Science

Focus	Number of Effect Sizes	Average Effect Size	Percentile Gain
Activate prior knowledge	14	0.08	3
Cognitive dissonance	11	0.80	29
Discussions regarding a central question	3	0.51	19

Note: Data from the 1993 Guzzetti, Snyder, Glass, & Gamas study.

Action Steps

Action Step 1. Teach Students About Effective Support

Because hypothesis testing and generation involve supporting a conclusion, a logical place to start is to provide students with information about effective support. Figure 4.4 provides a framework that is based on the work of Toulmin, Rieke, and Janik (1981) and Halpern (1984, 1996a, 1996b) but simplified for use with middle and high school students by Marzano and Kendall (2007).

Students do not have to understand the technical aspects of grounds, backing, and qualifiers (such as their names and defining characteristics). However, they should be aware that to be valid claims must be supported (grounds); the support should be explained and discussed (backing); and exceptions to the claims should be identified (qualifiers). To illustrate, assume that a health teacher distributes an article on the dangers of smoking. Students read the article and discuss whether they believe it provides a good argument. The teacher then presents the framework for constructing support and uses the article to demonstrate specific elements of the framework. She has prepared a poster of the various elements and displays it in a prominent place in the classroom. It serves as the general structure to examine the validity of information throughout the rest of the unit. Other than a general framework for support, students should be exposed to various types of errors in thinking that can occur when constructing support. The four categories of errors presented in Chapter 3's Action Step 2 can serve as a useful resource. They are faulty logic, attacks, weak reference, and misinformation. In addition, students can be presented with errors that are common to support that utilizes quantitative data. Based on the work of Abelson (1995) and Halpern (1996a, 1996b), Marzano and Kendall (2007)

FIGURE 4.4
Framework for Supporting a Claim

Grounds: Once a claim is made, it should be supported by grounds. Depending on the type of claim made, grounds may be composed of
- matters of common knowledge
- expert opinion
- experimental evidence
- other information considered "factual"

Backing: Backing establishes the validity of grounds and discusses the grounds in depth.

Qualifiers: Not all grounds support their claims with the same degree of certainty. Consequently, qualifiers state the degree of certainty for the claim and/or exceptions to the claim.

Source: Marzano & Kendall, 2007.

provide a list of such errors. These are reported in Figure 4.5. Again, students would be presented with clear examples of each. These examples would be displayed in the classroom and used as criteria for evaluating support that involves quantitative data.

FIGURE 4.5
Limits When Analyzing Statistical Information

Category	Description
Regression toward the mean	Being aware that an extreme score on a measure is most commonly followed by a more moderate score that is closer to the mean.
Errors of conjunction	Being aware that it is less likely that two or more independent events will occur simultaneously than it is that they will occur in isolation.
Keeping aware of base rates	Using the general or typical pattern of occurrences in a category of events as the basis on which to predict what will happen in a specific situation.
Understanding the limits of extrapolation	Realizing that using trends to make predictions (i.e., extrapolating) is a useful practice as long the prediction does not extend beyond the data for which trends have been observed.
Adjusting estimates of risk to account for the cumulative nature of probabilistic events	Realizing that even though the probability of a risky event might be highly unlikely, the probability of the event occurring increases with time and the number of events.

Source: Marzano & Kendall, 2007.

Action Step 2. Engage Students in Experimental Inquiry Tasks That Require Them to Generate and Test Hypotheses

Experimental inquiry is the quintessential task for generating and testing hypotheses. Many of the studies reported in Figure 4.2 dealt with experimental inquiry in part or in whole. In its purest form it involves making a prediction based on observations, designing an experiment to test that prediction, and then examining the results in light of the original prediction.

The first step in designing a good experimental inquiry task is to set up a situation in which students must observe some physical or psychological phenomenon or for the teacher to present such an observation. For example, assume that a social studies teacher has designed a unit focusing on the 1960s in America and the impact that decade had on the thinking and mores of the country. To introduce an experimental inquiry task, the teacher points out that one commonly accepted observation is that people who were teenagers in the United States during the 1960s lived through a period of great social upheaval. Rules and customs of all types were challenged.

Next the teacher invites hypotheses from the students regarding the behavior of those people today, many of whom are in their 60s. What predictions might be made about these individuals based on the fact that they grew up during a very liberal period in our history? Would they tend to be quite liberal today? Would they tend to be more conservative today, or would the fact that they grew up in a liberal era have no effect on their current behavior?

With their hypotheses generated, students collect data that allow them to test their hypotheses. One group of students does this by designing a questionnaire that they administer to people in the community who grew up in the 1960s. They collect this information and analyze it to determine which hypothesis it supports.

When reporting their conclusions, students are asked to state their original hypothesis and the logic that led them to this hypothesis, explain how the data they collected allowed them to test their hypothesis, and describe the results of their data collection and whether it supported or did not support their hypothesis. Finally students are asked to explain the changes the task produced in their initial thinking about the topic.

Action Step 3. Engage Students in Problem-Solving Tasks That Require Them to Generate and Test Hypotheses

Problem-solving tasks are those in which students must use knowledge in a highly unusual context or a situation that provides constraints. The defining feature of a problem-solving task is that students are challenged to determine what must be done differently given the unusual context or the constraint. To illustrate a problem situation that involves a constraint, assume that a language arts teacher has been working on the effective use of conjunctions in writing. As a problem-solving task, the teacher asks students to rewrite a paragraph leaving out all conjunctions but still conveying the basic message of the conjunctions. The constraint here is that students must convey specific meaning without using the common conventions for conveying that meaning. An example of a problem-solving task involving an unusual context is a basketball coach who makes his first team scrimmage against the second team. However, the second team is allowed to have seven players on the court as opposed to five players. The new context of seven players makes the team of five players reexamine its strategies and techniques.

Prior to engaging in a problem-solving task, students predict how the new context or the constraint will affect the situation. For example, students in the language arts class would make predictions about how the constraint of not using conjunctions will affect their writing. After the problem-solving task is completed, students restate their predictions and then contrast them with what actually occurred. They are asked to describe their conclusions using well-structured support.

Action Step 4. Engage Students in Decision-Making Tasks That Require Them to Generate and Test Hypotheses

Decision-making tasks require students to select among equally appealing alternatives. For example, students are engaged in a decision-making task when asked to determine which among the following list of literary works qualifies as a classic based on criteria provided by the teacher: *Romeo and Juliet, One Flew Over the Cuckoo's Nest, To Kill a Mockingbird, Failsafe, The Most Dangerous Game,* and *2001: A Space Odyssey.*

Typically, decision-making tasks require a fair amount of structuring on the teacher's part. The first step in designing a decision-making task is to identify or have students identify the alternatives to be considered. In the case of the sample task focusing on the literary works, alternatives are provided for students. An option is to provide some of the titles and ask students to supply two titles of their own. At this point students are presented with the overall decision-making task and asked to make their prediction as to which alternative will be selected.

The next step is addressing the criteria by which the alternatives will be judged. For the sample task, that teacher provides the following criteria:

- Is recognized by literary scholars as an example of good literature
- Is typically required reading in high school or college literature classes
- Has a story line that is applicable over decades

Again, an option would be to have students generate the criteria or provide some criteria for students and have them generate some on their own.

With alternatives and criteria identified, students can complete the decision-making process. Typically a matrix such as the one in Figure 4.6 is used. Note that three symbols have been used in Figure 4.6: an X indicates that the alternative possesses the criterion, a 0 means that it does not possess the criterion, and a question mark (?) indicates that the student is not sure. When the students count up the number of Xs for each alternative, they have a rank ordering of the alternatives in terms of the criteria. In the case of Figure 4.6, *Romeo and Juliet* has the most Xs.

Another option is more quantitative in nature but also more precise. In this system, each criterion is given a score indicating how important it is using the

Criteria	Alternatives					
	A	B	C	D	E	F
1	X	X	X	0	?	X
2	X	0	X	X	X	?
3	X	0	?	0	0	X

FIGURE 4.6
Decision Matrix

Alternatives: A = *Romeo and Juliet*; B = *One Flew Over the Cuckoo's Nest*; C = *To Kill a Mockingbird*; D = *Failsafe*; E = *The Most Dangerous Game*; F = *2001: A Space Odyssey*.

Criteria: 1 = Is recognized by literary scholars as an example of good literature; 2 = Is typically required reading as an example of good literature; 3 = Has a story line that is applicable over the decades.

X = possesses the criterion; 0 = does not possess the criterion; ? = not sure.

following scale: 3 = critically important, 2 = important but not critical, 1 = not very important. Similarly, each alternative is assigned scores indicating the extent to which it possesses each criterion using the following scale: 3 = completely possesses the criterion, 2 = possesses the criterion to a great extent but not completely, 1 = possesses the criterion a little bit, 0 = does not possess the criterion at all. This is depicted in Figure 4.7.

Note that each cell has two scores that are multiplied, and the product is displayed. The score in parentheses is the score for the criterion. The first criterion (Is recognized by literary scholars as an example of good literature) was assigned a weight of 2 by the student or students who completed this matrix. Every cell in the first row has the score of 2 in parentheses. The score it is multiplied by is the score the student or students have assigned for a given alternative relative to the criterion. Alternative A (*Romeo and Juliet*) has received a score of 3 for this criterion, indicating that *Romeo and Juliet* completely possesses the criterion. The product score is 6. Also notice that the product scores are summed for each alternative. When these products are summed the alternatives can again be rank ordered in terms of the extent to which they possess the criterion.

As before, to make decision-making tasks reap the benefits of generating and testing hypotheses, students must contrast their initial predictions with the actual outcomes of the activity. In this case, students would explain how the decision-making task confirmed or denied their original opinions. They would state their conclusions using proper support.

	FIGURE 4.7					
	Quantitative Method					
	Alternatives					
Criteria	A	B	C	D	E	F
1 (2)	(2) × 3 = 6	(2) × 2 = 4	(2) × 3 = 6	(2) × 1 = 2	(2) × 2 = 4	(2) × 3 = 6
2 (1)	(1) × 2 = 2	(1) × 1 = 1	(1) × 3 = 3	(1) × 3 = 3	(1) × 3 = 3	(1) × 1 = 1
3 (3)	(3) × 2 = 6	(3) × 1 = 3	(3) × 2 = 6	(3) × 0 = 0	(3) × 1 = 3	(3) × 3 = 9
Total	14	8	15	5	10	16

Alternatives: A = *Romeo and Juliet;* B = *One Flew Over the Cuckoo's Nest;* C = *To Kill a Mockingbird;* D = *Failsafe;* E = *The Most Dangerous Game;* F = *2001: A Space Odyssey.*

Criteria: 1 = Is recognized by literary scholars as an example of good literature; 2 = Is typically required reading as an example of good literature; 3 = Has a story line that is applicable over the decades.

Importance of Criterion: (3) = critically important, (2) = important but not critical, (1) = not very important.

Alternative Score: × 3 = completely possesses the criterion, × 2 = possesses the criterion to a great extent but not completely, × 1 = possesses the criterion a little bit, × 0 = does not possess the criterion at all.

Action Step 5. Engage Students in Investigation Tasks That Require Them to Generate and Test Hypotheses

Investigation is the process of testing hypotheses about past, present, or future events. Marzano (1992) refers to three types of investigation: historical, definitional, and projective investigation. Historical investigation involves answering questions such as, What really happened?, and Why did X happen? For example, students are engaged in historical investigation when they examine historical questions such as the following:

Why did *Homo sapiens* survive and flourish when Neanderthals died out?

How were the pyramids of Egypt built with the limited technology of the day?

Projective investigation involves answering questions such as, "What would happen if . . . ?" For example, students are engaged in projective investigation when they examine questions such as the following:

What would happen if the laws in the United States required a passport to travel from one state to another?

What would happen if the temperature of Earth rose 1 degree Fahrenheit over a five-year period of time?

Definitional investigation involves answering questions such as, "What are the important features of _____?" and "What are the defining characteristics of _____?" For example, students are engaged in definitional investigation when they examine questions such as the following:

> What are the defining characteristics of an "old-growth" forest?

> Pluto was recently downgraded from a planet to a dwarf planet. What are the defining characteristics of each?

The first step in designing an investigation task is to clearly identify the past event to be explained (historical investigation), the future or hypothetical event to be explained (projective investigation), or the concept to be defined (definitional investigation) and state the investigation task in the form of a question. Next, students are asked to make their initial predictions regarding these questions. As before, students record these predictions for future reference. With their predictions generated, students seek out information about what is already known or believed to be true about the topic, with special emphasis on identifying confusions or contradictions. For example, in the historical investigation task regarding Neanderthals and *Homo sapiens,* students attempt to find opinions of experts on this issue. Of course this would require consulting a variety of sources such as those found on the Internet, primary source material, video- and DVD-based material from the library, and so on. In all cases, students focus on identifying areas in which the experts' opinions differ. Finally, students contrast their conclusions at the completion of the task with their original predictions, presenting their conclusions using proper support.

Action Step 6. Have Students Design Their Own Tasks

The tasks described in Action Steps 2 through 5 are all designed by the teacher. Alternatively students can design their own tasks. To stimulate interest in student-designed tasks, the teacher would pose questions such as the following:

- Is there a particular experiment you would like to conduct using the information we have been studying?
- Is there a particular problem you would like to examine using the information we have been studying?
- Is there a particular decision you would like to examine using the information we have been studying?
- Is there a particular concept you would like to examine, past event you would like to examine, or hypothetical event you would like to examine using the information we have been studying?

Of course, students will be better able to address these questions if they have had some previous experience with experimental inquiry, problem-solving, decision-making, and investigation tasks designed by the teacher.

Action Step 7. Consider the Extent to Which Cooperative Learning Structures Will Be Used

Tasks involving hypothesis generation and testing are well suited to group interactions, particularly because all of these tasks require gathering information. Some information will be newly generated data, as in the experimental inquiry example involving people who grew up in the 1960s. Some information will be drawn from traditional archives such as the Internet, the library, and so on. The information-gathering component of each task can be done in small cooperative groups. For example, the teacher who assigned the historical investigation task involving Neanderthals and *Homo sapiens* might organize student in groups of five. Each group works together to gather information on this issue. Groups also work together to organize the information, take a position, and so on. In this example, the entire task is done by groups. It is also possible to split the task into parts that are done cooperatively and parts that are done individually. For example, students might work in cooperative groups to gather information and organize that information. However, they perform all other components of the task individually. That is, each student generates his or her own initial prediction, and each student contrasts his or her final conclusions with the initial prediction.

Summary

When considering the fourth design question—What will I do to help students generate and test hypotheses about new knowledge?—teachers should remember that hypothesis-generation and -testing tasks allow students to examine their thinking regarding knowledge being learned. This process stimulates major changes in their understanding. Also, teachers should be aware of the four types of hypothesis-generation and -testing tasks: experimental inquiry, problem solving, decision making, and investigation.

5

What will I do to engage students?

Arguably, keeping students engaged is one of the most important considerations for the classroom teacher. Although it is probably not the job of classroom teachers to entertain students, it is the job of every classroom teacher to engage students. One might argue that this is becoming increasingly more difficult in a society of fast-paced media and video games. In spite of these constraints, there are many things a teacher can do to engage students—many activities teachers can use to capture students' attention in a way that enhances their knowledge of academic content.

In the Classroom

Returning to our scenario, Mr. Hutchins sometimes recognizes that students are having difficulty paying attention. He considers this somewhat of an occupational hazard. He also realizes that at these moments he must do something to reengage students. At times he simply asks students to stand up and stretch, but more commonly his techniques focus on the content addressed in class. For example, sometimes he involves students in games that have the content of the unit as their focus. Quite a few of his engagement strategies are organized around questions. Students are never quite sure whom he will call on when Mr. Hutchins asks a question. This creates some anticipation and keeps all students on their toes. For the most part, Mr. Hutchins is constantly monitoring students' levels of engagement and immediately takes preventive action if that engagement is low.

Research and Theory

The focus of this design question is engagement. The importance of engagement to academic achievement is almost self-evident and has been commented on by a number of researchers and theorists (Connell, Spencer, & Aber, 1994; Connell & Wellborn, 1991; Marks, 2000; Skinner, Wellborn, & Connell, 1990). Figure 5.1 summarizes some research findings regarding engagement and achievement.

It is important to note that some of the researchers in Figure 5.1 use different terms for engagement. For example Bloom (1976) refers to participation, and Frederick (1980) refers to time on task. This is not a surprise. The term itself is used to mean very different things. Fredricks, Blumenfeld, and Paris (2004) explain that researchers have identified at least three types of engagement: behavioral, emotional, and cognitive. Reeve (2006) explains engagement the following way:

> Engagement includes on-task behavior, but it further highlights the central role of students' emotion, cognition, and voice. . . . When engagement is characterized by the full range of on-task behavior, positive emotions, invested cognition, and personal voice, it functions as the engine for learning and development. (p. 658)

Although it is very useful to think of engagement in this broad sense, this chapter focuses on on-task behavior, which is typically thought to be highly situated (Fredricks et al., 2004). Specifically, by engagement I refer to students attending to the instructional activities occurring in class. The dynamics of what causes or encourages students to engage in classroom behavior are most probably very complex. Indeed entire volumes have been written on the topic (see Pashler, 1999; Styles, 1997). With this complexity noted, the following

---

FIGURE 5.1
Research Findings Regarding Engagement and Achievement

Synthesis Study	Focus	Number of Effect Sizes	Average Effect Size	Percentile Gain
Bloom, 1976	General effects of engagement	28	0.75	27
Frederick, 1980	General effects of engagement	20	0.82	29
Lysakowski & Walberg, 1982	General effects of engagement	22	0.88	31
Walberg, 1982	General effects of engagement	10	0.88	31

Note: Effect sizes for studies are as reported in Fraser, Walberg, Welch, & Hattie, 1987.

five areas can provide useful insights into how teachers might increase student engagement:

- High energy
- Missing information
- The self-system
- Mild pressure
- Mild controversy and competition

The following sections describe these areas in a bit more detail.

High Energy as a Stimulus for Engagement

It makes intuitive sense that paying attention requires students to have a certain energy level. Research and theory point to a number of possible ways to boost energy. Physical activity is one of those ways. Jensen (2005) cites a number of studies linking physical activity to enhanced energy (Dwyer, Blizzard, & Dean, 1996; Dwyer, Sallis, Blizzard, Lazarus, & Dean, 2001). Jensen (2005) explains the reason in terms of oxygen: "Oxygen is essential for brain function, and enhanced blood flow increases the amount of oxygen transported to the brain. Physical activity is a reliable way to increase blood flow, and hence oxygen, to the brain" (p. 62). Jensen (2005) also notes, "Amazingly, the part of the brain that processes movement is the same part of the brain that processes learning" (p. 61).

The pacing of instruction appears to be another activity that affects energy in the classroom. Emmer and Gerwels (2006) explain that "the teacher needs to keep the activity moving and avoid interruptions to the activity flow by using good pacing" (p. 423). Pacing is particularly important during transitions from one activity to another. Slow transitions from activity to activity provide no stimulus that might capture students' attention. Arlin (1979) observes that poorly orchestrated translation can waste time and create a lull in classroom activity that makes it difficult for students to stay engaged. Effective transitions characteristically allow students to quickly respond to brief signals that have been taught and practiced. Smith (1985) makes similar observations.

Teacher enthusiasm and intensity also appear to affect students' energy levels and enhance engagement (Bettencourt, Gillett, Gall, & Hull, 1983). In his 1970 review of research, Rosenshine reports positive associations between teacher enthusiasm and student achievement. Research by Armento (1978) and McConnell (1977) demonstrates similar trends. Rosenshine (1970) postulates that teacher enthusiasm facilitates student achievement "because animated behavior arouses the attending behavior of pupils" (p. 510). Other studies support this notion (Coats & Smidchens, 1966; Land, 1980; Mastin, 1963; Williams & Ware, 1976, 1977; Wyckoff, 1973).

Missing Information as a Stimulus for Engagement

Human beings are typically interested in puzzles and games even though they may be of little consequence in terms of long-term goals or deeply held values; witness the number of people who do crossword puzzles and play video games in their leisure time. One possible reason for our interest in puzzles and games is that they tap into our sense of curiosity and anticipation. Jensen (2005) explains that "curiosity and anticipation are known as 'appetitive' states because they stimulate the mental appetite" (p. 77). He cites evidence that stimulation of this appetite activates one's attention (Kirsch, 1999).

Most probably, games and puzzles stimulate the human appetite because of a psychological principle known as clozentropy (see Broadhurst & Darnell, 1965; Darnell, 1970, 1972; Taylor, 1953; Weiner, 1967). The basic theory of clozentropy was popularized when Taylor (1953) developed a method of testing proficiency in English by systematically leaving out words from text. For example, consider the following:

Bill went to the _____ to buy some _____ to put on his cereal ___ they were out of stock.

As one reads this sentence, the mind naturally fills in the words *store, milk,* and *but.* Human beings tend to "fill in the blanks" when presented with incomplete information (Ebbinghaus, 1987).

This principle also has roots in cybernetic theory, which states that goal-seeking mechanisms such as human beings are always trying to lessen the discrepancy between what they predict will occur and what is actually occurring (Weiner, 1967). This might be the working dynamic underlying people's interest in games, puzzles, and questions. They pose missing information that the human mind has a hard time ignoring.

The Self as a Stimulus for Engagement

In terms of human motivation and engagement, one of the more powerful distinctions to come out of psychology is that of the self-system. It is the system that controls what we decide to attend to. Csikszentmihalyi (1990) describes it in the following way:

> The self is no ordinary piece of information. . . . In fact, it contains [almost] every-
> thing . . . that passes through consciousness: all the memories, actions, desires, plea-
> sures, and pains are included in it. And more than anything else, the self represents
> the hierarchy of goals that we have built up, bit by bit over the years. . . . At any
> given time we are usually aware of only a tiny part of it. (p. 34)

Since Csikszentmihalyi's comments, some psychologists have postulated that
the self-system is made up of two major structures—the "me" self and the "I" self
(McCaslin et al., 2006; McCombs, 2001; Roeser, Peck, & Nasir, 2006). According to McCaslin and colleagues:

> Self system structures consist of the "I" self and the "me" self. The "I" self is the
> source of more enduring, natural, and higher-order self-concept; the "me" self is
> more task or domain specific. . . . The "me" self is a sort of working self-concept that
> is the source of motivation and self-regulatory strategies in a particular context. The
> "me" self can get in the way of the "I" self. (p. 228)

The "me" self is fairly specific to situations. For example, from a "me" self perspective, a student may have a very low opinion of her ability to do well in a specific
mathematics class. Consequently, topics addressed in that particular mathematics
class would not be inherently engaging to her. The "I" self is a more generalized
construct that includes all those elements considered important to an individual
(McCombs, 2001). The "I" self is the composite of everything we find personally
interesting and valuable. For example, an individual might consider physical prowess or musical prowess as a part of the "I" self along with the values of honesty and
integrity. One might say that the "I" self is the focal point of human attention. Anything that is considered a component of the "I" self is of immediate interest.

Mild Pressure as a Stimulus for Engagement

It is certainly true that anxiety has a negative effect on people. Jensen (2005) cites
evidence that stressful events lead to the secretion of hormones that are deleterious
to not only learning but well-being in general (Ito, Larsen, Smith, & Cacioppo,
2001; Roozendaal, 2003). However, it is also true that under the right circumstances
mild pressure can have a positive influence on learning. The reason is that mild pressure forces attention on the source of the pressure. If pressure becomes too intense
or prolonged, thinking and learning are inhibited. Again, Jensen (2005) offers supporting evidence (Cahill, Gorski, & Lee, 2003; Shors, Weiss, & Thompson, 1992;
Van Honk et al., 2003). In terms of student engagement, then, pressure should be
at the right level of intensity and for the right duration of time.

Relative to classroom instruction, appropriate pressure can be generated during questioning. Specifically, if students realize that there is a moderate chance

of being called on to answer a question, it will likely raise their level of attention. This general notion is supported by a good deal of theory on effective teaching (Becker, 1988; Skinner, Fletcher, & Hennington, 1996). Indeed, increasing the rate at which students respond is a commonly mentioned technique for capturing students' attention and enhancing achievement (Good & Brophy, 2003).

Even after a question has been asked, the teacher can employ techniques that help hold students' attention. Specifically, a fair amount of research indicates that *wait time* focuses students' attention (Atwood & Wilen, 1991; Rowe, 1987; Tobin, 1987). Although wait time typically is thought of as the interval of time between a teacher's question and a student's answer, Stahl (1994) has identified a number of adaptations, which are reviewed in Action Step 3.

Mild Controversy and Competition as Stimuli for Engagement

When orchestrated well, mild controversy can enhance student engagement. Jensen (2005) refers to such behavior as "engineered controversy" (p. 79). He explains that when controversy is not too strong, such as in the form of a structured debate, it can enhance learning (Cahill, Prins, Weber, & McGaugh, 1994). Good & Brophy (2003) describe controversy strategies in the following way: "Controversy strategies include eliciting divergent opinions on an issue and then inviting students to resolve their discrepancies through sustained discussion" (p. 240).

Mild competition can also be used as an engagement activity. Good and Brophy (2003) describe the benefits of mild competition in the following way:

> The opportunity to compete can add excitement to classroom activities, whether the competition is for prizes or merely for the satisfaction of winning. Competition may be either individual (students compete against everyone else) or group (students are divided into teams that compete with one another). (p. 227)

As in the case of mild pressure, qualifications apply to the use of competition. First and foremost, it should not cause embarrassment for losing teams (Epstein & Harackiewicz, 1992; Moriarity, Douglas, Punch, & Hattie, 1995; Reeve & Deci, 1996). In response, members of losing teams might feel devalued and even scapegoat individuals they believe are responsible for the team loss (Ames, 1984; Grant & Dweck, 2001; Johnson & Johnson, 1985).

Action Steps

Action Step 1. Use Games That Focus on Academic Content

There are many types of games that can be used to engage students. Games stimulate attention because they involve missing information. Based on an analysis of

93 studies, Walberg (1999) reports an effect size of 0.35 for the use of games. This translates into a 14 percentile point gain. It is important to note that games should focus on academic content so that they represent a form of review. Marzano and Pickering (2005) have identified a number of formats around which games can be structured, and four of them are discussed here.

What Is the Question?

Just like the popular television game show *Jeopardy!* the game What Is the Question? requires a simple matrix like the one in Figure 5.2. A teacher can use a whiteboard, an overhead transparency, or presentation software such as PowerPoint to create this matrix. Words, or pictures, or a combination of both can be used in the cells; initially all cells are covered either by slips of paper or using software animation. As the teacher reveals each term, students indicate they understand the meaning by stating a question for which that concept would be the answer. For example, for the term *earthquake,* several questions would be acceptable, including, "What is measured on a Richter scale?" or "What do people in California fear will happen because of the San Andreas Fault?" For the answer "O. Henry," students could reply, "Who wrote *The Cop and the Anthem?*" or "What writer was known for surprise endings?" The teacher decides whether a student's question represents an adequate understanding of the term.

Name That Category

The game Name That Category is modeled after the television show *The $100,000 Pyramid.* This game helps students focus on the attributes of concepts represented by or associated with terms as they try to determine what the terms in a list have

FIGURE 5.2
Matrix for What Is the Question?

	Science	Math	Language Arts	Sports/Arts	General
100					
200					
300					
400					
500					

in common. In the example provided in Figure 5.3, a board game in the shape of a triangle is used (note the board can be of any shape). The object of the game is for the clue giver, who sees one category at a time on the game board, to list words that fit that category until teammates correctly identify the category name.

At the beginning of each round, the teacher hides the category names, perhaps with sticky notes or animation features. One player on each team, the clue giver, is able to see the game board. Other students, the guessers, cannot see the game board. As the teacher reveals the first category, clue givers begin to list terms that pertain to that category. For example, for the first category shown at the bottom of Figure 5.3, the clue giver might say, "water, milk, soda, tea, coffee" and keep listing terms until the guessers name the category—in this case, liquids.

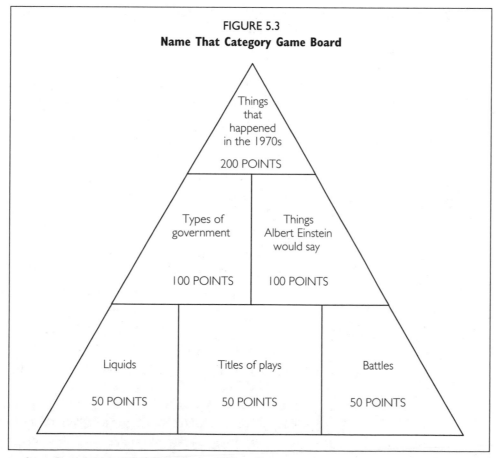

FIGURE 5.3
Name That Category Game Board

Things that happened in the 1970s
200 POINTS

Types of government
100 POINTS

Things Albert Einstein would say
100 POINTS

Liquids
50 POINTS

Titles of plays
50 POINTS

Battles
50 POINTS

Source: Reprinted from Marzano & Pickering, 2005, p. 60.

The teacher reveals the next category as soon as she sees that a team has correctly identified the first category and is ready to move to the next.

Talk a Mile a Minute

In this game, teams of students are given a list of terms that have been organized into categories. The words in the list represent related items such as parts of a circle or things associated with the planets. To play each round, each team designates someone as the talker, who receives a list of words under a category title, such as the one shown in Figure 5.4. The talker tries to get the team to say each of the words by quickly describing them. The talker is allowed to say anything about the terms while "talking a mile a minute" but may not use any words in the category title or any rhyming words. The talker keeps talking until the team members identify all terms in the category. If members of the team are having difficulty with a particular term, the talker skips it and comes back to it later. The first few teams to identify all terms receive points.

Classroom Feud

Classroom Feud is a game modeled after the popular television quiz show *Family Feud*. It can be played with teams put together on the spot by randomly organizing students into two teams. It can also be played with teams that have been set up for an extended period of time, such as for an entire unit. To prepare the game, the teacher constructs at least one question for every student in class. Any or all of the following question formats can be used: multiple choice, fill in the blank, and short answer. In general, if one type of question is asked of one team, then the same type of question should be asked of the other team. That is, if a multiple-choice question is asked of one team, a multiple-choice question should be asked of the other team. There should be an even number of questions of each type and at least enough questions to ask each student one question.

Questions are asked of each team in an alternating pattern. The teacher functions as the question asker and the judge of whether answers are deemed correct or incorrect. One student from each team serves as the responder for the group. Students on each team take turns being responders in some systematic fashion. For example, when first organized into groups, students might simply count off

---

FIGURE 5.4
Talk a Mile a Minute List

Types of Animals
mammal
reptile
amphibian
bird
insect
fish
spider

Source: Reprinted from Marzano & Pickering, 2005, p. 64.

1, 2, 3, and so on. The number each student receives represents his or her turn as responder.

The teacher presents a question to the responder for a team. The responder then turns to her team members and shares with them the answer she thinks is correct or tells her team that she does not know the answer. Team members either agree with the responder and provide support for her answer or offer suggestions as to the correct answer. The responder has 15 seconds to decide which answer to offer as the correct answer. When the answer is offered, the teacher determines whether it is acceptable as a correct answer or not. If the answer is acceptable as correct, the team receives a point. If the answer is not acceptable as correct, the other team has an opportunity to answer the question. The most recent responder for that team again acts as responder for the group. He or she has 15 seconds to come up with an alternative answer, again taking suggestions from the team. If the answer is correct, the other team gets the point and is asked the next question. If a correct answer is not offered by the challenging team, no point is awarded. When every student on both teams has functioned as the responder, the team with the most points wins.

Action Step 2. Use Inconsequential Competition

As its name implies, inconsequential competition means that students compete, but the competition is done in the spirit of fun. It draws on the principle of mild pressure discussed in the research and theory section. This is best accomplished if the teacher periodically organizes students in small groups. Group membership should be systemically changed so that students who exhibit high mastery of the content are matched with those who do not. In this way, over time every student will probably be on a winning team, and every student will probably be on a losing team. Inconsequential competition obviously aligns nicely with the use of games and puzzles (Action Step 1). As games are played, the top team or teams are assigned team points. For example, a teacher might play games two or three times a week and assign 5, 4, 3, 2, and 1 points, respectively, for the first five teams. At the end of the unit, team points are totaled, and the two (or more) teams with the highest points are singled out for some minimal reward such as coupons for movie rentals, coupons for fruit drinks from the cafeteria, and so on. As discussed in the research and theory section of the chapter, competition should be kept light and inconsequential. The purpose of the rewards is to stimulate fun.

Action Step 3. Manage Questions and Response Rates

Questions can stimulate engagement for two reasons at least. First, they are a form of missing information; second, they tend to put mild pressure on students. When used effectively, questioning techniques can be one of the most flexible and adaptive tools in a teacher's arsenal. This action step addresses four aspects of effective questioning: wait time, response cards, choral response, and response chaining.

Wait Time

Stahl (1994) has identified a number of types of wait time that can help focus students' attention. I describe five of them here:

- **Post-Teacher-Question Wait Time.** After teachers ask a question of a student, they typically wait from 0.7 to 1.4 seconds before continuing to talk or calling on another student. Teachers should allow at least three seconds for a student to respond. The teacher might even remind students to take a moment to think before they answer.
- **Within-Student Pause Time.** When students are answering a question, they sometimes pause. The general practice of teachers is to interrupt or cut students off from completing their response even when a pause is as short as 0.5 seconds. Students should be provided with adequate time to think during such pauses. Again, three seconds is advisable. The same situation occurs when students are asking a self-initiated question. Teachers will tend to interrupt when students pause even briefly during these questions. They should allow processing time to formulate or reformulate such questions.
- **Post-Student-Response Wait Time.** After a student has completed a response and while other students are considering volunteering their reactions, a small pause of a few seconds helps focus attention and sharpen students' thinking.
- **Teacher Pause Time.** This type of pause time occurs when a teacher is presenting new information and allows students a few seconds to process what was just presented and formulate their thoughts and questions.
- **Impact Pause Time.** Impact pause time occurs when the most dramatic way to focus attention at a given time is to provide uninterrupted silence. This creates a sense of anticipation on the part of students as to what will occur next.

Response Cards

Response cards can be a particularly powerful way to engage all students when asking questions (Narayan, Heward, Gardner, Courson, & Omness, 1990). To use response cards, every student must be equipped with a small (e.g., 12-inch by 12-inch) chalkboard or whiteboard and appropriate material for writing and erasing comments. If these reusable materials cannot be provided, the teacher might simply use blank pieces of paper on which students write their responses in pen or pencil. The backs of paper from discarded assignments can work well.

When the teacher asks a question, each student in class records his or her answer individually. (A variation is to organize students in dyads or triads. Responses are then recorded by each dyad or triad.) On a cue from the teacher, the students hold up their response cards. It is sometimes useful to have students present their response cards in such a way that only the teacher can see. In this way, students feel less threatened because their answers are not public. The teacher uses the group feedback from response cards to guide her subsequent interaction with students. Of course, the teacher must structure the questions to allow for short answers that can be written on a 12-inch by 12-inch response card. To this end, the most useful type of question is forced choice.

Forced-choice questions include true/false, multiple choice, and fill-in-the-blank formats. True/false questions require students to indicate whether a statement or statements are true or false. For example, a teacher reviewing the proper procedure for shooting free throws in basketball might pose the true/false question:

> Is this statement true or false? When shooting a free throw, the elbow of the hand that will actually push the ball toward the basket should be as far out to your side as possible. Write a T on your response card if you think it is true. If you think it is false, write F.

True/false questions are fairly easy to design while planning a lesson and can even be thought up spontaneously as a teacher interacts with the class.

Multiple-choice questions provide students with a series of options from which to choose. For example, a teacher focusing on a unit on the cell might present students with a question that has four options for the correct answer. Students record the letter of the option they believe to be accurate on the response card. Multiple-choice questions are very effective but require preparation before their use in class.

Fill-in-the-blank questions present students with a partial statement and require students to fill in the rest of the information. For example, a social studies teacher might provide students with the statement: "One characteristic of a constitutional democracy is_____." Students then record their responses on the response cards. As with true/false questions, fill-in-the-blank questions are easy to construct and can be designed on the spot.

A final variation on the response card is a class vote. Here students simply raise their hands to signal their acceptance of a specific response. No response cards per se are used in this technique, but the net effect is the same. Students signal the response they believe is correct. For example, if the teacher has provided a true/false statement, she simply asks for a show of hands from those who believe the statement is true and a show of hands from students who believe it is false. The same process is used with multiple-choice items. The teacher asks for a show of hands representing those who believe each alternative is correct. With fill-in-the-blank questions, voting is a little more difficult. The teacher must provide possible responses and ask students to vote for the response they believe is correct—in effect turning the fill-in-the-blank question into a multiple-choice question.

Choral Response

Unfortunately choral response (also referred to as unison response) is associated by some with ineffective didactic instruction. However, when used appropriately it can be an effective way of engaging students (Becker, 1988). It is best accomplished when important information is stated in a short phrase or sentence and students appear to be having difficulty with the information. To illustrate, assume that a social studies teacher has addressed the generalization that subcultures can be associated with regions, ethnic origins, social class, and values. She has asked a number of questions that can be answered with this generalization, but students seem confused and are not responding well. To use choral response effectively, she might engage in the following type of dialogue:

> We all seem to be missing the point here. Let me tell you the answer to the questions about subcultures: Subcultures can be associated with regions, ethnic origins, social class, and values. Now everyone say that all together. . . .
>
> Again. . . .
>
> One more time. . . .

It is important to note that the teacher would review and exemplify the various components of a subculture because the students' lack of response shows that they do not understand the range of subcultures. The purpose of choral response, then, is not to have students memorize verbatim answers. The purpose is to review an important generalization or principle about which there seems to be some confusion.

Response Chaining

Response chaining refers to linking or chaining students' responses. Response chaining begins by asking a question to which a specific student responds. The teacher then asks the class as a whole to vote regarding the accuracy of the student's response using three options: the answer was correct, partially correct, or incorrect. The teacher selects a student who has voted correctly. If the original student's response was incorrect, the teacher asks the newly selected student to make the necessary corrections in the first student's response. When the correction is made, a new question is asked. If the original student's response was partially correct, the teacher asks the newly selected student to identify what was correct about the response and what was incorrect and provide the missing correct information. Again, a new question is then asked. If the original student's response was completely correct, the newly selected student is asked another question.

Obviously, response chaining should be done in such a way that it does not embarrass students who have answered a question incorrectly. This means that the teacher must take care when responding to an incorrect answer. A number of techniques for doing so are described in Chapter 9.

A simple but highly engaging variation on response chaining is to use a small foam ball to signal the transfer of responsibility from one student to another. For example, the original student who has answered the questions starts with the foam ball that has been passed to her by the teacher. When a new student is selected to respond, the ball is thrown to him by the student who currently holds it.

Action Step 4. Use Physical Movement

Physical movement refers to any activity that allows students to move their body position. As discussed in the research and theory section, physical movement enhances student engagement because it increases their energy. There are a number of ways this might be done:

- **Stand up and stretch.** The most obvious way to promote physical movement is to periodically ask students to stand up and stretch. For example, noticing that students are particularly lethargic during a class, a teacher asks students to stand next to their desks and leads them through some simple stretches.
- **Body representations.** This technique refers to students briefly acting out important content. For example, in a mathematics class the teacher asks the whole class to stand. She then asks each student to act out the following: radius, diameter, and circumference. One student uses her left arm outstretched to show radius, both arms outstretched to signify diameter, and both arms forming a circle to show circumference. An alternative is to have dyads or triads act out specific terms.
- **Give one, get one.** This technique is best done when students are using academic notebooks. The entire activity should be done with students in

a standing position. Periodically, each student is asked to stand and find a partner with whom he compares notes. The students take a moment to identify the information they have recorded in common. Each student also identifies something he did not record but his partner did. This new information is then recorded in each student's notebook. In effect, each student gives one and gets one. A variation on this theme is for pairs to report out to the entire class regarding what they gave and what they got.

- **Vote with your feet.** Class votes were addressed in the previous action step within the discussion of response cards. Voting can be easily turned into an activity that involves physical movement by students. The teacher posts three signs in different parts of the room: the answer is incorrect; the answer is partially correct; the answer is totally correct. The teacher provides a possible answer to a question he has asked or a student has asked. Sometimes the teacher provides an answer that is correct; sometimes the teacher provides an answer that is partially correct; and sometimes the teacher provides an answer that is incorrect. The students "vote with their feet" by standing under the sign representing their perception of the accuracy of the teacher's response.

Action Step 5. Use Appropriate Pacing

Pacing and flow of activity are mentioned in almost every discussion of effective classroom management. Pacing will not be negatively affected if a teacher has well-established procedures for common administrative tasks such as the following: handing in assignments, distributing materials, storing materials after an activity, and getting organized into groups. Many of these rules and procedures are addressed in Chapter 6.

In addition to the effective execution of administrative tasks, pacing involves transitions from one activity to another. There should be an overall logic to the manner in which a lesson proceeds, and that logic should be discernable to students. The design of a good lesson is discussed in depth in Chapter 10. Briefly though, one might think of a lesson as involving segments. Typically, every lesson will involve administrative segments such as those just mentioned. Every lesson will also involve segments devoted to content knowledge. Sometimes these content segments will involve providing students with new information in the form of critical-input experiences (see Chapter 2); sometimes they will involve activities designed to help students practice and deepen their understanding of new knowledge (see Chapter 3); and sometimes those segments will be devoted to activities designed to help students generate and test hypotheses about new knowledge (see Chapter 4). Transitions between these content segments should have an internal logic. For example, if a teacher has begun class with a critical-input experience involving reading a textbook section on overpopulation, it would not make much sense to then jump to a segment devoted to providing practice in reading a contour map. It would make more sense for students to engage in some type of activity designed to deepen their understanding, such as creating metaphors involving overpopulation.

Action Step 6. Demonstrate Intensity and Enthusiasm for Content

Good and Brophy (2003) stress the importance of verbal and nonverbal behavior to communicate intensity and enthusiasm for content. They describe intensity in the following way:

> An intense presentation will begin with a direct statement of the importance of the message ("I am going to show you how to invert fractions—now pay close attention and make sure you understand these procedures"). Then, the message itself is presented using verbal and nonverbal public speaking techniques that convey intensity and cue attention: a slow-paced, step-by-step presentation during which key words are emphasized; unusual voice modulations or exaggerated gestures that focus attention on key terms or procedural steps; and intense scanning of the group following each step to look for signs of understanding or confusion (and to allow anyone with a question to ask it immediately). In addition to the words being spoken, *everything about the teacher's tone and manner communicates to the student that what is being said is important* and that they should give it full attention and ask questions about anything they do not understand. (2003, p. 238)

These behaviors should be reserved for those situations that are critical for student learning. If used too frequently or for content that is tangential, the impact of teacher intensity and enthusiasm might be diminished.

It is worth noting that Good and Brophy (2003) also point out what intensity and enthusiasm are not:

> In suggesting that teachers project enthusiasm we do not mean pep talks or unnecessary theatrics. Instead, we mean that *teachers identify their own reasons for viewing a topic as interesting, meaningful, or important and project these reasons to the students* when teaching about the topic. (p. 238)

They provide an example of a history teacher demonstrating enthusiasm for the topic being taught by his detailed knowledge and use of anecdotes and stories not found in the textbook.

Action Step 7. Engage Students in Friendly Controversy

As its name implies, friendly controversy refers to engaging students in dialogue regarding topics about which they have different opinions. It is important to emphasize the adjective *friendly* within this action step. The dialogue regarding differences of opinion should not become too heated. If so, the attention of students will be on their growing sense of frustration and anger as opposed to the content. Thus, to effectively execute this action step, a teacher must carefully select those issues about which to have a friendly controversy. For example, in a science class a teacher might realize that an upcoming section of the science text includes a detailed treatment of global warming. She is aware that although all students in class believe that global warming is in fact occurring, they disagree on how imminent the danger is and how quickly action should be taken. She plans to ask specific students their opinions regarding this issue, making sure she calls on two students with very different opinions on the matter.

The overall intent of a friendly controversy is to engage as many students as possible in the debate. A variation on this theme is to ask students who take one position on the issue to stand on the left side of the classroom and those who take the opposite position to stand on the right side of the classroom. Those who are not attached to either position are asked to stand in the middle. The teacher then asks students who represent one position to present their case. This is quite informal, in that any student who wishes to can provide support for the position. Students on the other side of the room representing the opposite position also are asked to provide support for their position. All throughout the discussion students from the middle can elect to go to one side of the room or the other, indicating that they have been persuaded by the evidence they heard from a particular side of the room. The discussion continues until all students in the middle have been convinced to move to one of the sides of the room. To ensure that the activity does not take up too much time, the teacher at any point can ask those in the middle to select one side or the other: "Even if you aren't totally convinced that one position is superior to the other, pick a side to go to right now that represents the one that you think gave the best evidence for their position."

Action Step 8. Provide Opportunities for Students to Talk About Themselves

The research and theory section of this chapter discussed the nature of the "I" self and its importance in motivation. People like to talk about themselves and those things that interest them. One simple technique for engaging students and enhancing their level of energy is to create situations that allow them to talk about their interests. A straightforward way to facilitate this discussion is to ask students to relate academic content to their interests. For example, assume that a physical education teacher has presented a technique for stretching before running. She might ask students to think of something they are interested in that is related to this technique in any way. A student who is interested in playing the trumpet might say that it is like warming up your lips before you begin to play. A student who is interested in cars might say that it is like getting all the tools out and organized before working on the car. A student who is interested in crossword puzzles might say that it is like getting a feel for the whole puzzle before trying to solve individual elements. These connections have two benefits. First, they relate academic content to students' personal interests. Second, and equally if not more important, they allow students to discuss something of personal interest. Ideally, the teacher capitalizes on this opportunity to learn about individual students. She might ask a student to provide more information, for example, about how the topic is like warming up your lips.

Action Step 9. Provide Unusual Information

Unusual information is a form of missing information. To illustrate, consider the following facts:

- Take your height and divide by eight. That is how tall your head is.
- No piece of paper can be folded in half more than seven times.
- The first product to have a bar code was Wrigley's gum.
- Earth is the only planet not named after a pagan god.
- A Boeing 747's wingspan is longer than the Wright brothers' first flight.
- Venus is the only planet that rotates clockwise.
- Three percent of pet owners give Valentine's Day gifts to their pets.
- Thirty-one percent of employees skip lunch entirely.
- According to research, Los Angles highways are so congested that the average commuter sits in traffic for 82 hours a year.
- The 1912 Olympics was the last Olympics that gave out gold medals that were made entirely out of gold.

Even though these facts have little practical value, they tend to capture one's attention. They fill in information for the reader that is unexpected. Teachers can systematically provide interesting facts related to topics being addressed in a unit of instruction.

For example, a literature teacher focusing on the book *The Old Man and the Sea* might begin lessons by telling students interesting anecdotes about Hemingway's personal life: Hemingway's mother wanted twins; when this did not happen, she dressed him and his sister in similar clothes with similar hairstyles. He received numerous awards, including the Silver Medal of Military Valor in World War I, the Bronze Star in 1947, the Pulitzer Prize in 1953, and the Nobel Prize in Literature in 1964 for *The Old Man and the Sea*. He suffered from myopia all his life, but he would not be fitted with glasses until he was 32.

As another example, a physical education teacher addressing how to play defense in basketball might tell students anecdotes about the history of basketball: Basketball was invented by Dr. James Naismith, a Canadian physician at McGill University and minister on the faculty of a college for YMCA professionals, in December 1891. He designed the game to help keep his students occupied and physically fit during New England's long winters. According to legend, basketball is an adaptation of a Mayan game. Naismith wrote the basic rules and nailed a peach basket onto the 10-foot elevated track of the YMCA gymnasium; balls scored into the peach basket had to be poked out with a long stick each time. The first official basketball game was played in the YMCA gymnasium on January 20, 1892, with nine players, on a court that was half the size of a present-day NBA court. The name *Basket ball* was suggested by one of Naismith's students.

The teacher is not the only one who can provide unusual information. Students can be asked to bring in interesting facts about the topic of a lesson or unit. At the beginning of class, time might be allotted for students to share the facts they have discovered. If students have been assigned to teams, the responsibility for bringing in interesting information might shift weekly from team to team.

On a lighter note, Jonas (2004, pp. 135–136) recommends connecting fun facts, such as the following, to content whenever possible:

- Falling is the most common nightmare.
- Americans consume five tons of aspirin a day.
- Most men part their hair to the left for no apparent reason.
- Sixty-seven percent of Americans think they are overweight.
- Americans throw away 27 percent of their food each year.
- Twenty-five percent of all people snoop in friends' medicine cabinets.
- People typically spend a year of their lives looking for things they have lost.
- One out of every 10 children sleepwalks.
- Thirty-six percent of people choose pizza for the one food they would eat if they could only eat one food.

Summary

When considering the fifth design question—What will I do to engage students?—teachers should think about stimulating students' on-task behavior via high energy, missing information, the self system, mild pressure, and mild controversy and competition. Teachers should plan to use action steps that can promote physical movement, challenge students' thinking, and stimulate their attention to the task at hand.

6

$\mathscr{W}$hat will I do to establish or maintain classroom rules and procedures?

Up to this point all design questions have dealt with content issues and instructional issues. This question deals with a staple of classroom management—the design and implementation of classroom rules and procedures. Regardless of how well behaved students in a given class might be, they still need rules and procedures. Although rules and procedures should be established at the beginning of a school year, there are many times throughout the year when students need reminders or when rules and procedures must be added or altered. Without effective rules and procedures, teaching (and consequently learning) is inhibited.

In the Classroom

In our classroom scenario, Mr. Hutchins spends substantial time crafting classroom rules and procedures during the first week. He announces to students that he has two rules only: treat each other with respect, and make the classroom a place of learning. He leaves it to the students to come up with specific behaviors, routines, and processes to ensure that these rules are followed.

On occasion throughout the year, he finds that one or more of the routines and processes require alterations. For example, initially he and the students establish the procedure that students must raise their hands and be called on before they can speak. However, he observes that this protocol seems to stifle discussions. He brings this up to students in a class meeting. Most students agree with his perception. As a result of a fairly lively discussion, the procedure is changed. Now when Mr. Hutchins signals, students are allowed to talk without raising their hands. If the discussion becomes chaotic, Mr. Hutchins immediately reinstates the original rule that students must raise their hands before speaking.

Research and Theory

The creation of rules and procedures is an important aspect of classroom management. In a study by Wang, Haertel, and Walberg (1993), classroom management receives a very strong endorsement. Specifically, their content analysis of 86 chapters from annual research reviews, 44 handbook chapters, 20 government and commissioned reports, and 11 journal articles produced a list of 228 variables affecting student achievement. They asked 134 education experts to rate the impact of each variable. Based on the experts' responses and other analyses, classroom management receives the top rating. This ranking makes intuitive sense—a classroom that is chaotic as a result of poor management not only does not enhance learning, it might even inhibit it. The next three chapters address classroom management issues. Chapter 7 deals with consequences; Chapter 8 deals with teacher–student relationships. This chapter deals with rules and procedures.

Rules identify general expectations or standards regarding student behavior. For example, a teacher might establish the rule that students should behave in a manner that makes the classroom conducive to learning. Procedures and routines describe those behaviors that will help realize the rules. For example, in the service of this rule, the teacher might establish the procedure that students cannot talk at all or can talk very quietly when someone in the class is involved in seatwork.

The need for classroom rules and procedures is almost self-evident. Emmer, Evertson, and Worsham (2003) explain that rules and procedures vary among classrooms but are evident in all effectively managed classrooms:

> It is just not possible for a teacher to conduct instruction or for students to work productively if they have no guidelines . . . inefficient procedures and the absence of routines for common aspects of classroom life . . . can waste large amounts of time and cause students' attention and interest to wane. (p. 17)

The importance of establishing rules and procedures is mentioned in virtually every discussion of effective classroom management. In fact, most of the 47 chapters in the *Handbook of Classroom Management: Research, Practice, and Contemporary Issues* (Evertson & Weinstein, 2006), which synthesizes more than five decades of research, contain explicit or implicit references to the need for rules and procedures. In a review of more than 100 studies, Marzano (2003a) estimates that establishing rules and procedures had an effect size of –0.76 with disruptive behavior. This effect size is interpreted differently from those mentioned in previous chapters. Whereas the effect sizes mentioned previously referred to *increases* in student achievement associated with certain practices, this effect size depicts an expected *decrease* in certain behaviors associated with a specific practice. To illustrate, consider the effect size of –0.76. It implies that the effective design of rules and procedures is associated with a decrease in disruptive behavior of 28 percentile points. Figure 6.1 shows the results of effectively executing rules and procedures at different grade-level intervals, as reported by Marzano (2003a).

Although the terms are used somewhat interchangeably, rules and procedures have important differences. Both refer to stated expectations in terms of student behavior. However, rules identify general expectations or standards, and procedures communicate expectations for specific behaviors (Emmer et al., 2003; Evertson, Emmer, & Worsham, 2003). For example, "treat others they way you would want them to treat you" would be a rule a teacher might establish, and "when the bell rings for recess, line up on the left side of the door after you have put on your coat" would be a procedure.

The research literature shows that the beginning of the school year is the most appropriate time to establish rules and procedures. Moskowitz and Hayman (1976) compared the beginning-of-the-year behavior of 14 highly effective junior high school teachers with that of 13 first-year junior high teachers. Their study found that the more effective teachers spent a great deal of time establishing and reinforcing rules and procedures, whereas first-year teachers spent relatively little time. Eisenhart (1977) reports the same finding with elementary students. The seminal studies on the beginning of the school year were conducted in the late 1970s

FIGURE 6.1 **Rules and Procedures**			
Focus	Number of Effect Sizes	Average Effect Size	Percentile Decrease in Disruptions
Design and implementation of rules and procedures in general	10	–0.76	28
High school	3	–0.77	28
Middle school/junior high	1	–0.62	23
Upper elementary	6	–0.77	28

Source: Marzano, 2003a.

and early 1980s at the Research and Development Center for Teacher Education in Austin, Texas (see Anderson, Evertson, & Emmer, 1980; Emmer, Evertson, & Anderson, 1980; Emmer, Sanford, Clements, & Martin, 1982; Emmer, Sanford, Evertson, Clements, & Martin, 1981; Evertson & Emmer, 1982; Evertson, Emmer, Sanford, & Clements, 1983; Sanford & Evertson, 1981). As a group, the early and more recent research (see Evertson & Weinstein, 2006) supports the generalization that effective teachers not only plan for classroom management before the beginning of the school year but also spend time at the beginning of the school year making sure that students understand the rules and procedures, that students generally accept the rules and procedures, and that students practice procedures enough to execute them in a routine fashion.

A link can be made between classroom rules and procedures and those established at home. In a study involving more than 69,000 pairs of parents and children, Fan and Chen (2001) report an effect size of 0.18 for the effect of rules and procedures at home (the researchers refer to this as supervision at home) on student academic achievement. This means that establishing rules and procedures at home as compared with not establishing rules and procedures at home is associated with a 10 percentile point gain in student academic achievement. Using research by Slicker (1998), one can estimate an effect size of –0.79. This implies that establishing rules and procedures at home as compared with not establishing rules and procedures at home is associated with a decrease in disruptive behavior at school of 29 percentile points. In contrast to these positive findings, other studies examining the impact of parental involvement on student achievement have reached different conclusions. Mattingly, Prislin, McKenzie, Rodriguez, and Kayzar (2002) challenge the strength of relationship between parental involvement and student achievement, noting methodological problems in the research. In a follow-up study, however, Jeynes (2005) estimates the effect size for parental involvement on a variety of academic variables to be 0.70 with urban elementary school students.

Some evidence shows that the utility of rules and procedures is enhanced if students have input into their design. For example, in a study of the management techniques of teachers who consistently produced gains in student achievement greater than expected, Brophy and Evertson (1976) found that the more successful teachers took pains to explain the rules and procedures as well as the reasons behind them. Good and Brophy (2003) describe the need for teachers to discuss the rationale for rules and procedures in the following way:

> Behavioral rules should be kept to a minimum and stated clearly with convicting rationales. They should be presented to the class as means, not ends in themselves.

For example, the rationale underlying rules about behavior during independent work times might stress that students should not disrupt concurrent group lessons or work by other students (because assignments require careful thinking and concentration). (p. 120)

The physical arrangement of the classroom is often overlooked when designing effective rules and procedures (Brophy, 2006; Weinstein, 1979). Brophy (2006) notes that

ecological theorists have coined the term 'synomorphy' to refer to the compatibility between the setting's design and the activities planned to take place in the setting (e.g., rows accommodate frontal teaching nicely but a circular seating pattern is better for a discussion). (p. 33)

Brophy further explains that scant research has been directed to this aspect of classroom management. One exception he notes is a study by Weinstein (1977) indicating that planned physical changes in the environment of an open classroom produced the desired effect on students' use of learning centers.

Action Steps

Action Step 1. Organize the Classroom for Effective Teaching and Learning

The physical setting of the classroom conveys a strong message regarding a teacher's approach to managing instruction and learning. Obviously, the teacher should consider the classroom's physical design before students come to class. The general principle guiding classroom organization is to create physical conditions that facilitate and support teaching and learning. Desk arrangements should provide access to any student within four steps from where the teacher spends most of his time. The arrangement should also allow easy storage of and access to materials and a clear traffic pattern for student movement. Finally, the physical arrangement should provide for flexibility in organizing students. Marzano, Gaddy, Foseid, Foseid, and Marzano (2005, pp. 139–140) have identified several areas to consider when organizing the classroom.

Access to Learning Centers, Technology, and Equipment

In the 21st-century classroom, learning centers, technology, and equipment are common considerations for many teachers. To this end, the following questions are useful:

- How many centers are needed?
- What are the primary patterns of movement around the class?
- Should some centers be close to particular books, materials, or other resources?

- What is the best placement for computers and printers?
- Do certain materials and equipment require special placement for safety reasons (for example, chemicals, lab equipment)?
- Where might bookshelves provide easy access but not create traffic jams?

Decorating the Room

To one degree or another, most teachers decorate their rooms. The following questions promote beneficial awareness regarding room decoration:

- Relative to the classroom door, what do you want students to see as they enter and leave the room?
- Are wall spaces available for bulletin boards, calendars, and displays to post learning goals, assignments, special announcements, and student work? What is the best placement for these things?
- Will you have posters with pockets for each student?
- How much empty space will be set aside for later use?

Materials

Depending on the grade level, content area, and types of lessons and units planned, the teacher might want to have the following materials prepared and organized:

- pens, pencils, and paper
- paper clips, staplers, and staples
- music and a CD player
- Band-Aids, tissues, and any other first-aid equipment the school requires
- attendance materials, class sheets, and seating charts
- in/out boxes for collected papers and transparencies
- an extra bulb for the overhead projector
- sticky notes and name tags

Students' Desks and Chairs and the Teacher's Work Area

The physical arrangement of desks and chairs can either inhibit or facilitate learning. The following questions represent useful considerations:

- How many students will be in the class?
- Does the room's layout present any safety issues?
- Where will whole-group instruction take place?
- Will all students be able to easily see the teacher during whole-class discussion or see other students who are making presentations?
- Where is the storage area for materials that will be used most frequently?

- Where is the blackboard or whiteboard located?
- What is the best placement for the overhead projector?
- What seating arrangements will best encourage student discussion and productive interaction?
- Can eye contact be made with each student?

Sample arrangements for elementary and secondary classrooms are presented in Figures 6.2 and 6.3.

Action Step 2. Establish a Small Set of Rules and Procedures

The research and theory section of this chapter alluded to the fact that in general teachers must establish rules and procedures. However, not every teacher must have

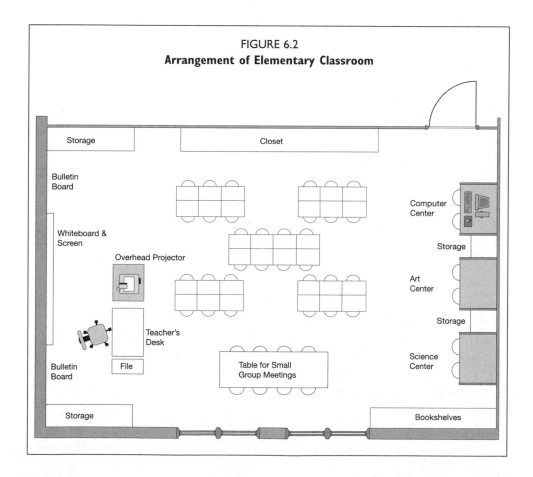

FIGURE 6.2
Arrangement of Elementary Classroom

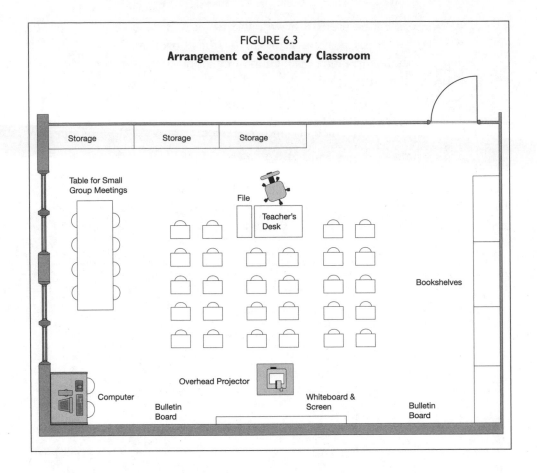

FIGURE 6.3
Arrangement of Secondary Classroom

the same rules and procedures. Emmer, Evertson, and Worsham (2003, p. 20) recommend that teachers employ only five to eight rules and procedures at the secondary level. Similarly, Evertson, Emmer, and Worsham (2003, p. 22) recommend that teachers at the elementary level employ five to eight rules and procedures. Examining the suggestions of Emmer and colleagues (2003), Evertson and colleagues (2003), Doyle (1986), and Good and Brophy (2003), Marzano (2003a) found that teachers might construct rules and procedures for the following areas.

General Classroom Behavior
Elementary level:

- Politeness and helpfulness when dealing with others
- Respecting the property of others

- Interrupting the teacher or others
- Hitting or shoving others

Secondary level:

- Bringing material to class
- Being in the assigned seat at the beginning of class
- Respecting and being polite to others
- Talking or not talking at specific times
- Respecting other people's property

Beginning and Ending of the School Day or the Period

Elementary level:

- Beginning the school day with specific social activities (e.g., acknowledging birthdays, important events in students' lives)
- Beginning the day with the Pledge of Allegiance
- Doing administrative activities (e.g., taking attendance, collecting lunch money)
- Ending the day by cleaning the room and individual tasks
- Ending the day by putting away materials

Secondary level:

- Taking attendance at the beginning of the period
- At the beginning of the period, addressing students who missed the work from the previous day because of absence
- Dealing with students who are tardy at the beginning of the period
- Ending the period with clear expectations for homework

Transitions and Interruptions

Elementary level:

- Leaving the room
- Returning to the room
- Use of the bathroom
- Use of the library and resource room
- Use of the cafeteria
- Use of the playground
- Fire and disaster drills
- Classroom helpers

Secondary level:

- Leaving the room
- Returning to the room
- Fire and disaster drills
- Split lunch period

Use of Materials and Equipment

Elementary level:

- Distributing materials
- Collecting materials
- Storage of common materials
- The teacher's desk and storage areas
- Students' desks and storage areas
- Use of the drinking fountain, sink, and pencil sharpener

Secondary level:

- Distributing materials
- Collecting materials
- Storage of common materials

Group Work

Elementary level:

- Movement in and out of the group
- Expected behaviors of students in the group
- Expected behaviors of students not in the group
- Group communication with the teacher

Secondary level:

- Movement in and out of the group
- Group leadership and roles in the group
- The relationship of the groups to the rest of the class or other groups in the class
- Group communication with the teacher

Seatwork and Teacher-Led Activities

Elementary level:

- Student attention during presentations
- Student participation

- Talking among students
- Obtaining help
- Out-of-seat behavior
- Behavior when work has been completed

Secondary level:

- Student attention during presentations
- Student participation
- Talking among students
- Obtaining help
- Out-of-seat behavior
- Behavior when work has been completed

Again, a small set of rules and procedures should be constructed from these selected areas. Marzano, Gaddy, Foseid, Foseid, and Marzano (2005, p. 12) provide examples of typical sets of rules and procedures at different grade levels. They are listed in Figure 6.4.

Action Step 3. Interact with Students About Classroom Rules and Procedures

When designing rules and procedures, it is important to interact with students about them from the outset. As noted, the best time to do this is the very beginning of the school year for elementary teachers or the beginning of a new term for secondary teachers.

Interactions can take a number of forms. Interactions might be as simple as explaining each rule and procedure to students and discussing with them the logic and need for the rules and procedures. For example, assume a teacher has established the following general rule for handling conflicts that might arise in class: "Forgive, forget, and move on." Because this is a rule, it is very general in nature. Interaction with students focuses on identifying the specific behaviors that operationalize this rule. As a result of classroom discussion, teachers and students generate the following procedures:

- Listen to the other person before doing or saying anything.
- Try to solve the conflict yourself before going to the teacher.
- If things start to get out of hand, back off and bring the issue to the teacher.

These student-generated procedures would be listed underneath the general rule and prominently posted in the classroom for future reference.

FIGURE 6.4
Example of Classroom Rules

Classroom Rules (1st Grade)
1. Be safe.
2. Be kind.
3. Be polite.

Classroom Rules (2nd Grade)
1. Listen carefully.
2. Follow directions.
3. Work quietly. Do not disturb others who are working.
4. Respect others. Be kind with your words and actions.
5. Respect school and personal property.
6. Work and play safely.

Classroom Rules (3rd Grade)
1. Be kind and respectful to others and to yourself.
2. All students have the right to be treated with respect.
3. Use your manners and be safe.
4. Keep your hands and mean words to yourself.
5. Have fun.

Our Basic Rights
1. All students have the right to be treated with respect.
2. All teachers have the right to be treated with respect.
3. Everyone has the right to feel safe in the teaching and learning environment.
4. Everyone must demonstrate a respect for the school's property.

Rules for Classroom Behavior (Secondary)
1. Respect one another at all times.
2. Maintain eye contact when communicating with others or when someone—a teacher or a classmate—is speaking.
3. Use your "6-inch" voice when working in small groups or pairs.
4. When working in groups, say "please" and "thank you"; praise each other and use good manners.
5. Remember: Only one person speaks at a time.

Making Our Classroom a Place for Learning
1. Respect others—when someone is speaking, listen.
2. Follow directions.
3. Keep hands, feet, objects, and unkind remarks to yourself.
4. Bring required materials to class.
5. Be in your seat when the bell rings.
6. Raise your hand.
7. Remember the rules we set for leaving your seat or leaving the classroom: Maintain respect and quiet, think before you act, and minimize disruptions to the learning process.

Source: Marzano, Gaddy, Foseid, Foseid, & Marzano, 2005.

Clearly, rules and procedures do not have to be generated by the teacher. Another option is to devote class time to designing rules and procedures from the ground up. In other words, the teacher shifts responsibility to the entire class for crafting their rules and the specific procedures associated with them. Quite obviously, this takes much more time. The interaction usually begins with a whole-class discussion regarding the characteristics of a class that facilitates learning. The teacher might then organize students into small groups that generate general rules that should govern behavior. In the context of a whole-class discussion, the students and teacher aggregate these lists into a single list. Students then identify the specific behaviors and procedures associated with the general rules. Although opening up the design of classroom rules and procedures to students certainly takes substantial time, it might significantly increase student ownership of the management of the classroom.

Action Step 4. Periodically Review Rules and Procedures, Making Changes as Necessary

Even when rules and procedures are well designed initially, they must be reviewed and adapted as time goes by. Review is necessary when students seem to be systematically violating or ignoring a rule or procedure. For example, a teacher might notice that students are becoming lax about using the identified procedure for handing in homework. Rather than trying to remedy the situation by enforcing some type of negative consequence (discussed in Chapter 7), the teacher calls the lapse in behavior to students' attention. Next, the teacher reviews the specifics of the procedure, perhaps modeling the steps or having students practice the steps.

On occasion a rule or procedure might have to be changed or dropped altogether. Using the example of the procedure for handing in homework, upon discussion with students the teacher might find that students believe the procedure is too cumbersome and punitive. The teacher and students jointly decide that the procedure should be changed.

As another example, assume that a procedure has been established for students leaving their seats during seatwork. It requires students to raise their hands and obtain permission from the teacher. Over time, the teacher and students recognize that this procedure simply does not work well. At times the teacher does not notice a student's raised hand for quite some time. Additionally, students assert that they can be trusted to leave their seats without disrupting the class. After discussion, the teacher and students agree to suspend the rule.

Action Step 5. Use Classroom Meetings

Classroom meetings can be useful in the design and maintenance of rules and procedures (Edwards & Mullis, 2003; Sorsdahl & Sanche, 1985). Classroom meetings might be scheduled regularly for 10 minutes on Friday every week or every other week. In these meetings, the teacher and students bring up issues relative to classroom management, including rules and procedures. For example, in a high school science class, students bring up the fact that the procedure for distributing lab equipment needs to be modified. If students do not feel comfortable volunteering issues in front of the entire class, then the teacher might institute a policy in which students suggest issues to the teacher individually and then the teacher introduces those issues at regularly scheduled class meetings. Even if rules and procedures are not altered, added, or deleted during these meetings, the message conveyed to students is that the management of the classroom is in their control. They can shape the environment to produce a classroom that is respectful of individuals and accommodates the learning process.

Summary

When considering the sixth design question—What will I do to establish or maintain classroom rules and procedures?—teachers should keep in mind that this is one of three critical aspects of classroom management. Establishing rules and procedures at the beginning of the year is important, as is modifying rules and procedures over time. Teachers should now be aware that they can take the following action steps: organizing the physical environment of the classroom, identifying a small set of rules and procedures, interacting with students about rules and procedures, reviewing and changing rules and procedures, and using classroom meetings.

7

*W*hat will I do to recognize and acknowledge adherence and lack of adherence to classroom rules and procedures?

Consequences are the other side of rules and procedures. When students do a good job at following rules and procedures, their willingness to be a positive influence in the class should be recognized and acknowledged. Conversely, when students do not follow classroom rules and procedures, their behavior that detracts from learning should be noted. In effect, consequences should be both positive and negative. As with rules and procedures, consequences should be established at the beginning of the school year. Unlike rules and procedures, consequences are typically addressed routinely and frequently. That is, the teacher frequently reinforces adherence to rules and procedures as opposed to taking it for granted, and the teacher also acknowledges lack of adherence to rules and procedures. Rules and procedures for which there are no consequences—positive and negative—do little to enhance learning.

In the Classroom

Let's return to our scenario. During the first week of class, Mr. Hutchins had students identify the consequences that would be enforced for not following rules and procedures. He was a little surprised at how harsh some of the students wanted those consequences to be. He also had students identify the positive consequences or acknowledgments they wanted when rules and procedures were followed. Again, he was surprised at how little students wanted in terms of positive consequences. Many students said they just wanted Mr. Hutchins to acknowledge that they were doing a good job.

Throughout the year, Mr. Hutchins makes sure that he acknowledges how well rules and procedures are being followed, never allowing positive behavior to go unnoticed. Many times he thanks students for their cooperation in making the classroom a positive learning environment. On the other hand, he also acknowledges violations of classroom rules and procedures immediately and employs the specific consequences that have been established. Students appreciate his straightforward and consistent approach. On Fridays, Mr. Hutchins provides a brief summary of his perceptions of how well students followed the rules and procedures throughout the week. Students are invited to share their perceptions. Frequently these Friday interludes turn into classroom discussions about what is going well in class and what can be improved.

Research and Theory

This design question relates to positive consequences for following classroom rules and procedures as well as negative consequences for not following classroom rules and procedures. A meta-analysis by Stage and Quiroz (1997) attests to the potential benefits of such an approach. These findings are reported in Figure 7.1.

Stage and Quiroz organize consequences into four general categories. *Reinforcement* involves straight positive consequences, recognizing adherence to rules and procedures. *Punishment* involves negative consequences, recognizing and evoking sanctions for lack of adherence to rules and procedures. As its name implies *no immediate consequence* does not involve immediate consequences. Rather, it involves many of the behaviors that Emmer and Gerwels (2006) refer to as "nonintrusive interventions" (p. 430), such as having a conference with the student after class

FIGURE 7.1
Research on Punishment, Reinforcement, or No Consequences

Disciplinary Technique	Number of Effect Sizes	Average Effect Size	Percentile Decrease in Disruptions
Punishment and reinforcement	12	−0.97	33
Reinforcement	101	−0.86	31
Punishment	40	−0.78	28
No immediate consequence	70	−0.64	24

Source: Adapted from Marzano, 2003a, p. 29. Data from Stage & Quiroz, 1997.

about the inappropriate behavior. The category *punishment and reinforcement* refers to a combination of positive and negative consequences.

At least two rather striking conclusions could be drawn from Figure 7.1. The first is that all four categories of strategies work. The lowest percentile decrease in disruptive behavior is 24, and the highest reported percentile decrease is 33. Stage and Quiroz (1997) reflect on their findings:

> In summary, this meta-analytic study demonstrates that interventions to reduce disruptive behavior work in public schools. . . . We hope that these findings serve to separate the myth that disruptive classroom behavior cannot be effectively managed from the reality that interventions widely used in our schools do, in fact, reduce disruptive behavior. (pp. 361–362)

The second conclusion is that a combination of positive and negative consequences appears to be the optimum approach. This conclusion is echoed by Miller, Ferguson, and Simpson (1998) in their review of the research literature: "Clearly, the results of these studies should permit schools to strike . . . a 'healthy balance' between rewards and punishments" (p. 56).

It is important to note that the topic of positive and negative consequences is a controversial one, at least as played out in the literature. This issue was introduced in Chapter 1 in the discussion of celebrating student success. It is discussed here in the context of recognizing and acknowledging student behavior.

Good and Brophy (2003) summarize much of the debate. They explain that some educational theorists oppose reinforcement even in principle. They note that early studies demonstrated that if you reward people for things they are already doing by their own volition, then they will begin to decrease their intrinsic motivation (Deci & Ryan, 1985). Additionally if students' attention becomes focused on external rewards as opposed to tasks in which they are engaged, their performance begins to diminish. Good and Brophy identify the following as particularly detrimental to performance and intrinsic motivation:

- Highly attractive awards presented in ways that call attention to them
- Rewards that are given simply for engaging in an activity as opposed to being contingent on achieving a specific goal
- Rewards that are tied to behavior as control devices

In the final analysis, Good and Brophy (2003) note that rhetoric regarding both sides of the issue is probably extreme:

> For now, we will emphasize that we believe that both the need for and the dangers of using reinforcement in the classroom have been exaggerated. It is becoming increasingly clear that the effects of reinforcement depend on the nature of the reinforcement used and especially on how it is presented. (p. 129)

In effect, both positive and negative consequences must be used in appropriate ways. This should be kept in mind when reading the remainder of this chapter. Most of the techniques suggested can be used to enhance student learning when used appropriately. When used inappropriately, they can be detrimental to learning.

With that caveat in mind, it is useful to consider effect sizes for various types of behavior computed by Marzano (2003a) and reported in Figure 7.2. Again, it is important to remember that a negative effect size is associated with a decrease in disruptive behavior.

Tangible recognition involves providing students with some symbol or token for appropriate behavior. Of all the interventions listed in Figure 7.2, tangible recognition is the one that can be most easily misused. Good and Brophy (2003) provide warnings regarding the potential negative consequences of tangible recognition but also acknowledge its utility:

> Students' accomplishments can be rewarded not only with high grades, but also with verbal praise, public recognition (hanging examples of good work for public display, describing accomplishments in the school newspaper), symbolic rewards (stars, happy faces, stickers), extra privileges or activity choices, or material rewards (snacks, prizes). (p. 127)

Token economies are a popular form of tangible recognition, with some research supporting their effectiveness (Kaufman & O'Leary, 1972; O'Leary, Becker, Evans, & Saudargas, 1969; Reitz, 1994). With token economies, students receive some type of chit for appropriate behavior or the cessation of inappropriate behavior.

FIGURE 7.2
Effect Sizes for Positive and Negative Consequences

Type of Intervention	Number of Effect Sizes	Average Effect Size	Percentile Decrease in Disruptions
Tangible recognition	20	−0.82	29
Teacher reaction	25	−1.00	34
"Withitness"	3	−1.42	42
Direct cost	7	−0.57	21
Group contingency	13	−0.98	34
Home contingency	3	−0.56	21

Token economies appear most powerful if chits are awarded for positive behavior and taken away for negative behavior.

Teacher reaction is probably the most general category of intervention listed in Figure 7.2. It includes verbal and nonverbal cues from the teacher that indicate whether a student's behavior is appropriate or not appropriate. Within this category is stimulus cueing (Carr & Durand, 1985; Lobitz, 1974). It involves providing a cue to students before inappropriate behavior occurs.

Withitness is one of the most well-recognized classroom management techniques. The term *withitness* was coined by Jacob Kounin (1983). Kounin describes withitness as follows:

> Classroom management is unrelated to how you handle misbehavior and how you handle misbehavior is unrelated to the amount of misbehavior you get. There is one exception. For example, two boys are in the back of the class during an arithmetic lesson. One of them grabs the other's paper and the second one grabs his paper. The first one pokes the second in the shoulder jokingly and the other one pokes the first, then they chase each other around the table laughing, then one pulls the shirt off the other and the second pulls his shirt off. Then he unzips the second guy's fly and he unzips the first guy's fly and the teacher says, "Boys, stop that!" We said that was too late. So it wasn't how she said "stop it" or whether she walked closer or didn't walk closer. Or whether she threatened or didn't threaten. It was whether she demonstrated to the class that she knew what was going on, that she had eyes in the back of her head. It was not whether she came in right away but whether she came in before something spread or became more serious. And we gave that the technical term of *withitness*. That is the only thing that correlated with management success. (1983, p. 7)

Brophy (1996) describes withitness in more technical and less anecdotal terms:

> Remaining "with it" (aware of what is happening in all parts of the classroom at all times) by continuously scanning the classroom, even when working with small groups or individuals. Also demonstrating this withitness to students by intervening promptly and accurately when inappropriate behavior threatens to become disruptive. This minimizes timing errors (failing to notice and intervene until an incident has already become disruptive) and target errors (mistakes in identifying the students responsible for the problem). (p. 11)

Direct cost includes those interventions that involve a direct and concrete consequence for misbehavior. Included in this category is isolation time-out, which involves the removal of a student from the classroom to a location reserved for disruptive students (Drabman & Spitalnik, 1973; Zabel, 1986). Overcorrection is another form of direct cost; it is used when a student misbehaves in such a way that destroys some physical aspect of the classroom (Foxx, 1978). For example, if a student damaged his textbook, overcorrection would involve the student fixing every textbook, not just his own.

Group contingency techniques are similar to tangible recognition techniques in that they involve some form of recognition for appropriate behavior. Such recognition might be taken away for inappropriate behavior. In addition, group contingency techniques target groups of students as opposed to individual students. Group contingency techniques that require every student in the group to meet the behavioral criterion appear to be particularly useful (Litow & Pumroy, 1975).

Home contingency involves bringing parents into the management process. If a student does not meet a behavior criterion in class, then the parents or guardians are involved. Interestingly, evidence shows that involving parents as a positive or negative consequence is a powerful intervention. For example, a number of studies have examined students' perceptions of the most important positive consequences as well as the most important negative consequences (Caffyn, 1989; Harrop & Williams, 1992; Houghton, Merrett, & Wheldall, 1988; Merrett & Tang, 1994; Miller, Ferguson, & Simpson, 1998; Sharpe, Wheldall, & Merrett, 1987). Notifying parents about students' positive behaviors is typically ranked quite high by students as a reward for positive behavior; similarly, notifying parents about negative behaviors is commonly ranked high as a powerful deterrent by students.

Action Steps

The action steps in this chapter are organized into two broad categories: those that acknowledge adherence to rules and procedures and those that acknowledge lack of adherence to rules and procedures.

Strategies That Acknowledge Adherence to Rules and Procedures

Action Step 1. Use Simple Verbal and Nonverbal Acknowledgment

One obvious way to provide positive reinforcement for adherence to rules and procedures is to use verbal and nonverbal forms of recognition. This might take the form of saying to the class as a whole or to specific students that they did a nice job carrying out a procedure. For example, during a lab class in science, a teacher notes that the entire class or a specific group of students did an exceptional job of putting away the lab equipment. Following up such comments with a thank-you is also useful. A variation on the theme is to recount specific student behaviors. For example, if students have done a particularly good job at handing in seatwork assignments at the end of class, the teacher might say:

> Nice job at handing in your seatwork. Notice that everyone was quiet while you did this. Assignments were passed from the back to the front and then from the row closest to the window to the row closest to the door. This keeps all assignments in the same order as my seating chart, and it saves me a lot of time reorganizing the papers. Thanks a lot.

This has the effect of reviewing the procedure while at the same time acknowledging students for their successful execution of the procedure.

Nonverbal acknowledgments are also quite effective. These take the form of smiles, nods, winks, thumbs-up signs, A-OK signs, and the like. For example, if a particular student has done a good job of raising his hand before asking a question, the teacher might simply smile and nod at the student. This keeps the interaction more private than verbal acknowledgments. For some students private types of interactions might be more appropriate if they are embarrassed by public acknowledgment.

In their book, *Discipline with Dignity,* Curwin and Mendler (1988) provide an interesting perspective on this issue. They recommend a strategy they refer to as "catching a student being good" (1988, p. 97). They explain in the following way:

> About every 15 to 20 minutes (2 or 3 times in a secondary class), catch a student being good . . . speak softly so no other student can hear. Tell the student you like the way he is paying attention, or that he did a nice job on his homework because it was very detailed, or that the questions he is asking in class are very thought provoking. . . . This strategy helps ensure the students' privacy because other students will never know if your private discussion was positive feedback or giving a consequence. The student might make the conversation public, but then it becomes his responsibility to deal with the loss of privacy. (1988, p. 97)

Action Step 2. Use Tangible Recognition When Appropriate

Tangible recognition is a broad term that describes any form of concrete recognition of student adherence to rules and procedures. Of course the research on token economies discussed in the research and theory section is the basis for this action step. In its purest form, a token economy assigns points to adherence to rules and procedures. For example, an elementary teacher might establish a system of points for adherence to rules and procedures throughout the day. At the end of the week, points are added up for each student. Students who have amassed a certain number of points are recognized with some nominal reward such as a certificate for a free fruit drink from the school cafeteria. At the secondary level, the recognition is typically much more symbolic, and the reward is delayed. For example, a high school science teacher has established a system whereby five points are allotted each day for adherence to rules and procedures. Each student is assigned five or less points depending on how well he or she followed the rules and procedures during the class period. At the end of the unit or grading period points accrued by each student are summed. Each student who amassed a certain number of points is provided with some concrete recognition of this accomplishment, such as a call home to the parents or guardians or a letter sent home.

A variation is for the teacher to distribute a form such as the one in Figure 7.3 to each student at the beginning of class each Monday. These forms are kept in the upper left-hand corner of each student's desk throughout the week. Each day, the student begins with 20 points in each of the five categories presented in the five rows of the matrix. If the student does not adhere to the behavior in a specific area, points are adjusted accordingly. For example, if the student comes late to class on Monday, then the teacher circles zero in the appropriate cell. If that same student works all period, then the teacher circles 20 in the appropriate cell. One useful aspect of this strategy is that the teacher can change a student's scores as the student's behavior changes throughout the day or period. For example, if a student is not being verbally respectful in class, the teacher circles a zero in that cell. However, if the student's behavior changes, then the teacher circles 10 to indicate that the student's negative behavior is being corrected. At the end of the class period, students tally their total points, and the teacher records their totals in a separate ledger that he keeps.

FIGURE 7.3 Daily Recognition Form					
Expectations	Monday	Tuesday	Wednesday	Thursday	Friday
Is on time to class	0-20	0-20	0-20	0-20	0-20
Is prepared for class	0-10-20	0-10-20	0-10-20	0-10-20	0-10-20
Works all period	0-10-20	0-10-20	0-10-20	0-10-20	0-10-20
Is verbally and physically respectful	0-10-20	0-10-20	0-10-20	0-10-20	0-10-20
Completes all seatwork	0-10-20	0-10-20	0-10-20	0-10-20	0-10-20

A final variation is to code student behavior. This is most common at the elementary level. For example, a teacher might establish a color code for behavior. A green card indicates exceptional attention and adherence to rules; the student is making an obvious effort to pay attention and behave. A yellow card indicates acceptable behavior, but improvement could be made. A brown card indicates unacceptable behavior. Students have all three cards on their desks in a stack with the one on top indicating the student's present level of behavior and attention. All students start with a green card on top at the beginning of class. During class, the teacher moves throughout the room, changing the color of the card exposed on each student's desk to indicate the level of behavior observed. A student whose exposed card has been changed from green to brown can have the green card returned if he reengages in the class at an appropriate level.

Action Step 3. Involve the Home in Recognition of Positive Student Behavior

Recognition of good behavior can extend beyond the classroom. As mentioned in the research and theory section of this chapter, students view the teacher or school contacting the home about their good behavior as a valued acknowledgment. This recognition can be done a number of ways.

Phone Calls Home

A phone call home is an obvious way to bring parents and guardians into the recognition process. A teacher might discipline herself to make one phone call home per day about some student's positive behavior. In this way, over a 180-day school year virtually every student receives a positive phone call about his or her behavior. Additionally, such phone calls do not have to take very long. Messages can be left on a voice mail system or answering machine:

> Hello Mr. and Mrs. Carleton. This is Mrs. Winning, your daughter Lindsay's algebra teacher. I just wanted to leave a message saying what a pleasure she has been in class today. She came well prepared, volunteered some great answers to tough questions, and even helped explain some difficult content to some students who were having a tough time understanding. Please let her know that I appreciate her behavior today. You might also think of giving her a pat on the back.

E-mails

Many homes have access to e-mail, and many teachers can send e-mail messages right from school. Teachers might systematically use this powerful technological tool as a way of communicating positive messages about student behavior. For example, at the end of each day an elementary teacher sends a brief message to parents or guardians:

> This is Mrs. Braun, Sarah's 3rd grade teacher. I wanted to let you know about some things Sarah did today that helped her learn and made my work much easier. She raised her hand each time she asked a question. She volunteered answers when I asked questions, and she was prepared for everything we did today.

If the teacher does not have the time to compose a personal message for each student, she might send a general message such as the following to students who demonstrated positive behavior in class: "This message is from Mrs. Braun, your child's 3rd grade teacher. I wanted you to know how well behaved your child was today. Please make mention of this tonight."

Notes Home and Certificates of Good Behavior

A low-tech but powerful way of communicating positive behavior to parents and guardians is to write a note home. The note might be as simple as, "Mr. and Mrs. Fenton: Please give your daughter Jennifer an extra hug tonight. Her behavior in class was excellent." Certificates of good behavior are less personalized but easier to administer. A teacher simply prints up a number of messages such as the following on colored paper: "Your child was a star today!" At the end of the day these certificates are passed out to students who have exhibited exceptional behavior.

Strategies That Acknowledge Lack of Adherence to Rules and Procedures

Action Step 4. Be With-It

Teacher awareness of potential problems and quick attention to those situations are at the core of effective classroom management. Such behavior defines withitness. Four general actions constitute withitness: being proactive, occupying the entire room, noticing potential problems, and using a series of graduated actions.

Being Proactive

Although not commonly associated with withitness in the research literature, being proactive about potential problems is a logical component behavior. This simply means that the teacher tries to be aware of incidents that have happened outside of class that might affect student behavior in class. For example, a high school teacher becomes aware of the fact that two students in her class have had an argument before school started, accompanied by typical threats regarding confrontations after class. To head off this potential problem, the teacher makes it a point to quietly and privately talk to both students before class starts and engage in brief conversations about expectations for the day:

> Mary and Sally, I know you two are upset about something today. Try your best to put all of that aside right now. Use your heads today. Don't just react to how you feel at the moment. We've got a lot of new information to cover in class today. Do your best to get involved, and things might look very different at the end of the period. If you want to talk, I'll be available to you both.

Stimulus cueing is another proactive behavior that is a form of forecasting problems. It involves providing a cue to selected students before inappropriate behavior occurs (Carr & Durand, 1985; Lobitz, 1974). For example, an elementary teacher notices that a particular student starts fidgeting prior to having an outbreak of disruptive behavior such as talking without permission or interrupting the class with an irrelevant comment. The teacher first talks to the student about this behavior in an attempt to come to an agreement that both teacher and student will work to extinguish the student's outbreaks. With the prior condition noted by the teacher and student, every time the student begins to fidget, the teacher places a mark on a notepad that is kept open on the student's desk. This is a private cue to the student that he is likely to engage in a type of behavior that will most likely result in negative consequences. Another form of stimulus cueing would be the teacher tapping on the student's desk as she walks by. Again, this would be a prearranged signal to the student to be aware of and exert control over his current behavior.

Occupying the Entire Room

A behavior typically associated with withitness is occupying the entire room either physically or visually. Occupying the entire room physically means that the teacher moves to all quadrants of the room systematically and frequently. This is not to say that it is inappropriate to spend a majority of the time in the front of the room while making presentations or guiding classroom interaction. However, even in these situations the teacher makes sure to walk to all areas of the room occasionally, paying particular attention to spots in the room that cannot be easily seen. Even when the teacher is standing still she can occupy the entire room by making eye contact with every student. For example, a middle school teacher occupies the entire room by making systematic sweeps of the class, trying to catch the gaze of every student.

Noticing Potential Problems

One reason for occupying the entire room is to recognize potential problems as quickly as possible. Such behavior is straightforward but not pleasant. No one likes conflict, and noticing potential problems smacks of conflict. Unfortunately, ignoring potential problems in the classroom can be catastrophic in terms of classroom management.

Noticing potential problems involves attending to unusual behavior by students. What is considered unusual behavior for one group of students might not be considered unusual behavior for another group of students. The following are examples of behavior that might indicate potential problems:

- Prior to class, several students are huddled together talking intensely.
- One or more students have not been engaged in class activity for an extended period of time.
- Students sitting in one area keep looking at each other and smiling.

- Members of the class keep looking at a specific location and smiling.
- Students giggle or smile whenever the teacher looks at or walks near a particular part of the room.
- When the teacher's back is turned toward the class, whispering or giggling can be heard, or unusual noises can be heard from a particular part of the room.

Using a Series of Graduated Actions

Once a potential problem has been identified, the teacher acts in a manner to seek out and extinguish the problem behavior immediately. This involves a series of graduated behaviors in terms of the extent to which the potential problem is confronted. Those graduated behaviors include looking at the suspected students, moving in the direction of students, and stopping the class to confront the behavior:

Looking at the suspected students. The first and least intrusive action is to look at the suspected students. This should be done in a way that elicits the attention of the suspected students; it might also elicit the attention of other students. For example, while responding to a question asked by a student, the teacher looks directly at the other side of the room to a group of students who are talking. The teacher continues to address the question but focuses her gaze on those students. While answering the question, the teacher does not raise her voice or use any physical gestures. Rather, she simply keeps looking in the direction of those students who are talking to let them know that she has noticed their behavior and that the behavior is not acceptable.

Moving in the direction of students. If the suspected behavior continues, the next step is to move in the direction of the offending students. At this point, the teacher continues to address the entire class; however, she does move toward and eventually stand right next to the student or students in question. A slightly more intrusive action is to quietly and privately talk to the offending students. This might be as simple as the teacher leaning toward the students and saying, "Mary. Bill. Sally. I need you to pay attention here. Whatever you are doing, please put it off until after class." At this point the interaction with students is as private and positive as possible. It is private in the sense that the teacher ensures that the students in question are not embarrassed in front of the rest of the class. It is positive in the sense that the teacher's comments are offered as a request as opposed to a demand. The underlying message to students should not be "pay attention or else." Rather, the underlying message is "would you please cease what you are doing and join in what we are doing in class; your participation is welcome and needed."

Stopping the class and confronting the behavior. If students still have not reengaged, then the teacher stops the class and addresses the students directly and publicly. This is done in a calm and polite manner. The teacher might say, "I'm sure whatever it is you are doing is important to you, but I need you to pay attention right now." The confrontation here is public and direct. At this stage there can also be an explicit statement of the consequences that will ensue if the current behavior continues. As much as possible the teacher communicates that the students have a decision to make. What occurs next is in their direct control:

> I assume you are aware of the rules relative to talking during a whole-class presentation. I'm going to have to use one of the consequences we agreed on for this particular issue. It's really up to you what happens. I hope you choose to join us. Your ideas could be very helpful.

Action Step 5. Use Direct-Cost Consequences

Direct cost involves explicit and concrete consequences for inappropriate behavior. Typically, direct-cost consequences are applied once a negative behavior has progressed beyond a point where it can be addressed by withitness. A number of negative consequences might be classified as direct-cost interventions. Two such consequences are addressed in this action step: time-out and overcorrection (for a more detailed discussion, see Marzano, Gaddy, Foseid, Foseid, & Marzano, 2005).

Time-Out

Time-out refers to a large array of techniques. In elementary school it is not uncommon to create a time-out seat in the classroom. Students who have demonstrated an inability to control themselves are asked to sit in the time-out seat, where they are not permitted to interact with any members of the class. They can, however, demonstrate their desire to reenter the class by attending to the academic activities that are occurring. A variation on this approach is for a school to set aside an area outside the classroom for time-out situations. For example, a school might designate a small office just outside the assistant principal's office as the time-out room. This room is constantly monitored by a teacher or administrator. Students are allowed to reenter their classrooms only after they demonstrate an awareness of the actions that led to their removal and have a concrete plan for avoiding similar negative behavior in the future. At the secondary level, time-out seats are not used, but variations of the time-out room are. Saturday school and detention are variations of the time-out room. Students who do not demonstrate an ability to manage their behavior in class lose the privilege of being in class but must make up the work they have missed.

It is important to note that time-out interventions can be easily abused. They should not be used simply to get rid of the more difficult students. Rather, they should be used only after other interventions have been exhausted, and their intent should be to help students understand and control their offending behavior so that they can return to regular classroom activities as soon as possible.

Overcorrection

Overcorrection involves engaging students in activities that overcompensate for inappropriate behavior. Overcorrection is employed when a student has done something to damage class property. In such cases, the student must not only pay for the damaged object or return it to its original state but also overcompensate by making things better than they were before. The following are examples of overcorrection:

- A student has ripped the pages of a book and is required to repair the pages of all books in the class.
- A student has drawn on the classroom wall and is required to clean marks on all the walls in the classroom, not just the one he vandalized.
- A student has thrown food across the classroom and is required to clean up the food she threw as well as sweep the floor of the entire classroom.

Overcorrection can also be applied to damage done to a class's opportunity to learn. To illustrate, assume a student has disrupted a presentation by the teacher, robbing his classmates of valuable information. As a form of overcorrection, the teacher requires the student to summarize the information contained in the presentation and provide a copy to every student in class.

Action Step 6. Use Group Contingency

Group contingency involves holding the class as a whole responsible for the behavior of any and all members of the class. The general message to the class is "you are all in this together. It is your responsibility to manage your behavior and help your classmates manage theirs." Two types of group contingency are discussed in the research literature: interdependent group contingency and dependent group contingency. With interdependent group contingency, the entire class receives positive consequences only if every student in the class meets a certain behavioral standard. With dependent group contingency, positive and negative consequences are dependent on the behavior of one student or a small group of students who have been singled out for behavioral change. The working principle behind dependent group contingency is that peer pressure will exert a strong influence on the behavior of the targeted students. Although peer pressure is a powerful short-term motivator, it is not a preferred method to be used in the typical classroom. Rather, it is usually reserved for clinical use with students who have severe behavioral problems (Litow & Pumroy, 1975). Interdependent group contingency, on the other hand, is frequently employed in regular classrooms.

Oftentimes, interdependent group contingency involves keeping track of the behavior of the class regarding some predetermined behavior. For example, assume the target behavior is students raising their hands before asking questions. Each time students fail to do so, the teacher records a mark on the blackboard or whiteboard. When a certain number of marks has been tallied, the entire class faces the consequence, such as the loss of some student privilege. Interdependent group contingency also can be used to reinforce positive behavior. For example, if students get through an entire class period with no marks on the board or only a few, a privilege is extended.

Action Step 7. Use Home Contingency

Involving parents and guardians was discussed in Action Step 3, which recommended that teachers recognize students' good behavior by notifying parents and guardians. Here the involvement is in the context of acknowledging and changing inappropriate behavior. Usually, teachers use home contingency only with those students who do not respond to the more general management techniques employed by the teacher.

Home contingency begins with a meeting among the parents or guardians, the teacher, and the student. The group discusses the student's problem behaviors, and the student has opportunities to explain or defend the behaviors in question. The purpose of this meeting or meetings is for all parties to agree on the specific negative behaviors that are to stop in class and the specific positive behaviors that are to be exhibited. For example, as a result of an initial meeting among a middle school student, her parents, and the teacher, the group determines that the targeted negative behavior for the student is acting out when she becomes frustrated. The targeted positive behavior is to increase her level of engagement during class. A record-keeping system is devised that allows both the teacher and student to keep track of instances of the targeted negative and positive behaviors. Positive and negative consequences are established. It is important that the student has some input into both types of consequences. For example, the student agrees that the positive consequence for changing her behavior is watching a favorite television program and the negative consequence is not being allowed to watch the program. On a weekly basis, the teacher communicates with the student's parents, summarizing the student's behavior as indicated by the daily records. As negative behaviors decrease and positive behaviors increase, the program is modified so that the student gradually does not require the external stimulus.

Action Step 8. Have a Strategy for High-Intensity Situations

One concern of a great many teachers is how to handle a situation in which a student is out of control—a student's behavior is so extreme that it threatens other students, the teacher, or both. Such situations are referred to as high-intensity situations. For example, a student becoming so upset that he begins to curse and throw things would constitute a high-intensity situation. It should be noted that ideally a classroom teacher should not have to address these situations. Rather, the teacher should be able to contact the principal or assistant principal, who in turn might contact the appropriate legal authorities trained to address situations involving physical danger. However, in case such help is not immediately available, teachers should have a strategy for diffusing these situations until help arrives. There are a number of actions that will help.

Recognize That the Student Is Out of Control

The first step is to recognize that the student is so upset that he or she is probably out of control. Trying to reason with a student makes sense only if the student is calm enough to think logically. When a student has "lost it," reasoning will provide little immediate relief for the situation.

Step Back and Calm Yourself

When a teacher becomes aware that a student has lost control, the first person she should attend to is herself. This involves establishing some physical space between the teacher and the student. In behavioral terms, the teacher simply takes a few steps backward if the student is standing near her. Such action signals to the student that the teacher does not intend any harm to the student. The teacher then immediately begins to calm herself down, breathing deeply and becoming aware of her thinking.

Listen Actively to the Student and Plan Action

Initially the teacher simply listens to the student in an active manner. This involves reflecting back what the student says and how he feels. For example, the teacher might say: "I see you're very upset, Mark. I wish I had realized this before. It seems that you're angry about the grade you received on the homework. Tell me why." The purpose of active listening is to communicate to students that their feelings are not discounted and that they are considered important by the teacher. It also reflects back to the students how they are being perceived. Sometimes an upset student is not aware of how threatening and intense his behavior is to other students and the teacher.

Active listening should continue until the student calms down. It also provides time for the teacher to think through her next actions. If it appears that the student still presents a physical threat, then the teacher might plan to get the student out of the classroom or get the other students out of the classroom. Ideally as a consequence of active listening on the part of the teacher, the student's level of anger will gradually decrease in intensity.

When the Student Is Calm, Repeat Simple Verbal Request

When the student becomes calmer, the teacher communicates a simple request intended to diffuse the situation. Typically, the request will involve the student and teacher leaving the classroom. The request should be repeated a number of times as if it were a broken record:

> Jonathan, I want you to go with me outside in the hallway to discuss this further. Can we please do that now? Jonathan, I want you to go with me outside in the hallway to discuss this further. Can we please do that now?

Action Step 9. Design an Overall Plan for Disciplinary Problems

The action steps discussed so far are very specific. Teachers should also find it useful to outline steps in an overall plan for resolving conflicts with students and improving disciplinary behavior. Good and Brophy (2003) describe the recommendations of a number of theorists regarding this issue. Glasser (1977, 1986) recommends an approach based on the assumption that students are ultimately responsible for their own behavior. Good and Brophy note that Glasser "emphasized that people are responsible for their own goals, decisions, and personal happiness in their lives and described methods for taking control of one's own life" (2003, p. 159). Glasser's suggested approach can be outlined as follows:

- List your typical reactions to student misbehavior.
- Analyze the list and determine which of your behaviors are effective and which are not.
- Make an attempt to improve your relationship with disruptive students.
- Meet with students and point out the specific behaviors that need to be curtailed.

- Make sure students understand and can describe the offending behavior.
- If the offending behavior continues, help the student develop an explicit plan to curtail it. Keep refining the plan as needed.
- If the offending behavior still persists, isolate the student from class until a renewed commitment is made on the part of the student.
- If the previous steps do not work, in-school suspension is the next step. The student is continually invited to develop and execute a plan.
- If the student remains out of control, parents are called, and the student goes home for the day.
- Students who do not respond to the previous steps are removed from school and referred to another agency.

Summary

When considering the seventh design question—What will I do to recognize and acknowledge adherence and lack of adherence to classroom rules and procedures?—teachers should remember the balanced approach, which involves acknowledgment of positive behavior and negative behavior. Teachers should now be aware of some action steps for acknowledging positive behavior: verbal and nonverbal acknowledgment, tangible recognition, and involving the home. In addition, action steps for acknowledging negative behavior include being with-it, using direct cost, using group contingency, using home contingency, having a strategy for high-intensity students, and designing an overall plan for discipline.

8

*W*hat will I do to establish and maintain
effective relationships with students?

Arguably the quality of the relationships teachers have with students is the keystone of effective management and perhaps even the entirety of teaching. There are two complementary dynamics that constitute an effective teacher–student relationship. The first is the extent to which the teacher gives students the sense that he is providing guidance and control both behaviorally and academically. In effect, the teacher must somehow communicate the message: "You can count on me to provide clear direction in terms of your learning and in terms of behavior. I take responsibility for these issues." The second dynamic is the extent to which the teacher provides a sense that teacher and students are a team devoted to the well-being of all participants. In effect, the teacher must somehow communicate the message: "We are a team here and succeed or fail as a team. Additionally, I have a stake personally in the success of each one of you."

In the Classroom

Looking in on our classroom scenario, Mr. Hutchins makes a concerted effort each day to ensure that students have the perception that he is concerned about the well-being of the class as a whole as well as each individual student. He realizes that it does not matter how he feels on a given day, but it does matter what he does. Students cannot know his thoughts and feelings, but they do interpret his actions, even seemingly insignificant ones. Consequently, each day he reminds himself to engage in behaviors such as meeting students at the door as they come into class, calling them by their first names, smiling at them, and even engaging in playful banter when appropriate. He finds that on days when he does not really feel like doing these things, his mood tends to change throughout the day as students respond positively to his overtures.

He is equally concerned that students have the perception that he is providing guidance both behaviorally and academically. Again he realizes that his behaviors, not his thoughts or feelings, communicate this message. Consequently, he reminds himself to engage in behaviors such as being clear about learning goals, being clear about rules and procedures, and being consistent about applying positive and negative consequences.

Research and Theory

If the relationship between the teacher and the students is good, then everything else that occurs in the classroom seems to be enhanced. Marzano (2003a) reports an effect size of -0.87 (p. 42) for teacher–student relationship. Recall that in this case a negative effect size indicates a decrease in student disruptions. The -0.87 effect size for teacher–student relationships is associated with a 31 percentile point decrease in such disruptions.

On an anecdotal level, Sheets and Gay (1996) note that many behavioral problems ultimately boil down to a breakdown in teacher–student relationship: "The causes of many classroom behaviors labeled and punished as rule infractions are, in fact, problems of students and teachers relating to each other interpersonally" (pp. 86–87). Plax and Kearney (1990) postulate that breakdowns in teacher–student relationships commonly occur because teachers put themselves in a "we–they" stance with students.

Although the importance of teacher–student relationships is fairly obvious, the components of an effective teacher–student relationship are more elusive. Researchers have identified some general characteristics, such as consideration, buoyancy, and patience (Barr, 1958; Good & Brophy, 1995). These are certainly important aspects of an effective teacher–student relationship, but they are not easy to state in behavioral terms. The work of Wubbels and his colleagues is, however, focused on behavior (see Brekelmans, Wubbels, & Creton, 1990; Wubbels, Brekelmans, den Brok, & van Tartwijk, 2006; Wubbels, Brekelmans, van Tartwijk, & Admiral, 1999; Wubbels & Levy, 1993). Wubbels postulates the interaction of two related dynamics—whether the teacher shows an appropriate amount of dominance and whether the teacher shows an appropriate amount of cooperation.

Dominance might sound like a harsh or even negative terms, but it is not intended as such. Dominance is characterized by clarity of purpose and strong guidance. Such purpose and guidance should be both academic and behavioral. In terms of academic guidance, the teacher provides strong direction regarding academic content. Attending to Design Question 1 (see Chapter 1)—What will I do to establish and communicate learning goals, track student progress, and celebrate success?—will go a long way to this end. Relative to behavioral guidance, attending to Design Questions 6 and 7 (see Chapters 6 and 7, respectively)— What will I do to establish or maintain classroom rules and procedures, and what will I do to recognize and acknowledge adherence and lack of adherence to classroom rules and procedures?—provides a sound foundation. In effect, the action steps in Chapters 1, 6, and 7 address many of Wubbels's recommendations for communicating a sense of dominance. Consequently, they will not be repeated in this chapter. However, another aspect of dominance not discussed previously, emotional objectivity, is addressed in this chapter.

Marzano (2003a) describes a teacher who has developed emotional objectivity as one who

> implements and enforces rules and procedures, executes disciplinary actions, and (even) cultivates effective relationships with students without interpreting violations of classroom rules and procedures, negative reactions to disciplinary actions, or lack of response to the teacher's attempts to forge relationships as a personal attack. (p. 68)

Nelson, Martella, and Galand (1998) address the same issue when they discuss the need for teachers to behave in an unemotional, matter-of-fact manner. Soar and Soar (1979) have made similar observations. In their study of teachers who consistently produced achievement gains greater than expected in comparison with a group of randomly related teachers, Brophy and Evertson (1976) observed behavior that qualifies as emotional objectivity, as defined here:

> The successful teachers usually had quite realistic attitudes toward students and teacher–student relationships. Although they liked the children and enjoyed interpersonal aspects of teaching, they took a professional view of their students, looking upon them primarily as young learners with whom they interacted within a teacher–student relationship. In contrast, the less successful teachers tended to take one of two contradictory extreme overreactions to students. The more common of these was a romanticized notion of the student as a warm, wonderful, lovely, precious, etc., person who was a great pleasure to be around. In our observations, teachers who painted this rosy picture of students were not more likely to be warm toward them or to appear to be enjoying their jobs any more than teachers with less romantic and more realistic views. In fact, a few of the more gushy teachers had highly chaotic classrooms . . . which occasionally became so out of control that the teacher exploded in anger and punitiveness in spite of herself. . . . There also were a few disillusioned and bitter teachers who looked upon students as "the enemy." (pp. 43–44)

Additionally, they note the following:

> We thought that the warmer, more affectionate teachers generally would be more effective than other teachers, particularly in low SES schools. As it turned out, teacher affectionateness did not show this relationship. It was unrelated, either linearly or curvilinearly, to students' learning gains. (1976, p. 106)

It is important to keep in mind that emotional objectivity does not imply being impersonal with or cool toward students. Rather, it involves keeping a type of emotional distance from the ups and downs of classroom life and not taking students' outbursts or even students' direct acts of disobedience personally.

Cooperation involves demonstrating concern for each student and building a sense of community within the classroom. There is a growing body of research and theory indicating how a sense of cooperation is established. First and perhaps foremost, students interpret the actions of the teacher as evidence for or against the teacher's desire for cooperation. Wubbels, Brekelmans, van Tartwijk, and Admiral (1999) explain in the following way:

> We consider every behavior that someone displays in the presence of someone else as communication, and therefore we assume that in the presence of someone else one cannot *not* communicate. . . . Whatever someone's intentions are, the other persons in the communication will infer meaning from that someone's behavior. If, for example, teachers ignore students' questions, perhaps because they do not hear them, then students may not only get this inattention but also infer that the teacher is too busy or thinks that the students are too dull to understand or that the questions are impertinent. The message that students take from the teacher's negation can be different from the teacher's intention. (pp. 153–154)

Teacher behavior, then, is the language of relationship. Students "listen" to every behavior made by the teacher as a statement of the type of relationship the teacher desires, even when the teacher's actions have no such intent.

In their meta-analysis, Harris and Rosenthal (1985) identify some salient aspects of this language of relationships, and their findings are reported in Figure 8.1. Figure 8.1 reports correlations along with the typical effect sizes listed in figures throughout the text thus far. The correlation coefficient and the effect size have a straightforward mathematical relationship. That is, the effect sizes reported in Figure 8.1 are computed using the correlations reported by Harris and Rosenthal (1985). (For a discussion, see Marzano, Waters, & McNulty, 2005.) It is also important to note that the effect sizes reported in Figure 8.1 include some outcomes other than academic achievement. As we shall see in Chapter 9, these same behaviors listed in Figure 8.1 become issues when a teacher is trying to communicate high expectations for all students.

	FIGURE 8.1			
	Research on Teacher Interactions with Students			
Behavior	Number of Effect Sizes	Average Correlation	Average Effect Size	Percentile Gain
Eye contact	7	.12	0.24	9
Gestures	3	.31	0.66	25
Smiles	3	.29	0.61	23
Encourages	1	.41	0.90	32
Touch	2	.05	0.10	4
Praise	11	.12	0.24	9
Frequency of interaction	3	.21	0.43	17
Duration of interaction	2	.47	1.07	36

Note: Data from Harris & Rosenthal, 1985.

As some of the behaviors listed in Figure 8.1 imply, there is an emotional component to an effective teacher–student relationship (see Anderman & Wolters, 2006; Perry, Turner, & Meyer, 2006). In general, positive emotions foster a sense of concern and cooperation. Teachers can use a variety of strategies to help stimulate positive emotions (Gettinger & Kohler, 2006). Moskowitz and Hayman (1976), for example, found that the most effective junior high teachers tended to joke with students and smiled quite frequently. This same general characteristic is noted by Rosenshine and Furst (1973). Another behavior that helps create a positive affective tone is teacher enthusiasm. As noted by Gettinger and Kohler (2006), when teachers project a positive and enthusiastic demeanor, students are likely to adopt the same general stance in class. In fact, Bettencourt, Gillett, Gall, and Hull (1983) found that training teachers in behaviors that communicate enthusiasm had positive effects on student engagement and achievement.

Action Steps

The action steps in this chapter are divided into two sections: those that communicate cooperation (which I refer to as concern and cooperation) and those that communicate an appropriate level of dominance (which I refer to as guidance and control).

Action Steps That Communicate an Appropriate Level of Concern and Cooperation

Action Step 1. Know Something About Each Student

Everyone likes to be known by others. If someone knows our interests and some details about our lives, we interpret this as an indication that they like us. Given the fact that teachers have many students in their class or classes, it is difficult if not impossible to obtain a great deal of personal information about every student. However, with a little strategic effort some information can be obtained on each student over the course of the year. It is useful to start with those students who seem to be disenfranchised, those students who do not engage in classroom activities, and those students who act out behaviorally.

One obvious way to obtain information about students is to use an adaptation of the time-honored interest inventory, which contains questions such as the following:

- Where were you born?
- How many brothers and sisters do you have?
- What are some things about your family about which you are proud?
- What are your hobbies?
- One person you admire is _____.
- What kinds of things do you do during summer vacation?
- What would you do if you knew you wouldn't fail?

Another option is to use part of each parent–teacher conference to ask about and listen for critical details regarding students, such as upcoming family get-togethers or vacations, transition points for siblings (such as graduations, marriages), or a move to a new home. Another useful source of information about students is the school newspaper, newsletter, and bulletins. Typically these sources report a variety of activities, including track or swim meets; debates; basketball, softball, and football games; clubs; school performances; and community volunteer activities.

Armed with personal information, a teacher can surprise students by engaging in discussions regarding aspects of their lives. For example, if a particular student is having some behavioral problems in class, the teacher might stop the student on the playground and make the following type of comment: "Juan, I understand your grandparents are visiting from Mexico City. Tell me about them."

In addition to knowing something about each student, it is helpful to be familiar with the local culture of students, including the following areas:

- Knowing popular recording artists and their works
- Knowing popular places where students like to gather

- Knowing about local events significant to students
- Knowing about rivalries between different groups of students
- Knowing popular terms and phrases used by students

To obtain information regarding these elements, a teacher might informally interview students in class, using prompts such as, "Tell me what's happening in your lives these days" or "What are some things students are talking about that teachers should be aware of?"

Action Step 2. Engage in Behaviors That Indicate Affection for Each Student

Teachers demonstrate affection for students in a myriad of small and seemingly insignificant ways, including the following:

- The teacher meets students at the door as they come into class each day, making an attempt to greet them by name. The teacher might also make positive comments while greeting students: "Hello Bill. Welcome back from your trip over the weekend. Mary. Looking forward to your comments today. Rosa. Good to have you here today. Hope you are feeling better from your cold."
- At the beginning of the year, the teacher takes pictures of each student and places them in a special section of the bulletin board. Under each student's picture are words and phrases written by the students that represent their thoughts about the class: "I'm lost," "I get this stuff," "I'm starting to catch on," "The KIING." Periodically, the teacher has students change the comment cards under their names to reflect their current thoughts and feelings. The students' comments provide a good deal of comic relief and lighten up the tone in class.
- With students who feel particularly alienated, the teacher takes the time to attend an after-school function in which the student participates. For example, let's say a student has been particularly negative toward the teacher and class, and the teacher becomes aware that the student is involved in junior varsity track. The teacher attends one of those track meets, notifying the student ahead of time: "Jeffrey. I'm going to the track meet tomorrow. Good luck in the relay. I'll be rooting for you." This, of course, would take time from the teacher's typical after-school routine, but it might pay big dividends in terms of future interactions with the student.

Elementary teachers might have 30 or more students each day in class. Secondary teachers might have 150 or more. It is difficult if not impossible to interact with each student personally in some friendly way every day. However, a teacher can develop a schedule that allows him to single out one or two students to talk with each day. This might be done in the lunchroom, during breaks between classes, right after school, or on any other occasion when students have some free time. In this way, every student will have some personalized, positive contact with the teacher at least once during the semester or year.

Action Step 3. Bring Student Interests into the Content and Personalize Learning Activities

An indirect but powerful way to communicate concern and cooperation is to involve student interests in class as much as possible. If the teacher has done well at Action Step 2, he will have information about each student and the class as a whole. He can then use this information to draft classroom tasks that include students' interests. Elements from Action Step 1 in Chapter 3 are particularly relevant to this point. Specifically, that action step addressed four tasks that emphasize similarities and differences: comparing, classifying, creating metaphors, and creating analogies. The latter two are perfect vehicles for designing tasks around student interests.

Metaphors require students to show how two seemingly different items are in fact similar at the abstract level. A teacher can ask students to construct metaphors that relate academic content to their personal interests. For example, assume that a health teacher has been focusing on the topic of disease. She presents students with a metaphor assignment by first listing the following elements as defining characteristics of diseases:

1. A small number of cells invade a host.
2. These cells multiply.
3. The host organism tries to fight the disease.

Next, with input from the class she translates the specific elements into more abstract elements or a more general pattern, such as the following:

1. A small number of things invade or affect something.
2. The things grow in number or strength.
3. The affected thing tries to fight back.

Then she gives the following directions to students: "Identify something you are interested in or something in your own life that has this same general pattern. Be ready to explain how the thing you have selected has each element of the general pattern."

Analogies are equally amenable to individual student interests. Recall from Chapter 3 that analogies have the following form:

core is to earth

as

nucleus is to atom

After thoroughly discussing the relationship that is common to the set *core* and *earth* and the set *nucleus* and *atom,* the teacher asks students to identify something they are interested in that has this same relationship.

Action Step 4. Engage in Physical Behaviors That Communicate Interest in Students

A teacher's physical actions are interpreted by students as indications of the teacher's mood and attitude toward students. Given that effective teaching by definition involves interacting with students in positive ways, the profession usually attracts people who quite naturally employ physical behaviors that are positive. It is safe to say, however, that not every teacher is equally skilled at or aware of such behaviors. Consequently, it is useful for every teacher to consciously practice and engage in behaviors such as the following:

- Smile at students at appropriate times.
- In an appropriate manner and at appropriate times, place a hand on a student's shoulder as a form of encouragement.
- When talking with students, look them in the eyes.
- When talking with students, stand close enough to communicate a sense of concern but not too close to violate personal space.
- Look interested in what students have to say.

Action Step 5. Use Humor When Appropriate

Teachers can provide a sense of concern and cooperation by periodically using humor (Gettinger & Kohler, 2006; Moskowitz & Hayman, 1976). Some teachers quite naturally use humor, and Jonas (2004) provides some simple guidelines for humor that can be used by teachers and administrators who may not be so inclined:

- Engage in playful banter with students when appropriate.
- Use historical and popular sayings to make a point, such as "I'll be back" (in the voice of Arnold Schwarzenegger) or "Four score and seven years ago. . . ."

- Keep a book of jokes or cartoons handy and read something funny at the beginning of class.
- Laugh at yourself.
- Laugh with your students.
- Play on words: "always avoid alliterations," "prepositions are not words to end sentences with," "be more or less specific," or "exaggeration is a billion times worse than understatement."

Action Steps That Communicate an Appropriate Level of Guidance and Control

Action Step 6. Consistently Enforce Positive and Negative Consequences

Establishing clear learning goals (Chapter 1), rules and procedures (Chapter 6), and positive and negative consequences related to those rules and procedures (Chapter 7) can go a long way toward creating an atmosphere of guidance and control with students. Students in a classroom that has well-articulated learning goals, rules and procedures, and related consequences get the strong impression that "this teacher is very clear about the behavior she expects."

To a great extent then, attending to the action steps addressed in Chapters 1, 6, and 7 can begin establishing a sense of guidance and control with students. However, these behaviors are not sufficient. If consequences are not executed consistently and fairly, their impact is negated. To ensure consistency, a teacher must be aware of the extent to which positive and negative consequences are applied to specific behaviors. For example, at the end of each day a middle school teacher mentally reviews the day, noting incidents of adherence to rules and procedures. She asks herself: "Did I provide proper acknowledgment when students followed the rules and procedures? Did I use proper consequences when students did not follow rules and procedures?" This systematic, informal checklist helps the teacher maintain consistency in the application of positive and negative consequences.

Action Step 7. Project a Sense of Emotional Objectivity

As described in the research and theory section, one way to communicate an appropriate level of guidance and control is to project a sense of emotional objectivity. This approach does not mean that teachers will be unemotional at all times. It does mean that teachers provide students with a consistent tone in the classroom. Marzano, Gaddy, Foseid, Foseid, and Marzano (2005) identify several aspects of emotional objectivity, including the following.

Recognize That Emotions Are Natural and Inevitable

The first step in projecting a sense of emotional objectivity is to realize that human beings are emotional animals. Having negative and positive emotions related to students is inevitable. Oftentimes, these emotions stem from past events in teachers' lives. For example, let's say a teacher has had a negative experience with a student who has a certain appearance. Years later another student who looks quite similar enters her classroom, and the negative emotions associated with the past events are activated. In effect, human beings are not accountable for how they feel. However, they are accountable for how they act. A teacher's thoughts and feelings toward a particular student are not changed easily. However, a teacher can control absolutely how he or she behaves toward a student. This concept provides great freedom to the classroom teacher. As human beings, we cannot be expected to have a natural affinity for every student in class. However, we can be expected to behave in a way that communicates care and concern equally for every student.

Monitor Your Thoughts and Emotions

It is true that a teacher's behaviors affect students and a teacher's thoughts do not. Still, it is important for teachers to be aware of those students for whom they harbor negative emotions so they might guard against related negative behavior. The following steps are useful to this end:

1. The teacher mentally reviews the students in her class, noting her emotional reaction to each student.
2. For those students who arouse negative thoughts or emotions, the teacher spends some time trying to determine the specific characteristics of the negative thoughts and emotions.
3. The teacher tries to determine past events that might be triggering the negative emotions or thoughts.

To illustrate, a middle school teacher spends some time reviewing the students in her class and discovers that she has a fairly strong negative reaction to a particular young woman named Aida (Step 1). In Step 2, the teacher tries to identify the specific characteristics of her thoughts and emotions. She determines that she feels angry whenever Aida enters the room and that she has thoughts about possible confrontations with Aida. In Step 3, the teacher links her negative thoughts about Aida to past events and discovers that Aida reminds her of a student she had many years ago with whom she had many confrontations. Being more aware of the source of her negative emotions and thoughts, the teacher is better able to behave in an objective manner with Aida.

Reframe

Reframing refers to explaining students' behaviors in terms that are not threatening or offensive to the teacher. To illustrate, assume that a teacher has had a negative experience with a particular student named Chris. Chris might have spoken disrespectfully to the teacher when the teacher asked if she had completed her homework. The teacher's first (and quite natural) thoughts are that Chris is challenging her authority and trying to disrupt the class. Such thoughts will quite naturally stimulate negative emotions in the teacher and potentially provoke further conflict. A more useful approach in terms of projecting a sense of emotional objectivity would be for the teacher to reexplain Chris's behavior to herself in more acceptable terms. For example, Chris could be upset because of an argument she had with her parents the night before class. Chris could be frustrated because she was working at her job after school and did not complete the homework assigned, and so on. Viewing the student's actions in a way that gives the student the benefit of the doubt provides the teacher with some emotional distance from the incident and consequently an opportunity for clearer thinking and more productive interactions.

Action Step 8. Maintain a Cool Exterior

A cardinal rule of emotional objectivity is that the teacher's demeanor in class avoids extremes. This is particularly true when a teacher becomes angry with a student. Even though a teacher is angry, he should resist the urge to demonstrate this emotion. Specifically, the teacher should guard against the following behaviors:

- Pointing a finger or shaking a fist at the offending student
- Raising the tone of voice toward the student
- Glaring or staring at the student
- Moving toward or hovering over the student
- Ridiculing the student

In place of these negative behaviors, the teacher should substitute assertive behaviors such as the following:

- Speaking directly to the student in a calm and respectful tone
- Looking directly at the student, without glaring or staring
- Maintaining an appropriate distance from the student
- Having a facial expression that is either neutral or positive

It is legitimate for the teacher to express anger in an appropriate manner, such as the following ways:

- Specifically pointing out the student's actions that were considered offensive as well as the reaction it elicited
- Using a calm and even tone
- Commenting on the student's behavior as opposed to his motives

Summary

In considering the eighth design question—What will I do to establish and maintain effective relationships with students?—teachers should think in terms of teacher behaviors as opposed to teacher thoughts or feelings. Teachers should now be aware of actions they can take to incorporate two critical components of effective relationships: (1) behaviors that communicate an appropriate level of concern and cooperation and (2) behaviors that communicate an appropriate level of guidance and control.

9

*W*hat will I do to communicate high

expectations for all students?

A teacher's beliefs about students' chances of success in school influence the teacher's actions with students, which in turn influence students' achievement. If the teacher believes students can succeed, she tends to behave in ways that help them succeed. If the teacher believes that students cannot succeed, she unwittingly tends to behave in ways that subvert student success or at least do not facilitate student success. This is perhaps one of the most powerful hidden dynamics of teaching because it is typically an unconscious activity.

In the Classroom

Returning to our classroom scenario, Mr. Hutchins realizes that he has different opinions about the abilities of the different students in the class. As a human being, it is difficult not to have such opinions. But he also realizes that these opinions can influence how he behaves toward individual students. To counteract the potential negative influence of his behaviors, he continually asks himself the following question, particularly when dealing with students for whom he has doubts about their chances for success in class: "If I believed this student was completely capable of learning this content, what would I be doing right now?"

This question serves as a trueing mechanism for him. He is amazed at how this approach provides clarity to his interactions. Invariably, he notices that with some students he tends to require a great deal of them—regardless of how they respond to a question—simply because he believes they can do better. He challenges their responses, asks them to explain, and stays with them until students have provided complete responses. With other students, he tends to back off and not probe their understanding, because he believes they cannot reach high levels of achievement. His intentions are good. He is not as demanding with low-expectancy students, because he does not want to embarrass them. However, the consequences are still negative. Low-expectancy students receive less attention than high-expectancy students. He realizes that it matters little whether his thoughts change regarding students, but it matters a great deal whether his behavior changes. Spurred on by these awarenesses, he tries to behave in ways that communicate high expectations for every student.

Research and Theory

The effect of teacher expectations on student achievement might be one of the most well-researched aspects of classroom instruction (see Ambady & Rosenthal, 1992; Brophy, 1981, 1983; Brophy & Good, 1970; Cooper & Good, 1983; Cooper & Hazelrigg, 1988; Dusek & Gail, 1983; Harris & Rosenthal, 1985; Raudenbush, 1984; Rosenthal & Jacobson, 1968; Smith, 1980). Weinstein's (2002) text, *Reaching Higher: The Power of Expectations in Schooling,* provides a comprehensive and panoramic view of this research. Weinstein explains that expectations theory took hold in 1956, when Robert Rosenthal's doctoral dissertation offered the hypothesis that an experimenter could have a subtle effect on the outcome of an experiment. He labeled this phenomenon as unconscious experimenter bias. Rosenthal wrote:

> The implication is that in some subtle manner, perhaps by tone, or manner, or gestures, or general atmosphere, the experimenter, although formally testing the success and failure groups in an identical way, influenced the success subjects to make lower initial ratings and thus increase the experimenter's probability of verifying his hypothesis. (cited in Weinstein, 2002, p. 43)

Weinstein notes that this observation started a research movement that was to influence almost every aspect of research in the behavioral sciences.

It spilled over into education when an elementary school principal named Lenore Jacobson contacted Rosenthal and encouraged him to examine the application of his theory to the effect teacher perceptions might have on student achievement. Rosenthal and Jacobson published the findings from their study in the book *Pygmalion in the Classroom* (1968). Their study involved administering a nonverbal intelligence test to students in an elementary school in May of the year before the experimental treatment, January and May of the experimental year, and two years later. At each grade level, about 20 percent of the students were randomly selected to be in the experimental group. Teachers were told that this 20 percent of students were thought to be "spurters" based on the results of the intelligence test they had taken the previous May and that teachers could expect to see the students' academic performance grow dramatically during the year.

At the end of the year, those students who had been identified as spurters outgained the 80 percent of students who were not identified as spurters on the IQ test. Although different patterns appeared from grade to grade, the results were considered quite startling. These results did not go unchallenged. As noted by Weinstein (2002), "Enormous controversy ensued over methodological problems such as the validity of the IQ test, the effects of multiple administrations of the same test, and the differences in the findings by grade level" (p. 44). A flood of studies followed, along with meta-analyses of these studies.

The meta-analysis by Raudenbush (1984) added a particularly interesting perspective to the general understanding of the effects of teacher expectancy. He found higher-expectancy effects in the 1st and 2nd grades as well as in 7th grade (entry into junior high school). He speculated that the expectancy effect is greater the less a teacher knows about a student. Stated differently, once a teacher has developed low expectations for a student, it is very difficult for the teacher to change his or her behavior toward the student. In a comment on the Raudenbush study, Weinstein (2002) poses the question, "What of the magnitude of these findings?" (p. 45). She explains that "in the seven credible experiments of expectancy induction highlighted by Raudenbush, an effect size of .29 would significantly improve the rate of favorable outcomes from 43 to 57 percent" (2002, p. 45).

Other studies have added some clarity to the issue of teacher expectations. Dusek and Gail (1983) conducted a meta-analysis of 77 studies that attempted to determine the sources of teachers' expectations of students. They identify a number of sources, and the following ones are most germane to the conversation here: cumulative folder, social class, race, and physical attractiveness. These findings are depicted in Figure 9.1.

In general, the studies addressed in the Dusek and Gail meta-analysis employed a similar technique. Subjects were provided information about a real or hypothetical student. For example, teachers were presented with cumulative folders regarding students (real or hypothetical). Teachers were then asked to rate students in terms of their chances for academic success. As shown in Figure 9.1, information in the cumulative folder, physical attractiveness, social class, and race influence expectations. Positive information in a student's cumulative folder (as opposed to negative information) is associated with a 30 percentile point gain in expectations regarding student academic performance. A student's physical attractiveness (as

FIGURE 9.1
Research on Sources of Teacher Expectancies

Source	Number of Effect Sizes	Average Effect Size	Percentile Gain in Expectancy
Cumulative folder	14	0.85	30
Physical attractiveness	11	0.30	11
Social class	20	0.47	18
Race	24	0.11	4

Note: Data from Dusek & Gail, 1983.

opposed to physical unattractiveness) is associated with an 18 percentile point gain in expectations regarding student academic achievement, and so on.

The importance of the research on teacher expectations was not lost on the world of K–12 education. There were immediate calls for teachers to expect all students to master complex content, and those calls persist today. However, changing expectations alone is not the ultimate outcome. Rather, changing the teacher behavior that comes with low expectations will most probably produce the desired effect on student achievement. To be sure, changing teacher beliefs and behaviors that constitute the overall expectancy effect is a tall order. Weinstein (2002) notes that even popular and robust staff development programs such as Teacher Expectations and Student Achievement do not have strong research supporting their positive effects on student achievement (Gottfredson, Marciniak, Birdseye, & Gottfredson, 1995).

A number of models address how teachers communicate expectations (for reviews, see Cooper, 1979; Weinstein, 2002). In simplistic terms, those models postulate that beginning early in the school year teachers form opinions or expectations about students' chances of succeeding academically. Based on these expectations, teachers treat high-expectation students differently from low-expectation students. These differences in treatment occur in what Ambady and Rosenthal (1992) refer to as thin slices of teacher behavior—a physical gesture, the turn of a phrase. Students interpret these messages coded in thin slices of behaviors as signals regarding how they are expected to behave in class. At a general level, there are two categories of thinly sliced teacher behaviors that communicate expectations: affective tone and quality of interactions with students.

Affective Tone

Affective tone refers to the extent to which the teacher establishes positive emotions in the classroom. Affective tone is obviously related to cooperative behavior, which is discussed in the section on teacher–student relationships in Chapter 8. Many of the action steps described as instrumental in communicating an appropriate level of concern and cooperation also generate a positive affective tone. In this chapter, the focus is on the differences in affective tone for high- versus low-expectancy students.

In general, when teachers interact with high-expectancy students they are more positive than when they interact with low-expectancy students. Cooper (1979)—discussing the findings of Chaiken, Sigler, and Derlega (1974), Page (1971), and Kester and Letchworth (1972)—explains that when working with high-expectancy students as opposed to low-expectancy students teachers tend to smile more, look students in the eye more, lean toward students more, and generally behave in a more friendly and supportive manner.

Research on affective tone, synthesized by Brophy (1983), can be organized in the following way:

- Teachers praise lows less frequently than highs for success (Babad, Inbar, & Rosenthal, 1982; Brophy & Good, 1970; Cooper & Baron, 1977; Firestone & Brody, 1975; Good, Cooper, & Blakey, 1980; Good, Sikes, & Brophy, 1973; Martinek & Johnson, 1979; Page, 1971; Rejeski, Darracott, & Hutslar, 1979).
- Teachers seat lows farther away (Rist, 1970).
- Teachers are less friendly with low-achieving students, including smiling less and using friendly nonverbal behaviors less (Babad et al., 1982; Chaikin et al., 1974; Kester & Letchworth, 1972; Meichenbaum, Bowers, & Ross, 1969; Page, 1971; Smith & Luginbuhl, 1976).
- Teachers give lows less eye contact and nonverbal communication of attention and responsiveness, such as leaning forward and using positive head nodding (Chaiken et al., 1974).

Quality of Interactions with Students

One of the most influential differences in teacher treatment of high- versus low-expectancy students is in the type and quality of interactions (Brophy & Good, 1974). About this general category of behavior, Cooper (1979) notes that "teachers often show more willingness to pursue an answer with highs than with lows. Furthermore, highs seem to create more output opportunities for themselves, while teachers vary in whether they equalize or accentuate contact frequency differences" (p. 395). Brophy's (1983) research synthesis on quality of interactions can be organized in the following way:

- Teachers wait less time for lows to answer questions (Allington, 1980; Taylor, 1979) and call on lows less frequently to answer questions (Mendoza, Good, & Brophy, 1972; Rubovits & Maehr, 1971).
- Teachers give lows answers or call on someone else to answer a question as opposed to trying to delve into the logic underlying the answer or improve on the answers of lows (Brophy & Good, 1970; Jeter & Davis, 1973).
- Teachers give lows briefer and less informative feedback on their responses (Cooper, 1979; Cornbleth, Davis, & Button, 1972).
- Teachers fail to give lows feedback for public responses (Brophy & Good, 1970; Good, Sikes, & Brophy, 1973; Jeter & Davis, 1973; Willis, 1970).
- Teachers generally pay less attention to lows and interact with them less frequently (Adams & Cohen, 1974; Blakey, 1970; Given, 1974; Kester & Letchworth, 1972; Page, 1971; Rist, 1970; Rubovits & Maehr, 1971).
- Teachers generally demand less from lows (Beez, 1968).
- Teachers make less use of effective but time-consuming instructional methods with lows when instructional time is running out (Swann & Snyder, 1980).

Many of these behaviors were discussed in the chapters on engagement (Chapter 5) and the active processing of information (Chapter 2). Here we consider their differential use with high- and low-expectation students.

Action Steps

The first two action steps in this section describe actions teachers can take to address expectations at a very general level. Action Step 3 addresses affective tone, and Action Steps 4 and 5 address quality of interactions.

Action Step 1. Identify Your Expectation Levels for Students

One of the first actions a teacher can take to address expectations is to become aware of his or her differential expectations for students. It is difficult, if not impossible, for a person to change his or her thinking about students. Yet it is entirely possible to change behavior toward students so that all students—regardless of the teacher's level of expectation for them—receive the same behavior in terms of affective tone and quality of interactions. To do so, a teacher might make a mental scan of her students, identifying those for whom she has high, medium, and low expectations. This can be done quite formally or informally. The important point is that the teacher becomes aware of those students she does not expect to perform well for one reason or another.

It is also useful for the teacher to determine if she has any systematic bias regarding low-expectancy students. Specifically, the teacher notes if she has any generalized low expectations for students because of their ethnicity, socio-economic status, and the like. It is important to remember that if a teacher does discover such patterns, it does not mean she is a racist or a bigot. To some extent, all adults probably have preconceived notions regarding groups of people, simply because those adults were influenced by the biases and generalizations of the people who raised them and the people with whom they interacted as children. These patterns of thought are very difficult to change because they are reactions that have been reinforced over many years. One might say that a bigot or a racist is one who knowingly or unknowingly behaves in accordance with such patterns. However, an individual who actively seeks to behave in a manner that is not controlled by biased patterns is anything but a bigot or racist. To this end then, a teacher can freely admit to himself or herself the existence of negative thought patterns, perhaps even try to ascertain the origin of these behaviors. For example, a teacher might discover that she has predetermined negative expectations for all students of a specific race and a specific socioeconomic status. Simply recognizing this tendency can provide some power over such patterns of thought.

Action Step 2. Identify Differential Treatment of Low-Expectancy Students

Once low-expectancy students are identified, it is useful for the teacher to spend some time taking stock of his differential treatment of lows. Relative to affective tone, the teacher would examine whether he treats low-expectancy students differently by

- Making less eye contact
- Smiling less
- Making less physical contact or maintaining less proximity
- Engaging in less playful or light dialogue

Relative to quality of interactions, the teacher would examine whether he treats low-expectancy students differently by

- Calling on them less
- Asking them less challenging questions

- Not delving into their answers as deeply
- Rewarding them for less rigorous responses

This information might be gathered using a simple observation form. In their book *Looking in Classrooms,* Good and Brophy (2003) discuss a number of observation strategies. For the purposes described here, a teacher might design a form such as the one in Figure 9.2. In this example, the teacher has taken brief notes at the end of the day or at the end of the period regarding selected students over one or two days. This teacher has identified possible negative patterns with both Andre and Sarah. With these negative patterns identified, the teacher can plan alternative behaviors.

FIGURE 9.2
Informal Observation Form

Student Name	My Behavior That Deals with Affective Tone	My Behavior Regarding Quality of Interactions
Andre	I notice I never kid around with Andre.	I typically never call on him unless he raises his hand.
Sarah	I think I treat students the same in this area. I don't notice anything different with Sarah.	I think I might be avoiding interaction with her.

Action Step 3. Make Sure Low-Expectancy Students Receive Verbal and Nonverbal Indications That They Are Valued and Respected

Once low-expectancy students have been identified, a teacher can focus on the affective tone for those students if he determines that this is an issue. (Quality of interactions for low-expectancy students is addressed in the next section. The two have been separated because they deal with different types of teacher behaviors.) Although it is important to change differential treatment of all low-expectancy students, focusing on the most severe cases will enhance the probability of seeing concrete progress. For these target students the teacher consciously and systematically engages in the following behaviors:

- Make eye contact with target students frequently.
- Smile at the target students at appropriate times.
- On occasion, make appropriate physical contact, such as putting a hand on the target student's shoulder.

- Maintain a proximity to target students that communicates interest but does not violate personal space.
- When appropriate, engage in playful dialogue with the target students.

The teacher should identify specific behaviors for specific students. For example, the teacher makes a commitment to smiling at a particular student. For another student, the teacher makes a commitment to stand closer to the student during interactions. When employing these behaviors, the teacher tries to gauge the reaction of each student. Not all behaviors will be equally effective for every student. Over time, the teacher discovers which behaviors are most useful for each low-expectancy student.

Action Step 4. Ask Questions of Low-Expectancy Students

Differential treatment for lows during questioning occurs in two ways: when students ask unsolicited questions and when the teacher asks a question and students respond. When students ask their own questions, it is important to address every student's question as much as possible. For example, a teacher has presented information about a hurricane during a critical-input experience in which students watched a videotape. A number of students ask questions about hurricanes that were not addressed in the video. Before moving on, the teacher addresses as many of these questions as time will allow but makes sure she calls on low-expectancy students. The teacher also acknowledges the usefulness and desirability of these questions by making comments such as, "Liam, thanks for asking that question. I'm sure others in the class had the same confusion."

When students are responding to questions the teacher has asked, it is common for a small group of the same students to raise their hands to volunteer answers. Unfortunately, low-expectancy students typically do not volunteer answers, particularly for the more challenging questions. To counteract this tendency, the teacher can employ a system of calling on students who have not raised their hands. This issue was partially addressed in the Chapter 5 discussion of student engagement. With this type of system, students have a sense that they can be called on at any time, even if they do not volunteer. For the purposes of this chapter, the technique would be modified to increase the probability of calling on low-expectancy students. For example, a teacher takes special note of her low-expectancy students in her seating chart and records a check mark next to the name every time she asks the student a question. In this way, the teacher makes sure that these students are not passed over. She also makes sure that low-expectancy students are systematically asked challenging questions. This approach helps create a culture of high expectations for all. Low-expectancy students are given the message that the teacher is confident that they can handle even the most difficult of questions.

Action Step 5. When Low-Expectancy Students Do Not Answer a Question Correctly or Completely, Stay with Them

When a low-expectancy student does not respond correctly to a question, the teacher should devote as much time with the incorrect or incomplete answer as he would with a high-expectancy student. Unfortunately, when a low-expectancy student answers a question incorrectly, teachers might have a natural tendency to try to elicit the correct answer as quickly as possible. However, if a teacher operates from the perspective that the student has answered the question from a system of logic (albeit flawed or based on faulty assumptions), then it makes good sense to identify the logic from which the student generated the answer. This can be done using the general framework of elaborative interrogations, as described in Chapter 2. Recall that elaborative interrogations have the general form, "How do you know this to be true?" To illustrate, a mathematics teacher asks a low-expectancy student, "Why is it that the mean, the median, and the mode will all be the same value in a normal distribution?" The low-expectancy student answers, "Because they all measure the same thing." The teacher then asks, "Tell me why you think this is so. What do you mean that they all measure the same thing?" To this the student responds, "They all tell you the point at which the same amount of numbers are above that point and the same amount of numbers are below that point." As a result of this interaction, the teacher has discovered the student's thinking and can comment on what is correct about that thinking and what is incorrect about it. The teacher says, "Good, you've correctly described what the median is. Nice job. But that does not describe the mean and the mode. Let's go back to the mode. Tell me what you remember about it."

These types of interactions allow the teacher to acknowledge what the student knows and delve more deeply into what the student does not understand. Finally, such interactions communicate to the student that her thinking is valued.

There are a number of other techniques that can be used with low-expectancy students (for a more comprehensive listing, see Good & Brophy, 2003). Some of them are listed here:

- **Demonstrate gratitude for students' responses.** Whenever students respond to a question in front of their peers, they put themselves at risk. A teacher can and should take the time to thank students for their responses. This can be done individually, particularly with a difficult question: "Arnold, thanks for taking on that question. I know it wasn't easy. You did a fine job." It can also be done with the class as a whole: "Thanks for your responses today. It was a great class. You were engaged. You worked hard and took on some tough questions I asked."

- **Do not allow negative comments from other students.** Part of the culture in a classroom regarding questioning is generated by the students. It is important to have and enforce rules about students commenting on other students' responses. A general classroom rule of behaving in a respectful manner to all members of the class (see Chapter 6 on rules and procedures) implies that negative comments from students regarding other students are unacceptable.

- **Point out what is correct and incorrect about students' responses.** Almost every response will contain some correct and some incorrect information. If both of these parts are systematically identified by the teacher, then being "wrong" will become a natural and acceptable part of learning. Along with this routine, it is useful to remind students that making mistakes is part of the learning process.

- **Restate the question.** If a student is having difficulty with a question, a teacher can restate the question or find a simpler question within the one asked. For example, a teacher has asked the question: "Why is it that the mean, median, and mode will always be the same value in a normal distribution?" A particular student says: "I don't know." In response the teacher comments, "OK, Lindsay, then tell me what you know about the mean. This was the first statistic we discussed. What do you remember about it?" By deconstructing the question into smaller, simpler parts, the teacher provides opportunities for Lindsay to demonstrate what she knows.

- **Provide ways to *temporarily* let students off the hook.** If a student becomes confused or embarrassed while being questioned, it is desirable to provide time for the student to compose himself. The teacher accomplishes this by telling the student that he will return to him later: "Mark. How about this? I'll give you a little time to think. Then I'll come back to you." When the teacher does return to the student, he asks a different question that is easier for the student to address. Or the teacher might ask the original question again, but this time the student has the benefit of hearing the responses of others and the extra time to think through an answer. Another variation is to allow students to call a friend as a humorous take off on the television show *Who Wants to Be* *a Millionaire*. The student then selects another class member to answer the question for her. However, the teacher comes back to the student who has called the friend and asks a question that has a higher probability of being answered.

Summary

When considering the ninth design question—What will I do to communicate high expectations for all students?—teachers should develop expectations for students' success in class and then behave in ways that are consistent with these expectations. Teachers should now be aware of actions they can take to avoid treating low-expectancy students differently from high-expectancy students in terms of communicating a positive affective tone. Teachers also should have strategies for ensuring consistency in terms of the quality of interactions with low- and high-expectancy students, particularly with regard to questions.

10

What will I do to develop effective lessons organized into a cohesive unit?

In this era of standards, many schools and school districts have identified specific content that should be taught at specific grade levels in specific courses. However, teachers are still free to organize this content into units of their design. Even when a school district or school identifies specific units that must be taught, teachers still have a great deal of flexibility in terms of how those units are structured.

There is no one best way to design a unit. This chapter addresses the various ways that a teacher might construct a unit and the lessons within that unit. To a great extent, this design question is a metaquestion. It organizes the previous nine.

In the Classroom

In our classroom scenario, Mr. Hutchins's well-structured unit on Hiroshima and Nagasaki did not happen by chance. Rather, he thought it through from beginning to end and planned accordingly. He started by identifying the focus of the unit. He concluded that this topic was particularly conducive to analyzing the beliefs and values that underlie political decisions—in this case the decision to use atomic weapons to end World War II. He knows there are no simple answers to such issues, but he also believes that such issues will continue to face humankind for the foreseeable future. He decides that the centerpiece of the unit will be a task that requires students to examine the values and beliefs that led to the decision to use atomic weapons and then requires them to take a position on whether those values and beliefs are still prevalent today. He creates a learning goal specifically for this task, along with a few more specific learning goals that support the overall focus.

Mr. Hutchins plans for specific critical-input experiences as well as activities that will deepen students' understanding of the content. He creates an outline for the three-week unit that identifies the activities for each day. He realizes that he will surely make changes as time goes by, but the outline provides a framework to guide his decisions. He also has a model for what an effective lesson should entail. Some lesson segments are devoted to routine procedures such as taking roll and acquiring and returning materials. Other lesson segments deal with content-specific activities such as providing students with a critical-input experience, providing students with some knowledge-deepening activity, or providing students with opportunities to work on the decision-making task that is the centerpiece of the unit. Finally, he realizes that every lesson involves some behaviors that he must be ready to execute immediately, such as applying consequences regarding rules and procedures and ensuring that he communicates the message of high expectations to every student. His framework for the unit and his model of lesson design provide a powerful structure, offering students guidance along with flexibility.

Research and Theory

Perhaps it was Benjamin Bloom (1976) who first validated the unit as the way teachers organize instruction. Bloom found that during a year in school, students encounter about 150 separate learning units. These units vary in length, some lasting a few weeks, others lasting a few days. In effect, teachers use these units to organize new content in ways that provide a cohesive framework for the entire semester or year. Doyle (1983) provides further insight into the organization of curriculum. Doyle notes that the academic task is the basic unit of organization within a lesson. He states that one must "view the curriculum as a collection of *academic* tasks" (1983, pp. 160–161). He explains that about 60 to 70 percent of class time is taken up by teacher-designed tasks. Doyle further demonstrates that the manner in which teachers design and organize these academic tasks affects student learning. Everything else being equal, a teacher who designs and organizes academic tasks well will produce better student learning than a teacher who does not.

Bennett and Desforges (1988) classify academic tasks into four broad categories: incremental, practice, restructuring, and enrichment. Their incremental and practice categories address the activities described in Chapter 3 on practice, review, and revision. Their restructuring and enrichment categories address the activities described in Chapter 4 on tasks involving hypothesis generation and testing. In a study of 4th and 6th grade classes, Blumenfeld and Meece (1988) corroborate Doyle's (1983) contention that task design has an effect on student achievement and that complex, well-designed tasks facilitate deeper levels of learning and higher engagement. Unfortunately, they also conclude that teachers tend not to design and implement these complex tasks even though the resources and materials are readily available.

Other researchers and theorists have addressed the issue of design from different perspectives. Leinhardt (1990) speaks of curriculum design in the context of craft knowledge. Drawing on a considerable amount of design theory (see Berliner, 1986; Doyle, 1986; Good, Grouws, & Ebmeier, 1983; Leinhardt & Greeno, 1986; and Stodolsky, 1983), Leinhardt notes the following:

> This research-based information points to the fact that lessons are constructed with multiple parts, or lesson segments, each of which has important characteristics. Each segment contains different roles for teachers and students. Each segment has multiple goals, which can be more or less successfully met by a variety of actions. Further, these segments are supported by fluid, well-rehearsed routines. (1990, pp. 21–22)

Leinhardt (1990) alludes to the fact that the manner in which lesson segments are designed and carried out in effect constitutes the craft knowledge of teaching. Miller and Meece (1997, 1999) tie the construction and implementation of effective lessons to student motivation. Interestingly, research indicates that the textbook might have less influence on the way teachers organize instructional segments than one might think. To illustrate, Freeman and Porter (1989) compared two elementary teachers who used the same textbook in the same district and found differences in the way teachers allocated their time: Teacher A allocated 17 percent of class time to concepts, 70 percent to skills, and 13 percent to applications; in contrast, Teacher B allocated 23 percent to concepts, 59 percent to skills, and 18 percent to applications (p. 413). Freeman and Porter (1989) note: "Do textbooks dictate the content of mathematics instruction in elementary schools? In a word, no" (p. 404).

Schoenfeld (1998, 2006) identifies the decisions teachers make inside and outside the classroom as a characteristic of craft knowledge. The decisions teachers make about the focus of units of instruction, the lessons within those units, and the segments within each lesson provide the infrastructure for effective or ineffective teaching. Additionally, the real-time decisions teachers make in the classroom are the point of contact between teacher and students. Clark and Peterson (1986) estimate that teachers make these real-time decisions about every two minutes. For maximum instructional effectiveness, both types of decisions must be well informed.

Finally, a case can be made that flexibility is a critical component of effective planning. This point is made by Berliner (1986) in his article "In Pursuit of the Expert Pedagogue." While discussing a study by Housner and Griffey (1985), Berliner notes the following:

> An example of skillful planning also shows up in the Housner and Griffey (1985) study. Experienced teachers were better able to anticipate situations that were likely to be encountered and were able to generate contingency plans based on those possibilities. In fact, about 1 out of 5 of the instructional strategy decisions of experienced teachers had to do with adaptations of instruction in case the planned lesson did not work out. That rate was about 1 out of 10 for novices. (1986, pp. 11–12)

Action Steps

Action Step 1. Identify the Focus of a Unit of Instruction

Each unit of instruction designed by a teacher is an entity in itself, and each teacher has his or her own style when it comes to designing these entities. One important distinction relative to a unit of instruction is its overall focus. This is probably the first decision a teacher should make in terms of unit design because it affects many other aspects of the unit. There are at least three basic areas of focus for a unit: (1) knowledge, (2) issues, and (3) student exploration.

A Focus on Knowledge

What might be referred to as the "traditional approach" to planning a unit of instruction focuses on specific elements of information and skill. In this era of state standards, this approach makes intuitive sense. States have standards documents that represent concrete expectations of what should be addressed in schools at different grade levels and for specific subject areas. These form the basis for curriculum design at the district and school level. Logically these standards should also form the basis for planning at the classroom level.

Marzano and Kendall (2007) provide an example of a teacher who is planning a unit of instruction around the topic of World War II, focusing on the use of atomic weapons by the United States. As we saw in Chapter 1 (Design Question 1), she would communicate these learning goals to students, track progress on these goals, and celebrate success relative to these goals. The following represent possible learning goals for that unit:

- **Goal 1.** Students will understand the major events leading up to the development of the atomic bomb, starting with Einstein's publication of the theory of special relativity in 1905 and ending with the development of the two bombs Little Boy and Fat Man in 1945.

- **Goal 2.** Students will understand the major factors involved in making the decision to use atomic weapons on Hiroshima and Nagasaki.
- **Goal 3.** Students will understand the effects that dropping atomic weapons had on the outcome of World War II and the Japanese people.

All activities in the unit would be geared toward helping students learn the content addressed in these goals. Critical-input experiences (see Design Question 2, Chapter 2) would provide information regarding these three goals. The teacher would schedule tasks designed to deepen students' knowledge regarding these three goals (see Design Question 3, Chapter 3), for example, having students create analogies regarding the information, make comparisons, and the like. The teacher might even engage students in a hypothesis-generation and -testing task (see Design Question 4, Chapter 4) such as the following:

> You are observing the interactions of those individuals who made the ultimate decision to drop the atomic bomb on Hiroshima and Nagasaki. What are some of the other alternatives the committee probably considered? What criteria did they use to evaluate the alternatives they were considering, and what value did they place on those criteria that led them to their final decision? Before you gather information about this issue, make your best guess at the alternatives and criteria you think they were considering.

Although this task requires students to go beyond the information contained in the three learning goals, its primary purpose within a focus on knowledge would be to add detail and sharpen understanding regarding those goals.

A Focus on Issues

When the focus of a unit is on issues, knowledge of state standards is still important. For example, the teacher might still identify the same three learning goals just discussed. In addition, though, the teacher would have a fourth goal such as the following:

> **Goal 4.** Students will be able to examine the values and beliefs that led to the decision to use atomic weapons.

This additional goal would be the centerpiece of instruction. To provide this focus, the teacher would design a hypothesis-generation and -testing task such as the following:

> Use of the atomic bomb on Hiroshima and Nagasaki during World War II was ultimately a decision made by a relatively small group of individuals. Part of your job throughout this unit will be to understand not only the people and events surrounding the use of nuclear weapons but also the values that guided those who made the decision. In addition, you will be asked to examine whether those values are still present

today. If you conclude that they are still present, you should explain how they affect current decisions made by those governing U.S. policy. If you conclude that they are not present, you should describe the difference between our current values and those present during World War II. Before you gather information about this issue, make your best guess regarding the beliefs and values that drove this decision.

To accomplish this task, students will certainly use the information acquired as a result of learning goals 1, 2, and 3, but the driving force of the unit is on an issue or central question. In this case, the question deals with the values—as opposed to the factual events—that led to the decision to use nuclear weapons and the extent to which those values are still present today. Wiggins and McTighe (1998) refer to such a question as an *essential question* and trace its use to John Dewey's (1916) view of schooling as the ultimate tool for a democratic society.

The focus of a unit has strong implications for the flow of activity. With a focus on knowledge, a hypothesis-generation and -testing task is typically presented at the middle or end of a unit, after students have had time to learn basic information and skills. With a focus on issues, the hypothesis-generation and -testing task might be presented at the start of the unit. For example, the task just discussed regarding the values that led to the use of atomic weapons might be presented the first week of class as an organizer for everything that occurs in the unit.

A Focus on Student Exploration

A unit focused on student exploration begins much like a unit that is focused on knowledge. That is, specific learning goals are identified, and the initial activities of the unit are designed to provide students with the information and skills critical to accomplishing these goals. However, once students begin to make progress on these goals students are asked to identify their own essential question, so to speak.

To facilitate students' selection of issues, the teacher might present them with questions such as the following:

- Relative to the content we have been studying, is there an important hypothesis you want to test?
- Relative to the content we have been studying, is there an important problem you want to examine?
- Relative to the content we have been studying, is there an important decision you want to examine?
- Relative to the content we have been studying, is there
  — An important concept you want to examine?
  — An important past event you want to study?
  — An important hypothetical or future event you want to examine?

When the focus is on student exploration, one of the teacher's primary jobs is to help students construct a task that allows them to explore an area of personal interest.

Action Step 2. Plan for Lesson Segments That Will Be Routine Components of Every Lesson

Although the overall unit provides the macrostructure for instruction, the individual lessons are the point of contact with students. Individual lessons are also the aspect of planning that is most observable in the sense that the school day is typically organized into periods, and lessons occur within these periods. An effective lesson has a definable structure.

Madeline Hunter (1984) is most commonly associated with a particular lesson structure that is referred to as lesson design. This is depicted in Figure 10.1. The elements of Hunter's lesson design are well articulated and quite useful. Indeed, the fact that Hunter's lesson design is still relevant today is a testament to her understanding of research and theory and her insights into the teaching–learning relationship. However, lesson design as depicted in Figure 10.1 does not apply equally well to all situations. It is best suited for lessons that address procedural knowledge, such as learning how to solve a specific type of mathematics problem. To illustrate, consider the description of guided practice. The figure states that "students practice their new knowledge or skill under direct teacher supervision." Although knowledge and skill are mentioned in this description, it is clear from the discussion in Chapter 3 that practice is more appropriate for procedural knowledge than it is for declarative knowledge. Additionally, lesson design as depicted in Figure 10.1 is not well suited for lessons involving hypothesis generation and testing, during which students might operate quite independently while gathering information for their projects or working in small groups.

An updated version of lesson design would necessarily account for the great variation in the nature and function of a lesson from day to day. Consequently, it is probably safe to say that no single design for a lesson will suffice for all situations. However, one can conceptualize a flexible form of lesson design that involves three elements: (1) segments that will most likely be part of every lesson, (2) segments that focus on content, and (3) segments that address actions that must be taken on the spot. This action step addresses the first aspect of flexible lesson design—planning for segments that generally will be part of every lesson.

Two of the design questions discussed in previous chapters address behaviors that typically are part of every lesson:

- **Design Question 1.** What will I do to establish and communicate learning goals, track student progress, and celebrate success?

FIGURE 10.1
Elements of Hunter's Lesson Design

Element	Description
Anticipatory set	A mental set that causes students to focus on what will be learned. It may also give practice in helping students achieve the learning and yield diagnostic data for the teacher. *Example:* "Look at the paragraph on the board. What do you think might be the most important part to remember?"
Objective and purpose	Not only do students learn more effectively when they know what they're supposed to be learning and why that learning is important to them, but teachers teach more effectively when they have that same information. *Example:* "Frequently, people have difficulty in remembering things that are important to them. Sometimes you feel you have studied hard and yet don't remember some of the important parts. Today, we're going to learn ways to identify what's important, and then we'll practice ways we can use to remember important things."
Input	Students must acquire new information about the knowledge, process, or skill they are to achieve. To design the input phase of the lesson so that a successful outcome becomes predictable, the teacher must have analyzed the final objective to identify knowledge and skills that need to be acquired.
Modeling	"Seeing" what is meant is an important adjunct to learning. To avoid stifling creativity, showing several examples of the process or products that students are expected to acquire or produce is helpful.
Checking for understanding	Before students are expected to do something, the teacher should determine that they understand what they are supposed to do and that they have the minimum skills required.
Guided practice	Students practice their new knowledge or skill under direct teacher supervision. New learning is like wet cement; it is easily damaged. An error at the beginning of learning can easily "set" so that correcting it later is harder than correcting it immediately.
Independent practice	Independent practice is assigned only after the teacher is reasonably sure that students will not make serious errors. After an initial lesson, students frequently are not ready to practice independently, and the teacher has committed a pedagogical error if unsupervised practice is expected.

Source: Adapted from Hunter, 1984.

- **Design Question 6.** What will I do to establish or maintain classroom rules and procedures?

Some aspects of rules and procedures (Design Question 6) are addressed as administrative necessities before and after the school day or class period; they include roll call, collecting lunch money, distributing materials, handing in homework, and reviewing what will occur during the day. At the end of the day or class period there are also routine activities that deal with rules and procedures, such as returning materials, collecting work done in class, and reviewing the expectations for the next day.

In addition to these administrative activities that deal with rules and procedures, teachers should address some aspects of learning goals (Design Question 1) systematically and perhaps daily—for example, reviewing the goals. Teachers do not need to review every learning goal every day, but it can help to review those that will be addressed during that particular day's lesson. In addition, teachers should routinely track student progress and celebrate success. On a systematic basis, the teacher might review how the class as a whole is doing relative to the learning goals for the unit. Students might also review their individual progress on their goals.

In summary, when planning a lesson, teachers should consider the following routine issues:

- **Rules and procedures.** What procedures and routines will be used? Will students be reminded of specific rules and procedures, or will new ones be established?
- **Communicating learning goals.** Will students be reminded about specific academic learning goals, or will new goals be set?
- **Tracking student progress on learning goals.** Will students be provided with feedback (e.g., a quiz, test, or informal assessment) on their progress on an academic learning goal? Will students be asked to record or reflect on their progress on learning goals?
- **Celebrating success on learning goals.** Will students be provided with some form of recognition for their progress on learning goals?

Action Step 3. Plan for Content-Specific Lesson Segments
The second component of flexible lesson design involves those segments that address academic content. Every lesson will address academic content in some way. Three of the design questions pertain to content-specific segments:

- **Design Question 2.** What will I do to help students effectively interact with new knowledge?
- **Design Question 3.** What will I do to help students practice and deepen their understanding of new knowledge?
- **Design Question 4.** What will I do to help students generate and test hypotheses about new knowledge?

These questions represent three distinct content lesson segments. It might be the case that only one content segment is addressed in a single lesson. If a class period is 50 minutes or less in duration, this will frequently be the case. However, it is also possible that multiple content segments might be addressed in a single lesson. This would most probably occur during extended class periods that are employed in block scheduling structures. For example, a lesson might begin with a critical-input experience in which new information is provided. It would then be followed by a segment that involves students in a comparison task regarding information that had been presented in a critical-input experience from the day before. The purpose of that segment would be to deepen students' understanding of knowledge. Still another lesson might begin with a critical-input experience and then be followed by a segment in which students work on a task involving hypothesis generation and testing.

When planning a lesson, then, teachers should determine:

- If students will be presented with a critical-input experience.
- If students will be presented with an activity that helps them practice or deepen their knowledge.
- If students will be presented with a hypothesis-generation and -testing task or asked to work on such a task that was started previously.

Each type of content segment brings with it important considerations.

Lesson Segments Devoted to Critical-Input Experiences

The action steps in Chapter 2 for Design Question 2 address how to help students interact with new knowledge during critical-input experiences. However, those action steps do not address the nature and format of the critical-input experience. When designing critical-input experiences, teachers should give some attention to the medium that will be used to provide new information. Of course there are a number of mediums that might be employed. These include the following:

- Lecture
- Materials students read

- Physical demonstrations
- Video or DVD presentations
- Field trips

It is probably safe to say that teachers most commonly rely on the first two, lectures and materials that students are asked to read. Although there is nothing wrong with these practices, it is also safe to say that teachers should seek variety in the mediums used for input experiences.

Another consideration regarding critical-input experiences is the structure of the content provided in the experience. Most textbooks present information in an expository format. However, as noted in the research and theory section of Chapter 2 (Design Question 2), the narrative format enhances student recall. This implies that teachers should seek to find stories that can be told to augment expository content. This is quite easily accomplished through the Internet. Specifically, Internet sources such as Wikipedia provide fascinating anecdotes and stories to accompany most academic content.

The teacher's role during critical-input experiences is an active one. The teacher previews the information with students, facilitates student processing of information after presenting small chunks of information, asks students questions that require them to elaborate on the content, engages students in activities that require them to summarize and re-present the content, and engages students in activities that require them to reflect on their learning. Consequently, it is useful for teachers to ask and answer the following questions regarding lesson segments that contain critical-input experiences:

- Am I being sensitive to the need for a variety of mediums for critical-input experiences?
- Will I augment the critical-input experience by using anecdotes and narratives?
- What specific techniques will I use to ensure that students actively process the new information, and what will my role be in those activities?
- How will grouping be used in those activities?

Lesson Segments Devoted to Practice and Deepening Students' Understanding of Content

If a lesson segment is devoted to practicing and deepening students' understanding of content, a major consideration is how much of the activity will be done in class and how much will be assigned as homework. Recall that for declarative knowledge, common tasks that help deepen students' understanding are comparing, classifying, creating metaphors, creating analogies, and analyzing errors. A teacher might begin these tasks in class and then ask students to complete the tasks as homework. With procedural knowledge, the issue of homework becomes more complex. As mentioned in Chapter 3, practice for procedural knowledge should not be assigned as homework until students have reached a level at which they can perform the procedure independently.

During segments devoted to practice and deepening students' understanding, the teacher takes on at least two roles: modeling and monitoring. Frequently, the teacher models a task for students. For example, if a metaphor task has been assigned, the teacher first explains the task to students and provides some examples. If a practice activity for procedural knowledge has been assigned, the teacher works through the procedure as it pertains to the practice task. After appropriate modeling, the teacher's role shifts to monitoring the progress of the tasks and providing help and guidance as needed.

Relative to lesson segments involving practice and knowledge-deepening activities, it is useful for teachers to ask and answer the following questions:

- What practice activities will I use, and what is my role during these activities?
- Am I using a variety of practice activities?
- What knowledge-deepening activities will I use, and what is my role during these activities?
- Am I using a variety of knowledge-deepening activities?
- What will the role of homework be in these activities?
- How will grouping be used in these activities?

Lesson Segments Devoted to Hypothesis-Generation and -Testing Tasks

By definition, hypothesis-generation and -testing tasks span a number of class periods. Depending on how involved these tasks are, they might take the entire unit to complete. In terms of daily lesson planning, one decision a teacher must consider is how much time will be provided for students to work on these tasks in class. During these segments, students might be going to the library to gather information, using the Internet to gather information, asking for feedback on certain aspects of their task, and generating rough drafts of various sections of their projects.

The teacher's role during such segments is quite different from that during the other two content lesson segments. Then the teacher is facilitating the processing of information, modeling a task, or monitoring the execution of a task. During hypothesis-generation and -testing segments, the teacher acts as a resource for students. A teacher might be stationed at her desk making herself available to students as needed. She might also circulate throughout the room asking students about the progress of their hypothesis-generation and -testing tasks and offering support and guidance.

Relative to lesson segments involving hypothesis-generation and -testing tasks, it is useful for teachers to ask and answer the following questions:

- What will I do to facilitate the hypothesis-generation and -testing task that has been assigned?
- What will my role be during these activities?
- What will the role of homework be during these activities?
- How will grouping be used during these activities?

Action Step 4. Plan for Actions That Must Be Taken on the Spot

The final type of lesson segment involves activities and behaviors that can be required at any point during a lesson. Four of the design questions deal with such activities and behaviors:

- **Design Question 5.** What will I do to engage students?
- **Design Question 7.** What will I do to recognize and acknowledge adherence and lack of adherence to classroom rules and procedures?
- **Design Question 8.** What will I do to establish and maintain effective relationships with students?
- **Design Question 9.** What will I do to communicate high expectations for all students?

Engagement (Design Question 5)

One of the central concerns of a teacher is engaging students. At any moment the teacher must be ready to employ one of the action steps described in Chapter 5 (Design Question 5). The teacher might remind himself of this need daily by considering a variety of engagement activities that can be used at a moment's notice. Variety is an important aspect of such considerations. If a game has been played one day, the next day the teacher should have a different technique available. On a daily basis, then, teachers might ask themselves the following:

- What techniques for engaging students should I be ready to use today?
- Am I being sensitive to the need for variety in these techniques?

Consequences for Rules and Procedures (Design Question 7)

Whereas the design of rules and procedures must be planned for and executed at the beginning of the school year or the beginning of a new course, providing consequences for adherence to and lack of adherence to rules and procedures is a day-to-day activity. On a daily basis vigilance is required to ensure that consequences are fairly and consistently applied. To this end a teacher might mentally track the consistency with which consequences are applied. If positive consequences have not been implemented in a while, it could be an indication that they are being neglected. The same is true for negative consequences. If one or more consequences have not been executed for an extended period of time, it might mean that students are adhering well to the rules and procedures or it might mean that those consequences are being neglected.

On a daily basis, teachers might ask themselves the following:

- What positive consequences should I be ready to implement today?
- What negative consequences should I be ready to implement today?
- Am I being sensitive to the need for variety in these activities?

Relationships (Design Question 8)

Establishing effective relationships with students is a daily concern. As discussed in Chapter 8 (Design Question 8), it involves communicating an appropriate level of guidance and control along with an appropriate level of concern and cooperation. One issue that should be monitored relative to teacher–student relationships is whether there is a balance between these two somewhat competing dynamics. Sometimes a teacher might place too much emphasis on behaviors that communicate guidance and control. At other times the teacher might place too much emphasis on behaviors that communicate concern and cooperation. Another area to monitor is the specific behaviors that might be used on a given day. Again, variety is important. If the teacher has used specific techniques the day before to forge effective relationships, other techniques should be considered.

Consequently, on a daily basis teachers might ask themselves the following:

- Are my actions balanced between communicating a sense of guidance and control and a sense of concern and cooperation?
- What actions should I be ready to take to communicate a sense of guidance and control?
- What actions should I be ready to take to communicate a sense of concern and cooperation?
- Am I being sensitive to the need for variety in these actions?

Expectations (Design Question 9)

The most obvious consideration relative to communicating high expectations for all students is whether low-expectancy students are being treated in the same manner as high-expectancy students. Consequently, teachers should ask the following question daily:

- Which students should I be paying particular attention to in terms of eliciting their participation?

In addition, the type and variety of techniques for affective tone and quality of interactions are important to keep in mind. Teachers should ask themselves the following questions daily:

- What techniques should I be ready to use to establish an appropriate affective tone for low-expectancy students?
- What techniques should I be ready to use to enhance quality of interactions with low-expectancy students?
- Am I being sensitive to the need for variety in these techniques?

Action Step 5. Develop a Flexible Draft of Daily Activities for a Unit

As mentioned more than once, there is no one way to choreograph a unit of instruction. A useful technique is to sketch out the major activities in the unit, as depicted in Figure 10.2. This figure depicts a three-week unit on Hiroshima and Nagasaki. It is probably best classified as having a focus on issues because the hypothesis-generation and -testing task is presented to students on Wednesday of the first week. Presumably, the teacher will assign this task in the context of asking students to examine the beliefs and values underlying the decision to use atomic weapons. Students will be organized into groups for these activities, and each group will make a brief presentation on the Thursday or Friday of the final week. The teacher plans to provide several input activities, using films, lectures, and readings. He will administer some type of formal assessment at the end of each week. He plans a number of knowledge-deepening activities, including a metaphor activity, an error analysis activity, and an activity in which students examine and revise the entries in their academic notebooks.

Finally, it is important to note that this outline does not provide great detail. The teacher has not made entries relative to routine administrative activities and behaviors, nor has he made entries regarding activities and behaviors that he will employ as needed. The unit outline is just that—an outline that maps out the overall picture of the unit but is easily changed as circumstances dictate.

Action Step 6. Review the Critical Aspects of Effective Teaching Daily

This book has described 10 broad design issues. One obvious conclusion from reading this book is that effective teaching is a complex endeavor involving many interacting components. Just as an airplane pilot consults a comprehensive

FIGURE 10.2
Sample Outline for Unit on Hiroshima and Nagasaki

Week	Monday	Tuesday	Wednesday	Thursday	Friday
1	Show film on Hiroshima and Nagasaki as input and intro to unit. Present students with four learning goals.	Present metaphor task for Hiroshima and Nagasaki as knowledge-deepening task.	Present students with hypothesis-generation and -testing task. Organize students into their data collection groups. Have students begin gathering data.	Give lecture on Einstein, Oppenheimer, and Manhattan Project as input.	Give test. Have groups gather data for hypothesis-generation and -testing task.
2	As input, have students read article about 1940 agreement between Japan and Germany and its impact.	As knowledge-deepening task, present error analysis activity regarding Allied and Axis decisions.	Present classification task for knowledge deepening.	Have students read article about Emperor Hirohito as input.	Give test. Have groups gather data for hypothesis-generation and -testing task.
3	Have students read articles about *Enola Gay* as input.	Have groups gather data for hypothesis-generation and -testing task.	Ask groups to review and revise entries in their academic notebooks for knowledge deepening. Have students watch film on aftermath of Japan's surrender as input.	Give test. Have groups present findings.	Have groups present findings. Celebrate knowledge gain and lessons learned.

checklist before every takeoff as a way of reminding herself of the complexities of flying, so too should a teacher remind himself of the complexities of teaching on a daily basis. To this end the daily questions outlined in this chapter can be used as a checklist for effective teaching. For convenience, these questions are presented as a group in Figure 10.3.

FIGURE 10.3

I. Lesson Segments Devoted to Routine Activities and Behaviors
Rules and procedures:
* What procedures and routines will be used?
* Will students be reminded of specific rules and procedures or will new ones be established?

Communicating learning goals:
* Will students be reminded about specific academic learning goals or will new goals be set?

Tracking student progress on learning goals:
* Will students be provided with feedback (e.g., a quiz, test, or informal assessment) on their progress on an academic learning goal?
* Will students be asked to record or reflect on their progress on learning goals?

Celebrating success on learning goals:
* Will students be provided with some form of recognition for their progress on learning goals?

II. Lesson Segments Devoted to Content
Critical-input experiences:
* Am I being sensitive to the need for a variety of mediums for critical-input experiences?
* Will I augment the critical-input experience by using anecdotes and narratives?
* What specific techniques will I use to ensure that students actively process the new information, and what will my role be in those techniques?
* How will grouping be used in those activities?

Knowledge practice and deepening activities:
* What practice activities will I use and what is my role during these activities?
* Am I using a variety of practice activities?
* What knowledge-deepening activities will I use and what is my role during these activities?
* Am I using a variety of knowledge-deepening activities?
* What will the role of homework be in these activities?
* How will grouping be used in these activities?

Hypothesis generation and testing tasks:
* What will I do to facilitate the hypothesis generation and testing tasks that have been assigned?
* What will my role be during these activities?
* What will the role of homework be during these activities?
* How will grouping be used during these activities?

III. Lesson Segments Devoted to Activities That Must Be Executed on the Spot
Engagement:
* What techniques for engaging students should I be ready to use today?
* Am I being sensitive to the need for variety in these activities?

Consequences for Rules and Procedures:
* What positive consequences should I be ready to implement today?
* What negative consequences should I be ready to implement today?
* Am I being sensitive to the need for variety in these activities?

Relationships:
* Are my actions balanced between communicating a sense of guidance and control and a sense of cooperation and concern?
* What actions should I be ready to take to communicate a sense of guidance and control?
* What actions should I be ready to take to communicate a sense of cooperation and concern?
* Am I being sensitive to the need for variety in these actions?

Expectations:
* Which students should I be paying particular attention to in terms of eliciting their participation?
* What techniques should I be ready to use to establish an appropriate affective tone for low-expectancy students?
* What techniques should I be ready to use to enhance quality of interactions with low-expectancy students?
* Am I being sensitive to the need for variety in these techniques?

Afterword

In this book, I have promoted the notion that effective teaching is part art and part science. The science part of effective teaching is founded on decades of research that has provided guidance for the general categories of behaviors that constitute effective teaching and for the specific techniques that can be employed within those general categories. The art part of teaching is founded on the dual realizations that research cannot provide answers for every student in every situation and that the same behaviors can be employed in a different order and fashion by two different teachers with equally beneficial results. I hope that I have succeeded in providing the necessary research base and practical suggestions to equip new and experienced teachers alike with the tools to enhance the art and science of effective teaching.

References

Abelson, R. P. (1995). *Statistics as principled argument.* Mahwah, NJ: Lawrence Erlbaum.

Adams, G., & Cohen, A. (1974). Children's physical and interpersonal characteristics that affect student–teacher interactions. *Journal of Experimental Education, 43,* 1–5.

Alexander, P. A. (1984). Training analogical reasoning skills in the gifted. *Roeper Review, 6*(4), 191–193.

Alexander, P. A., White, C. S., Haensly, P. A., & Crimmins-Jeans, M. (n.d.). *Training in analogical reasoning.* Tech. Report. College Station, GA: College of Education, Texas A&M University.

Alleman, J., & Brophy, J. (1998). Strategic learning opportunities during after-school hours. *Social Studies and the Young Learner, 62*(3), 10–13.

Allington, R. (1980). Teacher interruption behaviors during primary-grade oral reading. *Journal of Educational Psychology, 72,* 371–377.

Alvermann, D. E., & Boothby, P. R. (1986). Children's transfer of graphic organizer instruction. *Reading Psychology, 7*(2), 87–100.

Ambady, N., & Rosenthal, R. (1992). Thin slices of expressive behavior as predictors of interpersonal consequences: A meta-analysis. *Psychological Bulletin, 111*(2), 256–274.

Ames, C. (1984). Competitive, cooperative, and individualistic goal structures: A cognitive-motivational analysis. In R. Ames & C. Ames (Eds.), *Research on motivation in education: Vol. 1. Student motivation* (pp. 177–207). New York: Academic Press.

Anderman, E. M., & Wolters, C. A. (2006). Goals, values, and affect: Influences on student motivation. In P. Alexander & P. Winne (Eds.), *Handbook of educational psychology* (pp. 369–389). Mahwah, NJ: Erlbaum.

Anderson, J. R. (1982). Acquisition of cognitive skills. *Psychological Review, 89,* 369–406.

Anderson, J. R. (1983). *The architecture of cognition.* Cambridge, MA: Harvard University Press.

Anderson, J. R. (1995). *Learning and memory: An integrated approach.* New York: Wiley.

Anderson, J. R., Greeno, J. G., Reder, L. M., & Simon, H. A. (2000). Perspectives on learning, thinking, and activity. *Educational Researcher, 29*(4), 11–13.

Anderson, J. R., Reder, L. M., & Simon, H. A. (1995). Applications and misapplications of cognitive psychology to mathematics education. Unpublished paper, Carnegie Mellon University, Department of Psychology, Pittsburgh. Available from http://act.psy.cmu.edu/personal/ja/misapplied.html.

Anderson, J. R., Reder, L. M., & Simon, H. A. (1996). Situated learning and education. *Educational Researcher, 25*(4), 5–11.

Anderson, L., Evertson, C., & Emmer, E. (1980). Dimensions in classroom management derived from recent research. *Journal of Curriculum Studies, 12,* 343–356.

Anderson, L. W., Krathwohl, D. R., Airasian, P. W., Cruikshank, K. A., Mayer, R. E., Pintrich, P. R., et al. (Eds.). (2001). *A taxonomy for learning, teaching, and assessing: A revision of Bloom's taxonomy of educational objectives.* New York: Longman.

Anderson, V., & Hidi, S. (1988/1989). Teaching students to summarize. *Educational Leadership, 46,* 26–28.

Arlin, M. (1979). Teacher transitions can disrupt time flow in classrooms. *American Education Research Journal, 16,* 42–56.

Armbruster, B. B., Anderson, T. H., & Meyer, J. L. (1992). Improving content-area reading using instructional graphics. *Reading Research Quarterly, 26*(4), 393–416.

Armento, B. J. (1978, February). Teacher behavior and effective teaching of concepts. Paper presented at the Annual Meeting of the American Association of Colleges for Teacher Education, Chicago. (ERIC Document Reproduction Service No. ED 153 949).

Aronson, E., Blaney, N., Stephan, C., Sikes, J., & Snapp, M. (1978). *The jigsaw classroom.* Beverly Hills, CA: Sage.

Atwood, V. A., & Wilen, W. W. (1991). Wait time and effective social studies instruction: What can research in science education tell us? *Social Education, 55,* 179–181.

Aubusson, P., Foswill, S., Barr, R., & Perkovic, L. (1997). What happens when students do simulation-role-play in science. *Research in Science Education, 27*(4), 565–579.

Ausubel, D. P. (1968). *Educational psychology: A cognitive view.* New York: Holt, Rinehart, & Winston.

Babad, E., Inbar, J., & Rosenthal, R. (1982). Pygmalion, Galatea, and the Golem: Investigations of biased and unbiased teachers. *Journal of Educational Psychology, 74,* 459–474.

Baker, W. P., & Lawson, A. E. (1995). *Effect of analogical instruction and reasoning level on achievement in general genetics.* Tempe, AZ: Department of Zoology. (ERIC Document Reproduction Service No. 390 713).

Balli, S. J. (1998). When mom and dad help: Student reflections on parent involvement with homework. *Journal of Research and Development in Education, 31*(3), 142–148.

Balli, S. J., Demo, D. H., & Wedman, J. F. (1998). Family involvement with children's homework: An intervention in the middle grades. *Family Relations: Interdisciplinary Journal of Applied Family Studies, 47*(2), 149–157.

Balli, S. J., Wedman, J. F., & Demo, D. H. (1997). Family involvement with middle grades homework: Effects of differential prompting. *Journal of Experimental Education, 66*(1), 31–48.

Bangert-Drowns, R. L., Hurley, M. M., & Wilkinson, B. (2004). The effects of school-based writing-to-learn interventions on academic achievement: A meta-analysis. *Review of Educational Research, 74*(1), 29–58.

Bangert-Drowns, R. L., Kulik, C. C., Kulik, J. A., & Morgan, M. (1991). The instructional effects of feedback in test-like events. *Review of Educational Research, 61*(2), 213–238.

Bangert-Drowns, R. L., Kulik, J. A., & Kulik, C. C. (1991). Effects of classroom testing. *Journal of Educational Research, 85*(2), 89–99.

Barley, Z., Lauer, P. A., Arens, S. A., Apthorp, H. S., Englert, K. S., Snow, D., & Akiba, M. (2002). *Helping at-risk students meet standards: A synthesis of evidence-based classroom practices.* Centennial, CO: Mid-continent Research for Education and Learning.

Barr, A. S. (1958). Characteristics of successful teachers. *Phi Delta Kappan, 39,* 282–284.

Barrows, H. S., & Tamblyn, R. M. (1980). *Problem-based learning: An approach to medical education.* New York: Springer.

Becker, W. C. (Ed.). (1988). Direct instruction: Special issue. *Education and Treatment of Children, 11,* 297–402.

Beez, W. (1968). Influence of biased psychological reports on teacher behavior and pupil performance (Summary). *Proceedings of the 76th Annual Convention of the American Psychological Association, 3,* 605–606.

Bennett, N., & Desforges, C. (1988). Matching classroom tasks to students' attainments. *Elementary School Journal, 88*(3), 221–234.

Bennett, W. J., Finn, C. E., & Cribb, J. T. E. (1999). *The educated child: A parent's guide from preschool through eighth grade.* New York: Free Press.

Berliner, D. C. (1986). In pursuit of the expert pedagogue. *Educational Researcher, 15*(7), 5–13.

Berman, S. (2001). Thinking in context: Teaching for open-mindedness and critical understanding. In A. L. Costa (Ed.), *Developing minds: A resource book for teaching thinking* (pp. 11–17). Alexandria, VA: Association for Supervision and Curriculum Development.

Bettencourt, E. M., Gillett, M. H., Gall, M. D., & Hull, R. E. (1983). Effects of teacher enthusiasm training on student on-task behavior and achievement. *American Educational Research Journal, 20*(3), 435–450.

Black, P., & Wiliam, D. (1998). Assessment and classroom learning. *Assessment in Education, 5*(1), 7–75.

Blakey, M. (1970). The relationship between teacher prophesy and teacher verbal behavior and their effect upon adult student achievement. *Dissertation Abstracts International, 31,* 4615A. (UMI No. 4615A).

Bloom, B. S. (1976). *Human characteristics and school learning.* New York: McGraw-Hill.

Bloom, B. S. (1984). The search for methods of group instruction as effective as one-to-one tutoring. *Educational Leadership, 41*(8), 4–18.

Blumenfeld, P. C., & Meece, J. L. (1988). Task factors, teacher behavior, and students' involvement and use of learning strategies in science. *Elementary School Journal, 88*(3), 235–250.

Boud, D. (1987). Problem-based learning in perspective. In D. Boud (Ed.), *Problem-based learning in education for the professions* (pp. 13–18). Sydney: Higher Education Research and Development Society of Australia.

Bowen, C. W. (2000). A quantitative review of cooperative learning effects on high school and college chemistry achievement. *Journal of Chemical Education, 77*(1), 116–119.

Brandt, R. (1998). *Powerful learning.* Alexandria, VA: Association for Supervision and Curriculum Development.

Bransford, J. D., & Johnson, M. K. (1973). Considerations of some problems of comprehension. In W. G. Chase (Ed.), *Visual information processing* (pp. 383–438). New York: Academic Press.

Brekelmans, M., Wubbels, T., & Creton, H. A. (1990). A study of student perceptions of physics teacher behavior. *Journal of Research in Science Teaching, 27,* 335, 350.

Broadhurst, A., & Darnell, D. (1965). An introduction to cybernetics and information theory. *Quarterly Journal of Speech, 51,* 442–453.

Brooks, J. G., & Brooks, M. G. (1999). *In search of understanding: The case for the constructivist classroom.* Alexandria, VA: Association for Supervision and Curriculum Development.

Brooks, J. G., & Brooks, M. G. (2001). Becoming a constructivist teacher. In A. L. Costa (Ed.), *Developing minds: A resource book for teaching thinking* (3rd ed., pp. 150–157). Alexandria, VA: Association for Supervision and Curriculum Development.

Brophy, J., & Good, T. (1974). *Teacher–student relationships: Causes and consequences.* New York: Holt, Rinehart, & Winston.

Brophy, J. E. (1981). Teacher praise: A functional analysis. *Review of Educational Research, 51,* 5–32.

Brophy, J. E. (1983). Research on the self-fulfilling prophecy and teacher expectations. *Journal of Educational Psychology, 75*(5), 631–661.

Brophy, J. E. (1996). *Teaching problem students.* New York: Guilford.

Brophy, J. E. (2006). History of research in classroom management. In C. M. Evertson & C. S. Weinstein (Eds.), *Handbook of classroom management: Research, practice, and contemporary issues* (pp. 3–43). Mahwah, NJ: Lawrence Erlbaum.

Brophy, J. E., & Evertson, C. M. (1976). *Learning from teaching: A developmental perspective.* Boston: Allyn & Bacon.

Brophy, J. E., & Good, T. L. (1970). Teacher's communication of differential expectations for children's classroom performance: Some behavioral data. *Journal of Educational Psychology, 61*(5), 365–374.

Brown, J. S., & Burton, R. R. (1978). Diagnostic models for procedural bugs in basic mathematical skills. *Cognitive Science, 2,* 155–192.

Bruer, J. T. (1993). *Schools for thought: A science of learning in the classroom.* Cambridge, MA: The MIT Press.

Bruer, J. T. (1997). Education and the brain: A bridge too far. *Educational Researcher, 26*(8), 4–16.

Bruner, J. S. (1973). *Beyond the information given.* New York: W. W. Norton.

Butler, D. L., & Winne, P. H. (1995). Feedback and self-regulated learning: A theoretical synthesis. *Review of Educational Research, 65*(3), 245–281.

Caffyn, R. E. (1989). Attitudes of British secondary school teachers and pupils to rewards and punishments. *Educational Research, 31,* 210–220.

Cahill, L., Gorski, L., & Lee, K. (2003). Enhanced human memory consolidation with post learning stress: Interactions with the degree of arousal at encoding. *Learning and Memory, 10*(4), 270–274.

Cahill, L., Prins, B., Weber, M., & McGaugh, J. (1994). Adrenergic activation and memory of emotional events. *Nature, 371*(6399), 702–704.

Caine, R. N., & Caine, G. (1991). *Making connections: Teaching and the human brain.* Alexandria, VA: Association for Supervision and Curriculum Development.

Caine, R. N., & Caine, G. (1997). *Education on the edge of possibility.* Alexandria, VA: Association for Supervision and Curriculum Development.

Cameron, J., & Pierce, W. D. (1994). Reinforcement, reward, and intrinsic motivation: A meta-analysis. *Review of Educational Research, 64*(3), 363–423.

Carr, E. G., & Durand, V. M. (1985). Reducing behavior problems through functional communication training. *Journal of Applied Behavior Analysis, 18,* 111–126.

Chaikin, A., Sigler, E., & Derlega, V. (1974). Nonverbal mediators of teacher expectancy effects. *Journal of Personality and Social Psychology, 30*(1), 144–149.

Chen, Z. (1996). Children's analogical problem solving: The effects of superficial, structure, and procedural similarities. *Journal of Experimental Child Psychology, 62*(3), 410–431.

Chen, Z. (1999). Schema induction in children's analogical problem solving. *Journal of Educational Psychology, 91*(4), 703–715.

Chen, Z., Yanowitz, K. L., & Daehler, M. W. (1996). Constraints on accessing abstract source information: Instantiation of principles facilitates children's analogical transfer. *Journal of Educational Psychology, 87*(3), 445–454.

Chi, M. T. H., Feltovich, P. J., & Glaser, R. (1981). Categorization and representation of physics problems by experts and novices. *Cognitive Science, 5,* 121–152.

Clark, C., & Peterson, P. (1986). Teacher's thought processes. In M. C. Wittrock (Ed.), *Handbook of research on teaching* (3rd ed., pp. 255–296). New York: Macmillan.

Clement, J., Lockhead, J., & Mink, G. (1979). Translation difficulties in learning mathematics. *American Mathematical Monthly, 88,* 3–7.

Coats, W., & Smidchens, V. (1966). Audience recall as a function of speaker dynamism. *Journal of Educational Psychology, 57,* 189–191.

Cobb, P., Yackel, E., & Wood, T. (1992). A constructivist alternative to the representational view of mind in mathematics education. *Journal of Research in Mathematics Education, 23,* 2–33.

Cole, J. C., & McLeod, J. S. (1999). Children's writing ability. The impact of the pictorial stimulus. *Psychology in the Schools, 36*(4), 359–370.

Coleman, J. S., Campbell, E. Q., Hobson, C. J., McPartland, J., Mood, A. M., Weinfield, F. D., & York, R. L. (1966). *Equality of educational opportunity.* Washington, DC: U.S. Government Printing Office.

Collie, A., Maruff, P., Darby, D. G., & McStephen, M. (2003). The effects of practice on cognitive test performance of neurologically normal individuals assessed at brief test–retest intervals. *Journal of International Neuropsychology Society, 9*(3), 419–428.

Connell, J. P., Spencer, M. B., & Aber, J. L. (1994). Educational risk and resilience in African-American youth: Context, self, action, and outcomes in school. *Child Development, 65,* 493–506.

Connell, J. P., & Wellborn, J. G. (1991). Competence, autonomy, and relatedness: A motivational analysis of self-system processes. In M. Gunnar & L. A. Sroufe (Eds.), *Minnesota Symposium on Child Psychology* (Vol. 23, pp. 21–56). Chicago: The University of Chicago Press.

Cooper, H. (1989a). *Homework.* White Plains, NY: Longman.

Cooper, H. (1989b). Synthesis of research on homework. *Educational Leadership, 47*(3), 85–91.

Cooper, H., & Baron, R. (1977). Academic expectations and attributed responsibility as predictors of professional teachers' reinforcement behavior. *Journal of Educational Psychology, 69,* 409–418.

Cooper, H., & Hazelrigg, P. (1988). Personality moderators of interpersonal expectancy effects: An integrative research review. *Journal of Personality and Social Psychology, 55*(6), 937–949.

Cooper, H., Lindsay, J. J., Nye, B., & Greathouse, S. (1998). Relationships among attitudes about homework, amount of homework assigned and completed, and student achievement. *Journal of Educational Psychology, 90*(1), 70–83.

Cooper, H., Robinson, J. C., & Patall, E. A. (2006). Does homework improve academic achievement? A synthesis of research, 1987–2003. *Review of Educational Research, 76*(1), 1–62.

Cooper, H. M. (1979). Pygmalion grows up: A model for teacher expectation communication and performance influence. *Review of Educational Research, 49*(3), 389–410.

Cooper, H. M., & Good, T. L. (1983). *Pygmalion grows up: Studies in the expectation communication process.* New York: Longman.

Corkill, A. J. (1992). Advance organizers: Facilitators of recall. *Educational Psychology Review, 4,* 33–68.

Cornbleth, C., Davis, O., & Button, C. (1972). Teacher–pupil interaction and teacher expectations for pupil achievement in secondary social studies class. Paper presented at the Annual Meeting of the American Educational Research Association, Chicago.

Corno, L. (1996). Homework is a complicated thing. *Educational Researcher, 25*(8), 27–30.

Costa, A. L. (Ed.). (2001). *Developing minds: A resource book for teaching thinking* (3rd ed.). Alexandria, VA: Association for Supervision and Curriculum Development.

Crismore, A. (Ed.). (1985). *Landscapes: A state-of-the-art assessment of reading comprehension research: 1974–1984. Final report.* Washington, DC: U.S. Department of Education. (ED 261 350).

Cross, K. P. (1998). Classroom research: Implementing the scholarship of teaching. In T. Angelo (Ed.), *Classroom assessment and research: An update on uses, approaches, and research findings* (pp. 5–12). San Francisco: Jossey-Bass.

Csikszentmihalyi, M. (1990). *Flow: The psychology of optimal experience.* New York: Harper & Row.

Curwin, R. L., & Mendler, A. N. (1988). *Discipline with dignity.* Alexandria, VA: Association for Supervision and Curriculum Development.

Dagher, Z. R. (1995). Does the use of analogies contribute to conceptual change? *Science and Education, 78*(6), 601–614.

Darch, C. B., Carnine, D. W., & Kameenui, E. J. (1986). The role of graphic organizers and social structure in content area instruction. *Journal of Reading Behavior, 18*(4), 275–295.

Darnell, D. (1970). "Clozentropy": A procedure for testing English language proficiency of foreign students. *Speech Monographs, 37,* 36–46.

Darnell, D. (1972). Information theory: An approach to human communication. In R. Budd & B. Ruben (Eds.), *Approaches to human communication* (pp. 156–169). New York: Spartan.

Deci, E., Koestner, R., & Ryan, R. (2001). Extrinsic rewards and intrinsic motivation in education: Reconsidered once again. *Review of Educational Research, 71,* 1–27.

Deci, E., & Ryan, R. (1985). *Intrinsic motivation and self-determination in human behavior.* New York: Plenum.

Deci, E. L. (1971). Effects of externally medicated rewards on intrinsic motivation. *Journal of Personality and Social Psychology, 22,* 113–120.

Deci, E. L., Ryan, R. M., & Koestner, R. (2001). The pervasive effects of rewards on intrinsic motivation: Response to Cameron (2001). *Review of Educational Research, 71*(1), 43–51.

de Leeuw, J. (2004). Senior editor introduction. In R. A. Berk, *Regression analysis: A constructive critique* (pp. xi–xv). Thousand Oaks, CA: Sage.

Dewey, J. (1916). *Democracy and education: An introduction to the philosophy of education.* New York: Macmillan.

Doyle, W. (1983). Academic work. *Review of Educational Research, 53*(2), 159–199.

Doyle, W. (1986). Classroom organization and management. In M. C. Wittrock (Ed.), *Handbook of research on teaching* (3rd ed., pp. 392–431). New York: Macmillan.

Drabman, R., & Spitalnik, R. (1973). Social isolation as a punishment procedure: A controlled study. *Journal of Experimental Child Psychology, 5,* 236–249.

Druyan, S. (1997). Effects of the kinesthetic conflict on promoting scientific reasoning. *Journal of Research in Science Teaching, 34*(10), 1083–1099.

Dusek, J. B., & Gail, J. (1983). The bases of teacher expectancies: A meta-analysis. *Journal of Educational Psychology, 75*(3), 327–346.

Dwyer, T., Blizzard, L., & Dean., K. (1996). Physical activity and performance in children. *Nutrition Review, 54*(4), 27–31.

Dwyer, T., Sallis, J., Blizzard, L., Lazarus, R., & Dean, K. (2001). Relation of academic performance to physical activity and fitness in children. *Pediatric Exercise Science, 13,* 225–237.

Ebbinghaus, H. (1987). Regarding a new application of performance testing and its use with school children. *Journal of Psychology and Physiology, 13,* 225–237.

Edwards, D., & Mullis, F. (2003). Classroom meetings: Encouraging a climate of cooperation. *Professional School Counseling, 7*(1), 20–28.

Eisenhart, M. (1977, May). Maintaining control: Teacher competence in the classroom. Paper presented at the American Anthropological Association, Houston.

El-Nemr, M. A. (1980). Meta-analysis of outcomes of teaching biology as inquiry. *Dissertation Abstracts International, 40,* 5813A.

Embretson, S. E., & Reise, S. P. (2000). *Item response theory for psychologists.* Mahwah, NJ: Erlbaum.

Emmer, E. T., Evertson, C., & Anderson, L. (1980). Effective classroom management at the beginning of the school year. *Elementary School Journal, 80*(5), 219–231.

Emmer, E. T., Evertson, C. M., & Worsham, M. E. (2003). *Classroom management for secondary teachers* (6th ed.). Boston: Allyn & Bacon.

Emmer, E. T., & Gerwels, M. C. (2006). Classroom management in middle and high school classrooms. In C. Evertson, C. M. Weinstein, & C. S. Weinstein (Eds.), *Handbook of classroom management: Research, practice, and contemporary issues* (pp. 407–437). Mahwah, NJ: Erlbaum.

Emmer, E. T., Sanford, J. P., Clements, B. S., & Martin, J. (1982). *Improving classroom management and organization in junior high schools: An experimental investigation* (R & D Report No. 6153). Austin: Research and Development Center for Teacher Education, University of Texas. (ERIC Document Reproduction Service No. ED261053).

Emmer, E. T., Sanford, J. P., Evertson, C. M., Clements, B. S., & Martin, J. (1981). *The classroom management improvement study: An experiment in elementary school classrooms* (R & D Report No. 6050). Austin: Research and Development Center for Teacher Education, University of Texas. (ERIC Document Reproduction Service No. ED226452).

English, L. D. (1997). Children's reasoning in classifying and solving computational word problems. In L. D. English (Ed.), *Mathematical reasoning, analogies, metaphors, and images* (pp. 191–220). Mahwah, NJ: Lawrence Erlbaum.

Epstein, J. L. (1988). *Homework practices, achievement, and behaviors of elementary school students* (Rep. No. 26). Baltimore, MD: Johns Hopkins University, Center on Families, Communities, Schools, and Children's Learning.

Epstein, J. L. (1991). School programs and teacher practices of parent involvement in inner-city elementary and middle schools. *Elementary School Journal, 91*(3), 289–305.

Epstein, J. L. (2001). *School, family, and community partnerships: Preparing educators and improving schools.* Boulder, CO: Westview.

Epstein, J. L., & Becker, H. J. (1982). Teachers' reported practices of parent involvement: Problems and possibilities. *Elementary School Journal, 83,* 103–113.

Epstein, J. L., & Harackiewicz, J. (1992). Winning is not enough: The effects of competition and achievement orientation on intrinsic interest. *Personality and Social Psychology Bulletin, 18,* 128–138.

Epstein, J. L., Simon, B. S., & Salinas, K. C. (1997, September). *Involving parents in homework in the middle grades* (Research Bulletin 18). Bloomington, IN: Phi Delta Kappa, Center for Evaluation, Development, and Research.

Epstein, J. L., & Van Voorhis, F. L. (2001). More than minutes: Teachers' roles in designing homework. *Educational Psychologist, 36,* 181–194.

Evertson, C., & Weinstein, C. S. (Eds.). (2006). *Handbook of classroom management: Research, practice, and contemporary issues.* Mahwah, NJ: Erlbaum.

Evertson, C. M., & Emmer, E. T. (1982). Preventive classroom management. In D. Duke (Ed.), *Helping teachers manage classrooms* (pp. 2–31). Alexandria, VA: Association for Supervision and Curriculum Development.

Evertson, C. M., Emmer, E. T., Sanford, J. P., & Clements, B. S. (1983). Improving classroom management: An experiment in elementary classrooms. *Elementary School Journal, 84*(2), 173–188.

Evertson, C. M., Emmer, E. T., & Worsham, M. E. (2003). *Classroom management for elementary teachers* (6th ed.). Boston: Allyn & Bacon.

Fan, X., & Chen, M. (2001). Parental involvement and students' academic achievement: A meta-analysis. *Educational Psychology Review, 13*(1), 1–22.

Feltz, D. L., & Landers, D. M. (1983). The effects of mental practice on motor skill learning and performance: A meta-analysis. *Journal of Sport Psychology, 5,* 25–57.

Firestone, G., & Brody, N. (1975). Longitudinal investigation of teacher–student interactions and their relationship to academic performance. *Journal of Educational Psychology, 67*(4), 544–550.

Fishbein, H. D., Eckart, T., Lauver, E., Van Leeuwen, R., & Langmeyer, D. (1990). Learner's questions and comprehension in a tutoring setting. *Journal of Educational Psychology, 82*(1), 163–170.

Fitts, P. M., & Posner, M. I. (1967). *Human performance.* Belmont, CA: Brooks Cole.

Fitzgerald, J. (1987). Research on revision in writing. *Review of Educational Research, 57,* 481–506.

Flicek, M. (2005a, April). *Consistency of rubric scoring for common assessments for math that are a part of NCSD body of evidence (BoE) for high school graduation.* Assessment and Research Brief, 8. Casper, WY: Office of Assessment and Research, Natrona County School District #1.

Flicek, M. (2005b, July). *Moving toward a valuable and reliable teacher judgment of student performance on standards.* Assessment and Research Brief, 14. Casper, WY: Office of Assessment and Research, Natrona County School District #1.

Flick, L. (1992). Where concepts meet percepts: Stimulating analogical thought in children. *Science and Education, 75*(2), 215–230.

Foxx, R. M. (1978). An overview of overcorrection. *Journal of Pediatric Psychology, 3,* 97–101.

Fraser, B. J., Walberg, H. J., Welch, W. W., & Hattie, J. A. (1987). Synthesis of educational productivity research. Special issue. *International Journal of Educational Research, 11*(2), 145–252.

Frederick, W. C. (1980). Instructional time. *Evaluation in Education, 4,* 117–118.

Fredricks, J. A., Blumenfeld, P. C., & Paris, A. H. (2004). School engagement: Potential of the concept, state of the evidence. *Review of Educational Research, 74*(1), 49–109.

Freeman, D., & Porter, A. (1989). Do textbooks dictate the content of mathematics instruction in elementary school? *American Educational Research Journal, 26,* 403–421.

Fuchs, L. S., & Fuchs, D. (1986). Effects of systematic formative evaluation: A meta-analysis. *Exceptional Children, 53*(3), 199–208.

Ganske, L. (1981). Note-taking: A significant and integral part of learning environments. *Education Communication and Technology Journal, 29*(3), 155–175.

Gentner, D., & Markman, A. B. (1994). Structural alignment in comparison: No difference without similarity. *Psychological Science, 5*(3), 152–158.

Gettinger, M., & Kohler, K. M. (2006). Process-outcome approaches to classroom management and effective teaching. In C. Evertson, C. M. Weinstein, & C. S. Weinstein (Eds.), *Handbook of classroom management: Research, practice, and contemporary issues* (pp. 73–95). Mahwah, NJ: Erlbaum.

Gick, M. L., & Holyoak, K. J. (1980). Analogical problem solving. *Cognitive Psychology, 12,* 306–353.

Gick, M. L. & Holyoak, K. J. (1983). Schema induction and analogical transfer. *Cognitive Psychology, 15,* 1–38.

Gijbels, D., Dochy, F., Van den Bossche, P., & Segers, M. (2005). Effects of problem-based learning: A meta-analysis from the angle of assessment. *Review of Educational Research, 75*(1), 27–61.

Gijselaers, W. (1995). Perspectives on problem-based learning. In W. Gijselaers, D. Tempelaar, P. Keizer, J. Blommaert, E. Bernard, & H. Kasper (Eds.), *Educational innovation in economics and business administration: The case of problem-based learning* (pp. 39–52). Norwell, MA: Kluwer.

Gill, B. P., & Schlossman, S. L. (2000). The lost cause of homework reform. *American Journal of Education, 109,* 27–62.

Gilovich, T. (1991). *How we know what isn't so.* New York: Free Press.

Given, B. (1974). Teacher expectancy and pupil performance: The relationship to verbal and nonverbal communication by teachers of learning disabled children. *Dissertation Abstracts International, 35,* 1529A.

Glasser, W. (1977). Ten steps to good discipline. *Today's Education, 66,* 61–63.

Glasser, W. (1986). *Control theory in the classroom.* New York: Harper & Row.

Good, T., Cooper, H., & Blakey, S. (1980). Classroom interaction as a function of teacher expectations, student sex, and time of year. *Journal of Educational Psychology, 72,* 378–385.

Good, T., Sikes, J., & Brophy, J. (1973). Effects of teacher sex and student sex on classroom interaction. *Journal of Educational Psychology, 65,* 74–87.

Good, T. L., & Brophy, J. E. (1995). *Contemporary educational psychology* (5th ed.). White Plains, NY: Longman.

Good, T. L., & Brophy, J. E. (2003). *Looking in classrooms* (9th ed.). Boston: Allyn & Bacon.

Good, T. L., Grouws, D. A., & Ebmeier, H. (1983). *Active mathematics teaching* (Research on Teaching monograph series). New York: Longman.

Gottfredson, D. C., Marciniak, E. M., Birdseye, A. T., & Gottfredson, G. D. (1995). Increasing teacher expectations for student achievement. *Journal of Educational Research, 88,* 155–163.

Gottfried, G. M. (1998). Using metaphors as modifiers: Children's production of metaphoric compounds. *Journal of Child Language, 24*(3), 567–601.

Grant, H., & Dweck, C. (2001). Cross-cultural response to failure: Considering outcome attributions with different goals. In F. Salili, C. Chiu, & Y. Hong (Eds.), *Student motivation: The culture and context of learning* (pp. 203–219). New York: Kluwer Academic/Plunum.

Graue, M. E., Weinstein, T., & Walberg, H. J. (1983). School-based home instruction and learning: A quantitative synthesis. *Journal of Educational Research, 76,* 351–360.

Griffin, C., Simmons, D. C., & Kameenui, E. J. (1992). Investigating the effectiveness of graphic organizer instruction on the comprehension and recall of science content by students with learning disabilities. *Journal of Reading, Writing and Learning Disabilities International, 7*(4), 355–376.

Guzzetti, B. J., Snyder, T. E., Glass, G. V., & Gamas, W. S. (1993). Promoting conceptual change in science: A comparative meta-analysis of instructional interventions from reading education and science education. *Reading Research Quarterly, 28*(2), 117–155.

Haas, M. (2005). Teaching methods for secondary algebra: A meta-analysis of findings. *NASSP Bulletin, 89*(642), 24–46.

Hall, L. E. (1989). The effects of cooperative learning on achievement: A meta-analysis. *Dissertation Abstracts International, 50,* 343A.

Haller, E. P., Child, D. A., & Walberg, H. J. (1988). Can comprehension be taught? A quantitative synthesis of "metacognitive studies." *Educational Researcher, 17*(9), 5–8.

Halpern, D. F. (1984). *Thought and knowledge: An introduction to critical thinking.* Hillsdale, NJ: Lawrence Erlbaum.

Halpern, D. F. (1996a). *Thinking critically about critical thinking.* Mahwah, NJ: Lawrence Erlbaum.

Halpern, D. F. (1996b). *Thought and knowledge: An introduction to critical thinking* (3rd ed.). Mahwah, NJ: Lawrence Erlbaum.

Halpern, D. F., Hansen, C. & Reifer, D. (1990). Analogies as an aid to understanding and memory. *Journal of Educational Psychology, 82*(2), 298–305.

Hamaker, C. (1986). The effects of adjunct questions on prose learning. *Review of Educational Research, 56,* 212–242.

Hargrove, T. Y., & Nesbit, C. (2003). *Science notebooks: Tools for increasing achievement across the curriculum.* Columbus, OH: ERIC Clearinghouse for Science Mathematics and Environmental Education. (ERIC Document Reproduction Service Number ED 482720).

Harris, M. J., & Rosenthal, R. (1985). Mediation of interpersonal expectancy effects: 31 meta-analyses. *Psychological Bulletin, 97*(3), 363–386.

Harrop, A., & Williams, T. (1992). Rewards and punishments in the primary school: Pupils' perceptions and teachers' usage. *Educational Psychology in Practice, 7,* 211–215.

Hattie, J., Biggs, J., & Purdie, N. (1996). Effects of learning skills interventions on student learning: A meta-analysis. *Review of Educational Research, 66*(2), 99–136.

Hattie, J. A. (1992). Measuring the effects of schooling. *Australian Journal of Education, 36*(1), 5–13.

Haycock, K. (1998). Good teaching matters . . . a lot. *Thinking K–16, 3*(2), 1–14.

Hayes, B. K., Foster, K., & Gadd, N. (2003). Prior knowledge and subtyping effects in children's category learning. *Cognition, 88*(2), 171–199.

Hayes, J. R. (1981). *The complete problem solver.* Philadelphia: Franklin Institute.

Henk, W. A., & Stahl, N. A. (1985). A meta-analysis of the effect of notetaking on learning from lecture. Paper presented at the 34th Annual Meeting of the National Reading Conference, St. Petersburg Beach, FL. (ERIC Document Reproduction Service No. ED258533).

Hidi, S., & Anderson, V. (1987). Providing written summaries: Task demands, cognitive operations, and implications for instruction. *Reviewing Educational Research, 56,* 473–493.

Hillocks, G. (1986). *Research on written composition.* Urbana, IL: ERIC Clearinghouse on Reading and Communication Skills and National Conference on Research in English.

Hofstetter, C. R., Sticht, T. G., & Hofstetter, C. H. (1999, February). Knowledge, literacy, and power. *Communication Research, 26*(1), 58–80.

Hoover-Dempsey, K. V., Bassler, O. C., & Burow, R. (1995). Parents' reported involvement in students' homework: Strategies and practices. *Elementary School Journal, 95*(5), 435–450.

Horton, S. V., Lovitt, T. C., & Bergerud, D. (1990). The effectiveness of graphic organizers for three classifications of secondary students in content area classes. *Journal of Learning Disabilities, 23*(1), 12–22.

Houghton, S., Merrett, F., & Wheldall, F. (1988). The attitudes of British secondary school pupils to praise, rewards, punishments, and reprimands. *New Zealand Journal of Educational Psychology, 23,* 203–214.

Housner, L. D., & Griffey, D. C. (1985). Teacher cognition: Differences in planning and interactive decision-making between experienced and inexperienced teachers. *Research Quarterly for Exercise and Sport, 56,* 45–53.

Hunter, M. (1984). Knowing, teaching, and supervising. In P. Hosford (Ed.), *Using what we know about teaching* (pp. 169–192). Alexandria, VA: Association for Supervision and Curriculum Development.

Hyerle, D. (1996). *Visual tools for constructing knowledge.* Alexandria, VA: Association for Supervision and Curriculum Development.

Ito, T. A., Larsen, J. T., Smith, N. K., & Cacioppo, J. T. (2001). Negative emotion weighs more heavily on the brain: The negativity bias in evaluative categorizations. In J. Cacioppo (Ed.), *Foundations in social neuroscience* (pp. 576–597). Cambridge, MA: The MIT Press.

Jensen, E. (2005). *Teaching with the brain in mind* (2nd ed.). Alexandria, VA: Association for Supervision and Curriculum Development.

Jeter, J., & Davis, O. (1973). Elementary school teachers' differential classroom interaction with children as a function of differential expectations of pupil achievements. Paper presented at the Annual Meeting of the American Educational Research Association, New Orleans.

Jeynes, W. H. (2005). A meta-analysis of the relation of parental involvement to urban elementary school student academic achievement. *Urban Education, 40*(3), 237–269.

Johnson, D., & Johnson, R. (1985). Motivational processes in cooperative, competitive, and individualistic learning situations. In C. Ames & R. Ames (Eds.), *Research in motivation and education: Vol. 2. The classroom milieu* (pp. 249–286). Orlando, FL: Academic Press.

Johnson, D., Maruyama, G., Johnson, R., Nelson, D., & Skon, L. (1981). Effects of cooperative, competitive, and individualistic goal structures on achievement: A meta-analysis. *Psychological Bulletin, 89*(1), 47–62.

Johnson, D. W., & Johnson, R. T. (1999). *Learning together and alone: Cooperative, competitive, and individualistic learning.* Boston: Allyn & Bacon.

Johnson-Laird, P. N. (1983). *Mental models.* Cambridge, MA: Harvard University Press.

Johnson-Laird, P. N. (1985). Logical thinking: Does it occur in daily life? In S. F. Chapman, J. W. Segal, & R. Glaser (Eds.), *Thinking and learning skills: Research and open questions* (Vol. 2, pp. 293–318). Hillsdale, NJ: Lawrence Erlbaum.

Johnson-Laird, P. N., & Byrne, R. M. J. (1991). *Deduction*. Hillsdale, NJ: Lawrence Erlbaum.

Jonas, P. M. (2004). *Secrets of connecting leadership and learning with humor*. Lanham, MD: Scarecrow Education.

Joyce, B., & Weil, M. (1986). *Models of teaching* (3rd ed.). Englewood Cliffs, NJ: Prentice-Hall.

Kaufman, K. F., & O'Leary, K. D. (1972). Reward, cost, and self-evaluation procedures for disruptive adolescents in a psychiatric hospital at school. *Journal of Applied Behavior Analysis, 5,* 293–309.

Kavale, K. (1988). Using meta-analysis to answer the question: What are the important, manipulable influences on school learning? *School Psychology Review, 17*(4), 644–650.

Kester, S., & Letchworth, G. (1972). Communication of teacher expectations and their effects on achievement and attitudes of secondary school students. *Journal of Educational Research, 66,* 51–55.

Kintsch, W. (1974). *The representation of meaning in memory*. Hillsdale, NJ: Lawrence Erlbaum.

Kintsch, W. (1979). On modeling comprehension. *Educational Psychologist, 1,* 3–14.

Kirsch, I. (1999). The response expectancy: An introduction. In I. Kirsch (Ed.), *How expectancies shape experiences* (p. 7). Washington, DC: American Psychological Association.

Kohn, A. (2006). *The homework myth: Why your kids get too much of a bad thing*. Cambridge, MA: DaCapo Press.

Kounin, J. S. (1983). *Classrooms: Individual or behavior settings? Micrographs in teaching and learning* (General Series No. 1). Bloomington: Indiana University, School of Education. (ERIC Document Reproduction Service No. ED240070).

Kralovec, E., & Buell, J. (2000). *The end of homework: How homework disrupts families, overburdens children, and limits learning*. Boston: Beacon.

Kumar, D. D. (1991). A meta-analysis of the relationship between science instruction and student engagement. *Education Review, 43*(1), 49–66.

LaBerge, D., & Samuels, S. J. (1974). Toward a theory of automatic information processing in reading. *Cognitive Psychology, 6,* 293–323.

Land, M. L. (1980, February). *Joint effects of teacher structure and teacher enthusiasm on student achievement*. Paper presented at the annual meeting of the Southwest Educational Research Association, San Antonio, TX. (ERIC Document Reproduction Service No. ED182310).

Lee, A. Y. (n.d.). *Analogical reasoning: A new look at an old problem*. Boulder: University of Colorado, Institute of Cognitive Science.

Leinhardt, G. (1990). Capturing craft knowledge in teaching. *Educational Researcher, 19*(2), 18–25.

Leinhardt, G., & Greeno, J. (1986). The cognitive skill of teaching. *Journal of Educational Psychology, 78*(2), 75–95.

Linden, D. E., Bittner, R. A., Muckli, L., Waltz, J. A., Kriegekorte, N., Goebel, R., Singer, W., & Munk, M. H. (2003). Cortical capacity constraints for visual working memory: Dissociation of FMRI load effects in a fronto-parietal network. *Neuroimage, 20*(3), 1518–1530.

Lindsay, P. H., & Norman, D. A. (1977). *Human information processing*. New York: Academic Press.

Linn, M. C., & Eylon, B. (2006). Science education: Integrating views of learning and instruction. In P. Alexander & P. Winne (Eds.), *Handbook of educational psychology* (2nd ed., pp. 511–544). Mahwah, NJ: Erlbaum.

Lipsey, M. W., & Wilson, D. B. (1993). The efficacy of psychological, educational, and behavioral treatment. *American Psychologist, 48*(12), 1181–1209.

Litow, L., & Pumroy, D. K. (1975). A brief review of classroom group-oriented contingencies. *Journal of Applied Behavior Analysis, 8,* 341–347.

Lobitz, W. C. (1974). A simple stimulus cue for controlling disruptive classroom behavior. *Journal of Abnormal Child Psychology, 2,* 143–152.

Lott, G. W. (1983). The effect of inquiry teaching and advanced organizers upon student outcomes in science education. *Journal of Research in Science Teaching, 20*(5), 437–451.

Lou, Y., Abrami, P. C., Spence, J. C., Paulsen, C., Chambers, B., & d'Apollonio, S. (1996). Within-class grouping: A meta-analysis. *Review of Educational Research, 66*(4), 423–458.

Lovelace, M. K (2005). Meta-analysis of experimental research based on the Dunn & Dunn model. *The Journal of Educational Research, 98*(3), 176–183.

Luiten, J., Ames, W., & Ackerson, G. (1980). A meta-analysis of the effects of advance organizers on learning and retention. *American Educational Research Journal, 17*(2), 211–218.

Lysakowski, R. S., & Walberg, H. J. (1981). Classroom reinforcement in relation to learning: A quantitative analysis. *Journal of Educational Research, 75*, 69–77.

Lysakowski, R. S., & Walberg, H. J. (1982). Instructional effects of cues, participation, and corrective feedback: A quantitative synthesis. *American Educational Research Journal, 19*(4), 559–578.

Macklin, M. C. (1997). Preschoolers' learning of brand names for visual cues. *Journal of Consumer Research, 23*(3), 251–261.

Markman, A. B., & Gentner, D. (1993a). Splitting the differences: A structural alignment view of similarity. *Journal of Memory and Learning, 32*, 517–535.

Markman, A. B., & Gentner, D. (1993b). Structural alignment during similarity comparisons. *Cognitive Psychology, 25*, 431–467.

Marks, H. M. (2000). Student engagement in instructional activity: Patterns in the elementary, middle, and high school years. *American Educational Research Journal, 37*, 153–184.

Martinek, T., & Johnson, S. (1979). Teacher expectations: Effects on dyadic interaction and self-concept in elementary-age children. *Research Quarterly, 50*, 60–70.

Marzano, R. J. (1992). *A different kind of classroom: Teaching with dimensions of learning.* Alexandria, VA: Association for Supervision and Curriculum Development.

Marzano, R. J. (2001). *Designing a new taxonomy of educational objectives.* Thousand Oaks, CA: Corwin Press.

Marzano, R. J. (2002). A comparison of selected methods of scoring classroom assessments. *Applied Measurement in Education, 15*(3), 249–268.

Marzano, R. J. (with Marzano, J. S., & Pickering, D. J.) (2003a). *Classroom management that works: Research-based strategies for every teacher.* Alexandria, VA: Association for Supervision and Curriculum Development.

Marzano, R. J. (2003b). *What works in schools: Translating research into action.* Alexandria, VA: Association for Supervision and Curriculum Development.

Marzano, R. J. (2006). *Classroom assessment and grading that work.* Alexandria, VA: Association for Supervision and Curriculum Development.

Marzano, R. J., Gaddy, B. B., Foseid, M. C., Foseid, M. P., & Marzano, J. S. (2005). *A handbook for classroom management that works.* Alexandria, VA: Association for Supervision and Curriculum Development.

Marzano, R. J., Gnadt, J., & Jesse, D. M. (1990). *The effects of three types of linguistic encoding strategies on the processing of information presented in lecture format.* Unpublished manuscript. Denver: University of Colorado at Denver.

Marzano, R. J. & Haystead, M. (In press). *Making standards useful to classroom teaching.* Alexandria, VA: Association for Supervision and Curriculum and Development.

Marzano, R. J., & Kendall, J. S. (2007). *The new taxonomy of educational objectives.* Thousand Oaks, CA: Corwin Press.

Marzano, R. J., Norford, J. S., Paynter, D. E., Pickering, D. P., & Gaddy, B. B. (2001). *A handbook for classroom instruction that works.* Alexandria, VA: Association for Supervision and Curriculum Development.

Marzano, R. J., Paynter, D. E., & Doty, J. K. (2003). *The pathfinder project: Exploring the power of one: Teacher's manual.* Conifer, CO: Pathfinder.

Marzano, R. J., & Pickering, D. J. (2005). *Building academic vocabulary: Teacher's manual.* Alexandria, VA: Association for Supervision and Curriculum Development.

Marzano, R. J. & Pickering, D. J. (2007a). Errors and allegations about research on homework. *Ph. Delta Kappan.*

Marzano, R. J. & Pickering, D. J. (2007b). The case for and against homework. *Educational Leadership.*

Marzano, R. J. & Pickering, D. J. (2007c). Response to Kohn's allegations. Centennial, CO: Marzano and Associates.com/documents/kohnrepsonse.pdf.

Marzano, R. J., Pickering, D. J., & Pollock, J. E. (2001). *Classroom instruction that works: Research-based strategies for increasing student achievement.* Alexandria, VA: Association for Supervision and Curriculum Development.

Marzano, R. J., Waters, T., & McNulty, B. A. (2005). *School leadership that works: From research to practice.* Alexandria, VA: Association for Supervision and Curriculum Development.

Mason, L. (1994). Cognitive and metacognitive aspects in conceptual change by analogy. *Instructional Science, 22*(3), 157–187.

Mason, L. (1995). Analogy, meta-conceptual awareness and conceptual change: A classroom study. *Educational Studies, 20*(2), 267–291.

Mason, L., & Sorzio, P. (1996). Analogical reasoning in restructuring scientific knowledge. *European Journal of Psychology of Education, 11*(1), 3–23.

Mastin, V. (1963). Teacher enthusiasm. *Journal of Educational Research, 56,* 385–386.

Mattingly, D. J., Prislin, R., McKenzie, T. L., Rodriguez, J. L., & Kayzar, B. (2002). Evaluating evaluations: The case of parent involvement programs. *Review of Educational Research, 72*(4), 549–576.

Mayer, R. E. (1979). Can advance organizers influence meaningful learning? *Review of Educational Research, 49,* 371–383.

Mayer, R. E. (1989). Models of understanding. *Review of Educational Research, 59,* 43–64.

Mayer, R. E. (2003). *Learning and instruction.* Upper Saddle River, NJ: Merrill, Prentice Hall.

McCaslin, M., Bozack, A. R., Napoleon, L., Thomas, A., Vasquez, V., Wayman, V., & Zhang, J. (2006). Self-regulated learning and classroom management: Theory, research, and consideration for classroom practice. In C. Evertson, C. M. Weinstein, & C. S. Weinstein (Eds.), *Handbook of classroom management: Research, practice, and contemporary issues* (pp. 223–252). Mahwah, NJ: Erlbaum.

McClelland, D. C. (1994). The knowledge-testing educational complex strikes back. *American Psychologist, 49,* 66–69.

McCombs, B. L. (2001). Self-regulated learning and academic achievement: A phenomenological view. In B. J. Zimmerman & D. H. Schunk (Eds.), *Self-regulated learning and academic achievement: Theoretical perspectives* (2nd ed., pp. 67–124). Mahwah, NJ: Erlbaum.

McConnell, J. W. (1977, April). *The relationship between selected teacher behaviors and attitudes and achievement of algebra classes.* Paper presented at the annual meeting of the American Educational Research Association, New York. (ERIC Document No. ED141118).

McDaniel, M. A. & Donnelly, C. M. (1996). Learning with analogy and elaborative interrogation. *Journal of Educational Psychology, 88*(3), 508–519.

McLaughlin, E. M. (1991, March). Effects of graphic organizers and levels of text difficulty on less-proficient fifth-grade readers' comprehension of expository text. *Dissertation Abstracts International,* Vol. 51 (9-A), 3028.

McVee, M. B., Dunsmore, K., & Gavelek, J. R. (2005). Schema theory revisited. *Review of Educational Research, 75*(4), 531–566.

Medin, D., Goldstone, R. L., & Markman, A. B. (1995). Comparison and choice: Relations between similarity processes and decision process. *Psychonomic Bulletin & Review, 2*(1), 1–19.

Meichenbaum, D., Bowers, K., & Ross, R. (1969). A behavioral analysis of teacher expectancy effect. *Journal of Personality and Social Psychology, 13,* 306–316.

Mendoza, S., Good, T., & Brophy, J. (1972). *Who talks in junior high classrooms?* (Report No. 68). Research and Development Center for Teacher Education, University of Texas at Austin.

Mergendoller, J. R., Markham, T., Ravitz, J., & Larmer, J. (2006). Pervasive management of project based learning: Teachers as guides and facilitators. In C. Evertson, C. M. Weinstein, & C. S. Weinstein (Eds.), *Handbook of classroom management: Research, practice, and contemporary issues* (pp. 583–615). Mahwah, NJ: Erlbaum.

Merrett, F., & Tang, W. M. (1994). The attitudes of British primary school pupils to praise, rewards, punishments and reprimands. *British Journal of Educational Psychology, 64,* 91–103.

Miller, A. M., Ferguson, E., & Simpson, R. (1998). The perceived effectiveness of rewards and sanctions in primary schools: Adding in the parental perspective. *Educational Psychology, 18*(1), 55–64.

Miller, G. A., Galanter, E., & Pribram, K. H. (1960). *Plans and the structure of behavior.* New York: Holt, Rinehart, & Winston.

Miller, S. D., & Meece, J. L. (1997). Enhancing elementary students' motivation to read and write: A classroom intervention study. *Journal of Educational Research, 90,* 286–300.

Miller, S. D., & Meece, J. L. (1999). Third graders' motivational preferences for reading and writing tasks. *Elementary School Journal, 100,* 19–35.

Moriarity, B., Douglas, G., Punch, K., & Hattie, J. (1995). The importance of self-efficacy as a mediating variable between learning environments and achievement. *British Journal of Educational Psychology, 65,* 73–84.

Moskowitz, G., & Hayman, J. L. (1976). Success strategies of inner-city teachers: A year-long study. *Journal of Educational Research, 69,* 283–289.

Muehlherr, A., & Siermann, M. (1996). Which train might pass the tunnel first? Testing a learning context suitable for children. *Psychological Reports, 79*(2), 627–633.

Narayan, J. S., Heward, W. L., Gardner, R., Courson, F. H., & Omness, C. K. (1990). Using response cards to increase student participation in an elementary classroom. *Journal of Applied Behavioral Analysis, 23,* 483–490.

National Council of Teachers of Mathematics. (2000). *Principals and standards for school mathematics.* Reston, VA: Author.

Nelson, J. R., Martella, R., & Galand, B. (1998). The effects of teaching school expectations and establishing a consistent consequence on formal office disciplinary actions. *Journal of Emotional and Behavioral Disorders, 4*(3), 153–161.

Nesbit, J. C., & Adesope, O. O. (2006). Learning with concept and knowledge maps: A meta-analysis. *Review of Educational Research, 76*(3), 413–448.

Newby, T. J., Ertmer, P. A., & Stepich, D. A. (1995). Instructional analogies and the learning of concepts. *Educational Technology Research and Development, 43*(1), 5–18.

Newton, D. P. (1995). Pictorial support for discourse comprehension. *British Journal of Educational Psychology, 64*(2), 221–229.

Nuthall, G. (1999). The way students learn: Acquiring knowledge from an integrated science and social studies unit. *Elementary School Journal, 99*(4), 303–341.

Nuthall, G., & Alton-Lee, A. (1995). Assessing classroom learning: How students use their knowledge and experience to answer classroom achievement test questions in science and social studies. *American Educational Research Journal, 32*(1), 185–223.

Nye, B., Konstantopoulos, S., & Hedges, L. V. (2004). How large are teacher effects? *Educational Evaluation and Policy Analyses, 26*(3), 237–257.

O'Donnell, A. M. (2006). The role of peers and group learning. In P. Alexander & P. Winne (Eds.), *Handbook of educational psychology* (2nd ed., pp. 781–802). Mahwah, NJ: Erlbaum.

O'Donnell, A. M., Dansereau, D. F., Hall, R. H., Skaggs, L. P., Hyhecker, V. I., Peel, J. L., & Rewey, K. L. (1990). Learning concrete procedures: Effects of processing strategies and cooperative learning. *Journal of Educational Psychology, 82*(1), 171–177.

Ogle, D. (1986). K-W-L: A teaching model that develops active reading of expository text. *Reading Teacher, 39*(6), 564–570.

O'Leary, K. D., Becker, W. C., Evans, M. B., & Saudargas, R. A. (1969). A token reinforcement program in a public school: A replication and systematic analysis. *Journal of Applied Behavior Analysis, 2,* 3–13.

Ozgungor, S., & Guthrie, J. T. (2004). Interactions among elaborative interrogation, knowledge, and interest in the process of constructing knowledge from text. *Journal of Educational Psychology, 96*(3), 437–443.

Page, S. (1971). Social interaction and experimenter effects in a verbal conditioning experiment. *Canadian Journal of Educational Psychology, 25,* 463–475.

Paivio, A. (1969). Mental imagery in associative learning and memory. *Psychological Review, 76,* 241–263.

Paivio, A. (1971). *Imagery and verbal processing.* New York: Holt, Rinehart, & Winston.

Paivio, A. (1990). *Mental representations: A dual coding approach.* New York: Oxford University Press.

Palincsar, A. S. (1986). Metacognitive strategy instruction. *Exceptional Children, 53,* 118–124.

Palincsar, A. S., & Brown, A. L. (1984). Reciprocal teaching of comprehension-fostering and comprehension-monitoring activities. *Cognition and Instruction, 1,* 117–175.

Palincsar, A. S., & Herrenkohl, L. R. (2002). Designing collaborative learning contexts. *Theory into Practice, 41,* 26–32.

Paschal, R. A., Weinstein, T., & Walberg, H. J. (1984). The effects of homework on learning: A quantitative synthesis. *Journal of Educational Research, 78,* 97–104.

Pashler, H. E. (1999). *The psychology of attention.* Cambridge, MA: The MIT Press.

Perkins, D. N., Allen, R., & Hafner, J. (1983). Difficulties in everyday reasoning. In W. Maxwell (Ed.), *Thinking: The expanding frontier* (pp. 177–189). Philadelphia: Franklin Institute Press.

Perkins, P. G., & Milgram, R. B. (1996). Parental involvement in homework: A double-edged sword. *International Journal of Adolescence and Youth, 6*(3), 195–203.

Perry, N. E., Turner, J. C., & Meyer, D. K. (2006). Classrooms as contexts for motivating learning. In P. Alexander & P. Winne (Eds.), *Handbook of Educational Psychology* (pp. 327–348). Mahwah, NJ: Erlbaum.

Pflaum, S. W., Walberg, H. J., Karegianes, M. L., & Rasher, S. P. (1980). Reading instruction: A quantitative analysis. *Educational Researcher, 9*(7), 12–18.

Piaget, J. (1971). *Genetic epistemology* (E. Duckworth, Trans.). New York: Norton.

Plax, T. G., & Kearney, P. (1990). Classroom management: Structuring the classroom for work. In J. Daly, G. Friedrich, & A. Vangelesti (Eds.), *Teaching communication: Theory, research, and methods* (pp. 223–236). Hillsdale, NJ: Erlbaum.

Powell, G. (1980, December). *A meta-analysis of the effects of "imposed" and "induced" imagery upon word recall.* Paper presented at the annual meeting of the National Reading Conference, San Diego, CA. (ERIC Document Reproduction Service No. 199644).

Pressley, M. (1998). *Reading instruction that works: The case for balanced teaching.* New York: Guilford Press.

Pressley, M., Wood, E., Woloshyn, V., Martin, V., King, A., & Menke, D. (1992). Encouraging mindful use of prior knowledge: Attempting to construct explanatory answers facilitates learning. *Educational Psychologist, 27,* 91–109.

Pruitt, N. (1993). *Using graphics in content area subjects.* M.A. thesis, Kean College of New Jersey. (ERIC Document Reproduction Service No. ED355482).

Raphael, T. E. & Kirschner, B. M. (1985). *The effects of instruction in compare/contrast text structure in sixth-grade students' reading comprehension and writing products.* Lansing, MI: The Institute for Research on Teaching (Research Series, No. 161).

Ratterman, M. J., & Gentner, D. (1998). More evidence for a relation shift in the development of analogy: Children's performance on a causal-mapping task. *Cognitive Development, 13*(4), 453–478.

Raudenbush, S. W. (1984). Magnitude of teacher expectancy effects on pupil IQ as a function of credibility of expectancy induction: A synthesis of findings from 18 experiments. *Journal of Educational Psychology, 76*(1), 85–97.

Reder, L. M. (1980). The role of elaboration in the comprehension and retention of prose: A critical review. *Review of Educational Research, 50*(1), 5–53.

Redfield, D. L., & Rousseau, E. W. (1981). A meta-analysis of experimental research on teacher questioning behavior. *Review of Educational Research, 51*(2), 237–245.

Reeve, J. (2006). Extrinsic rewards and inner motivation. In C. Evertson, C. M. Weinstein & C. S. Weinstein (Eds.), *Handbook of classroom management: Research, practice, and contemporary issues* (pp. 645–664). Mahwah, NJ: Erlbaum.

Reeve, J., & Deci, E. (1996). Elements of competitive situations that affect intrinsic motivation. *Personality and Social Psychology Bulletin, 22,* 24–33.

Reitz, A. L. (1994). Implementing comprehensive classroom-based programs for students with emotional and behavioral problems. *Education and Treatment of Children, 17,* 312–331.

Rejeski, W., Darracott, C., & Hutslar, S. (1979). Pygmalion in youth sport: A field study. *Journal of Sports Psychology, 1,* 311–319.

Reynolds, D., & Teddlie, C. (with Hopkins, D., & Stringfield, S.). (2000). Linking school effectiveness and school improvement. In C. Teddlie & D. Reynolds (Eds.), *The international handbook of school effectiveness research* (pp. 206–231). New York: Falmer Press.

Riehl, C. (2006). Feeling better: A comparison of medical research and education research. *Educational Researcher, 35*(5), 24–29.

Ripoll, T. (1999). Why this made me think of that. *Thinking and Reasoning, 4*(1), 15–43.

Rist, R. (1970). Student social class and teacher expectations: The self-fulfilling prophesy in ghetto education. *Harvard Educational Review, 40,* 411–451.

Robinson, D. H., & Keiwra, K. A. (1996). Visual argument: Graphic organizers are superior to outlines in improving learning from text. *Journal of Educational Psychology, 87*(3), 455–467.

Roderique, T. W., Polloway, E. A., Cumblad, C. L., Epstein, M. H., & Bursuck, W. H. (1994). Homework: A survey of policies in the United States. *Journal of Learning Disabilities, 27*(8), 481–487.

Roeser, R. W., Peck, S. C., & Nasir, N. S. (2006). Self and identity processes in school motivation, learning, and achievement. In P. Alexander & P. Winne (Eds.), *Handbook of Educational Psychology* (pp. 391–424). Mahwah, NJ: Erlbaum.

Roozendaal, B. (2003). Systems mediating acute glucocorticoid effects on memory consolidation and retrieval. *Progress in Neuropsychopharmacology Biological Psychiatry, 27*(8), 1213–1223.

Rosenshine, B. (1970). Enthusiastic teaching: A research review. *School Review, 78,* 499–514.

Rosenshine, B. (2002). Converging findings on classroom instruction. In A. Molnar (Ed.), *School reform proposals: The research evidence.* Tempe, AZ: Arizona State University Research Policy Unit. Retrieved June 2006 from http://epsl.asu.edu/epru/documents/EPRU%202002-101/Chapter%2009-Rosenshine-Final.rtf.

Rosenshine, B., & Furst, N. (1973). The use of direct observation to study teaching. In R. Traverss (Ed.), *Handbook of research on teaching* (2nd ed., pp. 263–298). Chicago: Rand McNally.

Rosenshine, B., Meister, C., & Chapman, S. (1996). Teaching students to generate questions: A review of the intervention studies. *Review of Educational Research, 66*(2), 181–221.

Rosenshine, B., & Meister, C. C. (1994). Reciprocal teaching: A review of the research. *Review of Educational Research, 64*(4), 479–530.

Rosenthal, R. (1956). An attempt at an experimental induction of the defense mechanism of projection. PhD dissertation, University of California at Los Angeles.

Rosenthal, R., & Jacobson, L. (1968). *Pygmalion in the classroom.* New York: Holt, Rinehart & Winston.

Ross, B. H. (1987). This is like that: The use of earlier problems and the separation of similarity effects. *Journal of Experimental Psychology, 13*(4), 629–639.

Ross, J. A. (1988). Controlling variables: A meta-analysis of training studies. *Review of Educational Research, 58*(4), 405–437.

Ross, J. A., Hogaboam-Gray, A., & Rolheiser, C. (2002). Student self-evaluation in grade 5–6 mathematics: Effects on problem-solving achievement. *Educational Assessment, 8*(1), 43–59.

Rovee-Collier, C. (1995). Time windows in cognitive development. *Developmental Psychology, 31*(2), 147–169.

Rowe, M. B. (1987). Wait time: Slowing down may be a way of speeding up. *American Educator, 11,* 38–43.

Rubovits, P., & Maehr, M. (1971). Pygmalion analyzed: Toward an explanation of the Rosenthal-Jacobson findings. *Journal of Personality and Social Psychology, 19,* 197–203.

Ruiz-Primo, M. A., Li, M., & Shavelson, R. J. (2001). *Looking into students' science notebooks: What do teachers do with them?* National Center for Research on Evaluation Standards, and Student Testing. Retrieved June 10, 2003, from http://www.stanford.edu/dept/SUSE/SEAL/Reports_Papers/Cresst2001No2.pdf.

Sadoski, M., & Paivio, A. (2001). *Imagery and text: A dual coding theory of reading and writing.* Mahwah, NJ: Lawrence Erlbaum.

Sanford, J. P., & Evertson, C. M. (1981). Classroom management in a low SES junior high: Three case studies. *Journal of Teacher Education, 32*(1), 34–38.

Schoenfeld, A. H. (1998). Toward a theory of teaching-in-context. *Issues in Education, 4*(1), 1–94.

Schoenfeld, A. H. (2006). Mathematics teaching and learning. In P. Alexander & P. Winne (Eds.), *Handbook of educational psychology* (2nd ed., pp. 479–510). Mahwah, NJ: Erlbaum.

Schunk, D. H., & Cox, P. D. (1986). Strategy training and attributional feedback with learning disabled students. *Journal of Educational Psychology, 73*(3), 201–209.

Schwanenflugel, P. J., Stahl, S. A., & McFalls, E. L. (1997). *Partial word knowledge and vocabulary growth during reading comprehension* (Research Report No. 76). University of Georgia, National Reading Research Center.

Sharpe, P., Wheldall, K., & Merrett, F. (1987). The attitudes of British secondary school pupils to praise and rewards. *Educational Studies, 13,* 293–302.

Sheets, R. H., & Gay, G. (1996, May). Student perceptions of disciplinary conflict in ethnically diverse classrooms. *NASSP Bulletin,* 84–93.

Shors, T., Weiss, C., & Thompson, R. (1992). Stress induced facilitation of classical conditioning. *Science, 257,* 537–539.

Silver, H., & Strong, R., & Perini, M. (in press). *Teaching styles and strategies.* Alexandria, VA: Association for Supervision and Curriculum Development.

Skinner, C. H., Fletcher, P. A., & Hennington, C. (1996). Increasing learning rates by increasing student response rates. *School Psychology Quarterly, 11,* 313–325.

Skinner, E. A., Wellborn, J. G., & Connell, J. P. (1990). What it takes to do well in school and whether I've got it: The role of perceived control in children's engagement and school achievement. *Journal of Educational Psychology, 82,* 22–32.

Slicker, E. K. (1998). Relationship of parenting style to behavioral adjustment in graduating high school seniors. *Journal of Youth and Adolescence, 27*(13), 345–372.

Smith, F., & Luginbuhl, J. (1976). Inspecting expectancy: Some laboratory results of relevance for teacher training. *Journal of Educational Psychology, 68,* 265–272.

Smith, H. (1985). The marking of transitions by more and less effective teachers. *Theory Into Practice, 24,* 57–62.

Smith, M. (1980). Teacher expectations. *Evaluation in Education, 4,* 53–55.

Soar, R. S., & Soar, R. M. (1979). Emotional climate and management. In P. L. Peterson & H. J. Walberg (Eds.), *Research on teaching: Concepts, findings, and implications* (pp. 97–119). Berkeley, CA: McCutchan.

Solomon, I. (1994). Analogical transfer and "functional fixedness" in the science classroom. *Journal of Educational Research, 87*(6), 371–377.

Sorsdahl, S. N., & Sanche, R. P. (1985). The effects of classroom meetings on self-concept and behavior. *Elementary School Guidance and Counseling, 20*(1), 56–59.

Sousa, D. (2001). *How the brain learns* (2nd ed.). Thousand Oaks, CA: Corwin Press.

Stage, S. A., & Quiroz, D. R. (1997). A meta-analysis of interventions to decrease disruptive classroom behavior in public education settings. *School Psychology Review, 26*(3), 333–368.

Stahl, R. J. (1994). *Using "think-time" and "wait-time" skillfully in the classroom* (ERIC Digest). Bloomington, IN: ERIC Clearinghouse for Social Studies/Social Science Education. (ERIC Reproduction Service No. ED370885).

Stahl, S. A. (1999). *Vocabulary development.* Cambridge, MA: Brookline.

Stahl, S. A., & Fairbanks, M. M. (1986). The effects of vocabulary instruction: A model-based meta-analysis. *Review of Educational Research, 56*(1), 72–110.

Sternberg, R. J. (1977). *Intelligence, information processing, and analogical reasoning: The componential analysis of human ability.* Hillsdale, NJ: Erlbaum.

Sternberg, R. J. (1978). *Toward a unified componential theory of human reasoning* (Tech. Rep. No. 4). New Haven, CT: Yale University, Department of Psychology. (ERIC Document Reproduction Service No. ED154421).

Sternberg, R. J. (1979). *The development of human intelligence* (Tech. Rep. No. 4, Cognitive Development Series). New Haven, CT: Yale University, Department of Psychology. (ERIC Document Reproduction Service No. ED174658)

Stickgold, R., James, L., & Hobson, J. (2000). Visual discrimination requires sleep after training. *Nature Neuroscience, 3,* 1237–1238.

Stipek, D. J., & Weisz, J. R. (1981). Perceived personal control and academic achievement. *Review of Educational Research, 51*(1), 101–137.

Stodolsky, S. (1983). *Classroom activity structures in the fifth grade* (Final report, NIE contract No. 400-77-0094). Chicago: University of Chicago. (ERIC Document Reproduction Service No. ED 242412).

Stone, C. L. (1983). A meta-analysis of advanced organizer studies. *Journal of Experimental Education, 51*(7), 194–199.

Stronge, J. H. (2002). *Qualities of effective teachers.* Alexandria, VA: Association for Supervision and Curriculum Development.

Styles, E. A. (1997). *The psychology of attention.* East Sussex, UK: Psychology Press.

Swann, W., & Snyder, M. (1980). On translating beliefs into action: Theories of ability and their application in an instructional setting. *Journal of Personality and Social Psychology, 38,* 879–888.

Sweitzer, G. L., & Anderson, R. D. (1983). A meta-analysis of research in science teacher education practices associated with inquiry strategy. *Journal of Research in Science Teaching, 20,* 453–466.

Sylwester, R., & Margulies, N. (1998). *Discover your brain.* Tucson, AZ: Zephyr Press.

Taylor, M. (1979). Race, sex, and the expression of self-fulfilling prophesies in a laboratory teaching situation. *Journal of Personality and Social Psychology, 37,* 897–912.

Taylor, W. (1953). "Cloze procedure": A new tool for measuring readability. *Journalism Quarterly, 30,* 415–433.

Tennenbaum, G., & Goldring, E. (1989). A meta-analysis of the effect of enhanced instruction: Cues, participation, reinforcement, and feedback and correctives on motor skill learning. *Journal of Research and Development in Education, 22*(3), 53–64.

Tennyson, R. D., & Cocchiarella, M. J. (1986). An empirically based instructional design theory for teaching concepts. *Review of Educational Research, 56,* 40–71.

Tobin, K. (1987). The role of wait time in higher cognitive level learning. *Review of Educational Research, 57,* 69–95.

Toulmin, S., Rieke, R., & Janik, A. (1981). *An introduction to reasoning.* New York: Macmillan.

van Dijk, T. A. (1977). *Text and context.* London: Longman.

van Dijk, T. A. (1980). *Macrostructures.* Hillsdale, NJ: Laurence Erlbaum.

van Dijk, T. A., & Kintsch, W. (1983). *Strategies of discourse comprehension.* Mahwah, NJ: Lawrence Erlbaum.

Van Honk, J., Kessels, R. P., Putnam, P., Jager, G., Koppeschaar, H. P., & Postma, A. (2003). Attentionally modulated effects of cortisol and mood on memory for emotional faces in healthy young males. *Psychoneuroendocrinology, 28*(7), 941–948.

Van Voorhis, F. (2003). Interactive homework in middle school: Effects on family involvement and science achievement. *Journal of Educational Research, 96,* 323–338.

Walberg, H. J. (1982). What makes schooling effective? A synthesis and critique of three national studies. *Contemporary Education Review, 1,* 23–34.

Walberg, H. J. (1999). Productive teaching. In H. C. Waxman & H. J. Walberg (Eds.), *New directions for teaching practice research,* 75–104. Berkeley, CA: McCutchen.

Wang, M. C., Haertel, G. D., & Walberg, H. J. (1993). Toward a knowledge base for school learning. *Review of Educational Research, 63*(3), 249–294.

Weiner, N. (1967). *The human use of human beings.* New York: Avon.

Weinstein, C. (1977). Modifying student behavior in an open classroom through changes in the physical design. *American Educational Research Journal, 14,* 249–262.

Weinstein, C. (1979). The physical environment of the school: A review of the research. *Review of Educational Research, 49,* 557–610.

Weinstein, R. S. (2002). *Reaching higher: The power of expectations in schooling.* Cambridge, MA: Harvard University Press.

Welch, M. (1997, April). *Students' use of three-dimensional modeling while designing and making a solution to a technical problem.* Paper presented at the annual meeting of the American Educational Research Association, Chicago.

West, L. H. T., & Fensham, P. J. (1976). Prior knowledge or advance organizers as affective variables in chemical learning. *Journal of Research in Science Teaching, 13,* 297–306.

White, R., & Gunstone, R. (1992). *Probing understanding.* New York: Falmer Press.

Wiggins, G., & McTighe, J. (1998). *Understanding by design.* Alexandria, VA: Association for Supervision and Curriculum Development.

Wilkinson, S. S. (1981). The relationship of teacher praise and student achievement: A meta-analysis of selected research. *Dissertation Abstracts International, 41,* 3998A.

Williams, R. G., & Ware, J. E., Jr. (1976). Validity of student ratings of instruction under different incentive conditions: A further study of the Dr. Fox effect. *Journal of Educational Psychology, 68,* 48–56.

Williams, R. G., & Ware, J. E., Jr. (1977). An extended visit with Dr. Fox: Validity of student ratings of instruction after repeated exposure to a lecturer. *American Educational Research Journal, 14,* 449–457.

Willis, B. (1970). The influence of teacher expectation on teachers' classroom interaction with selected children. *Dissertation Abstracts, 30,* 5072A.

Willms, J. D. (1992). *Monitoring school performance: A guide for educators.* Washington, DC: Falmer Press.

Willoughby, T., Desmarias, S., Wood, E., Sims, S., & Kalra, M. (1997). Mechanisms that facilitate the effectiveness of elaboration strategies. *Journal of Educational Psychology, 89*(4), 682–685.

Willoughby, T., & Wood, E. (1994). Elaborative interrogation examined at encoding and retrieval. *Learning and Instruction, 4,* 139–149.

Winne, P. H. (1979). Experiments relating teachers' use of higher cognitive questions to student achievement. *Review of Educational Research, 49,* 13–50.

Winograd, T. (1975). Frame representations and the declarative-procedural controversy. In D. G. Bobrow & A. M. Collins (Eds.), *Representation and understanding: Studies in cognitive science.* New York: Academic Press.

Wise, K. C., & Okey, J. R. (1983). A meta-analysis of the effects of various science teaching strategies on achievement. *Journal of Research in Science Teaching, 20*(5), 415–425.

Wolfe, P. (2001). *Brain matters: Translating research into classroom practice.* Alexandria, VA: Association for Supervision and Curriculum Development.

Wubbels, T., Brekelmans, M., & den Brok, P., & van Tartwijk, J. (2006). An interpersonal perspective on classroom management in secondary classrooms in the Netherlands. In C. Evertson & C. S. Weinstein (Eds.), *Handbook of classroom management: Research, practice, and contemporary issues* (pp. 1161–1191). Mahwah, NJ: Erlbaum.

Wubbels, T., Brekelmans, M., van Tartwijk, J., & Admiral, W. (1999). Interpersonal relationships between teachers and students in the classroom. In H. C. Waxman & H. J. Walberg (Eds.), *New directions for teaching practice and research* (pp. 151–170). Berkeley, CA: McCutchen.

Wubbels, T., & Levy, J. (1993). *Do you know what you look like? Interpersonal relationships in education.* London: Falmer Press.

Wyckoff, W. L. (1973). The effect of stimulus variation on learning from lecture. *Journal of Experimental Education, 41,* 85–96.

Zabel, M. K. (1986, November). Timeout use with behaviorally disordered students. *Behavioral Disorders,* 15–21.

Index

About the Author

Robert J. Marzano is a senior scholar at Mid-continent Research for Education and Learning in Aurora, Colorado; an associate professor at Cardinal Stritch University in Milwaukee, Wisconsin; and president of Marzano & Associates. He has developed programs and practices used in K–12 classrooms that translate current research and theory in cognition into instructional methods. An internationally known trainer and speaker, Marzano has authored 26 books and more than 150 articles and chapters in books on such topics as reading and writing instruction, thinking skills, school effectiveness, restructuring, assessment, cognition, and standards implementation. Recent titles include *Classroom Instruction That Works: Research-Based Strategies for Increasing Student Achievement* (ASCD, 2001), *Classroom Management That Works: Research-Based Strategies for Every Teacher* (ASCD, 2003), *What Works in Schools: Translating Research into Action* (ASCD, 2003), *Building Background Knowledge for Academic Achievement* (ASCD, 2004), *School Leadership That Works* (ASCD, 2005), *Classroom Assessment and Grading That Work* (ASCD, 2006), and *The New Taxonomy of Educational Objectives* (Corwin, 2007). Marzano received his bachelor's degree in English from Iona College in New York, a master's degree in education in reading/language arts from Seattle University, and a doctorate in curriculum and instruction from the University of Washington. Address: 7127 S. Danube Court, Centennial, CO 80016 USA. Telephone: (303) 796-7683. E-mail: robertjmarzano@aol.com.

Related ASCD Resources: The Art and Science of Teaching

Audiotapes
Instructional Approaches of Superior Teachers by Lloyd Campbell (#299202)
Putting Best Practices to Work on Behalf of Improving Student Learning
    by Kathleen Fitzpatrick (#298132)
Teaching for the 21st Century by Linda Darling-Hammond (#297247)

Print Products
*Classroom Instruction That Works: Research Based Strategies for Increasing
    Student Achievement* by Robert J. Marzano, Debra J. Pickering, Jane E. Pollock
    (#101010)
Classroom Management That Works: Research Based Strategies for Every Teacher by
    Robert J. Marzano, Jana S. Marzano, Debra J. Pickering (#103027)
Grading and Reporting Student Learning by Robert J. Marzano and Tom Guskey
    (Professional Inquiry Kit; # 901061)
A Handbook for Classroom Instruction That Works by Robert J. Marzano,
    Jennifer S. Norford, Diane E. Paynter, Debra J. Pickering, Barbara B. Gaddy
    (#101041)

Videotapes
"Helping Students Acquire and Integrate Knowledge" Series with Robert J. Marzano
    (5 videos; #496065)
How to Use Graphic Organizers to Improve Student Thinking
    (Tape 6 of the "How To" Series; #499048)
Library of Teaching Strategies Parts I & II (#614178)
What Works in Schools: School Factors with Robert J. Marzano
    (Tape 1; # 403048)
What Works in Schools: Teacher Factors with Robert J. Marzano
    (Tape 2; #403049)

For more information: send e-mail to member@ascd.org; call 1-800-933-2723
or 703-578-9600, press 2; send a fax to 703-575-5400; or write to Information
Services, ASCD, 1703 N. Beauregard St., Alexandria, VA 22311-1714 USA.